T0377193

Wired Youth

This fully updated new edition offers a research-based analysis of the online social world of adolescence, incorporating additional research findings that have appeared during the last decade. Talmud and Mesch take a realistic, sociological approach to online adolescents' communication, demonstrating how online sociability is embedded in the larger social structure and in technological affordances.

Combining perspectives from sociology, psychology, and education with a focus on social constructionism, technological determinism, and social networking, the authors present an empirically anchored review of the field. The book covers topics such as youth sociability, relationship formation, online communication, and cyberbullying to examine how young people use the Internet to construct or maintain their interpersonal relationships. This new edition also incorporates new research findings on online adolescents' behavior in general, and specifically in relation to social apps, providing a more updated outlook regarding various dimensions of adolescents' online interactions.

Wired Youth is essential reading for advanced students of adolescent psychology, youth studies, media studies, and the psychology and sociology of interpersonal relationships, as well as undergraduate students in developmental psychology, social psychology, youth studies, media studies, and sociology.

Ilan Talmud is an Associate Professor in the Department of Sociology, University of Haifa, Israel.

Gustavo Mesch is a Professor of Sociology and the Rector of the University of Haifa, Israel.

Adolescence and Society
Series Editor: John C. Coleman
Department of Education, University of Oxford

In the 20 years since it began, this series has published some of the key texts in the field of adolescent studies. The series has covered a very wide range of subjects, almost all of them being of central concern to students, researchers and practitioners. A mark of its success is that a number of books have gone to second and third editions, illustrating its popularity and reputation.

The primary aim of the series is to make accessible to the widest possible readership important and topical evidence relating to adolescent development. Much of this material is published in relatively inaccessible professional journals, and the objective of the books has been to summarise, review and place in context current work in the field, so as to interest and engage both an undergraduate and a professional audience.

The intention of the authors is to raise the profile of adolescent studies among professionals and in institutions of higher education. By publishing relatively short, readable books on topics of current interest to do with youth and society, the series makes people more aware of the relevance of the subject of adolescence to a wide range of social concerns.

The books do not put forward any one theoretical viewpoint. The authors outline the most prominent theories in the field and include a balanced and critical assessment of each of these. Whilst some of the books may have a clinical or applied slant, the majority concentrate on normal development.

The readership rests primarily in two major areas: the undergraduate market, particularly in the fields of psychology, sociology and education; and the professional training market, with particular emphasis on social work, clinical and educational psychology, counselling, youth work, nursing and teacher training.

Also in this series:

Wired Youth: The Online Social World of Adolescence
Ilan Talmud and Gustavo S. Mesch

Youth and Internet Pornography
Richard Joseph Behun and Eric W. Owens

https://www.routledge.com/Adolescence-and-Society/book-series/
SE0238

Wired Youth
The Online Social World of Adolescence

Second Edition

Ilan Talmud and Gustavo Mesch

LONDON AND NEW YORK

Second edition published 2020
by Routledge
2 Park Square, Milton Park, Abingdon, Oxon, OX14 4RN

and by Routledge
52 Vanderbilt Avenue, New York, NY 10017

Routledge is an imprint of the Taylor & Francis Group, an informa business

© 2020 Ilan Talmud and Gustavo Mesch

The right of Ilan Talmud and Gustavo Mesch to be identified as authors of this work
has been asserted by them in accordance with sections 77 and 78 of the Copyright,
Designs and Patents Act 1988.

All rights reserved. No part of this book may be reprinted or reproduced or utilised
in any form or by any electronic, mechanical, or other means, now known or
hereafter invented, including photocopying and recording, or in any information
storage or retrieval system, without permission in writing from the publishers.

Trademark notice: Product or corporate names may be trademarks or registered trademarks,
and are used only for identification and explanation without intent to infringe.

First edition published by Routledge 2010

British Library Cataloguing-in-Publication Data
A catalogue record for this book is available from the British Library

Library of Congress Cataloging-in-Publication Data
A catalog record has been requested for this book

ISBN: 978-0-8153-7883-9 (hbk)
ISBN: 978-0-8153-7884-6 (pbk)
ISBN: 978-1-351-22774-2 (ebk)

Typeset in Bembo
by Newgen Publishing UK

Contents

Preface		vii
1	The information age, youth, and social networks	1
2	The Internet at home	24
3	Sociability and Internet use	50
4	Online relationship formation	69
5	ICT and existing social ties	89
6	The impact of ICT on social network structure	114
7	Online communication and negative social ties	136
8	Conclusion	154
	Bibliography	168
	Index	202

Preface

The book is an updated, second edition of the previous version that was published ten years ago. During this period, social media and smartphone social applications have become ubiquitous. Similarly to the previous edition, the current edition discusses the emergence of online social apps, which have materialized as a dominant vehicle for adolescents' online communication. The convergence between online and face-to-face networks is nowadays more prominent, requiring conceptual elaboration. Furthermore, this updated edition incorporates additional research findings that have appeared in the last decade. From the outset, we have adopted a realistic, sociological approach to online adolescents' communication, where online sociability is embedded in the larger social structure and in technological affordances.

In the last few decades, a great number of sophisticated empirical studies, examining the social implications of adolescents' online conduct have been published. We have incorporated research findings on online adolescent's behavior in general, and social apps in particular. These studies have provided a more up-to-date outlook regarding various dimensions of adolescents' online use, from the digital divide to tie formation, maintenance, and dissolution, to the convergence of online and offline behavior, especially on social apps and smartphones. It seems, however, that our basic premise, that adolescents' online networks are embedded in the larger social structure, and that the social effects of ICT on adolescents' online conduct are mixed, is corroborated even more by this new body of research.

1 The information age, youth, and social networks

Introduction

The Internet is all around us. Adolescents and youth are continuously exposed to it, using it most of the day, every day. The vast proliferation of Information and Communication Technologies (ICTs) is raising public debate and scholarly discussions regarding the nature and effects of ICT on adolescents. This chapter describes the social implications for adolescents of the rapid penetration of ICTs. It is organized through a discussion of the place of ICTs in the information society, the rise of the network society, and the parallel emergence of "networked individualism," adolescence as a developmental life stage, the ways in which adolescents' Internet use is immersed in family tension, and the association of technology and social relationships. To help us understand how adolescents are using ICT, we describe the general network structure and the attributes of online and offline social networks.

In most Western countries, the use of ICTs in the workplace, at home, and on smartphones has become common. These technologies have been integrated into the daily activities of most individuals, not as a novel or extraordinary activity but to forge new paths for both ordinary and extraordinary activities to be accomplished. Many search for news, information, jobs, and products; people communicate online and offline, diversifying their sources of information, communication, and social support in their daily lives (Dutton, Blumler, and Kraemer, 1987; Wellman and Haythornthwaite, 2002; Katz and Rice, 2002a; Miller, 2016; boyd, 2017; Hampton and Wellman, 2018). The integration of these technologies into everyday life seems to be an imperative of the information age, a historical period in which information and knowledge are produced and reproduced at an unprecedented high rate. Information and communication technologies are the current tools that facilitate access to opportunities, knowledge, resources, and social capital which

2 Information age, youth, social networks

might otherwise be difficult to acquire. The Internet is a global network that links computers, and, through them, governments, organizations, and individuals, supporting economic, social, and information activity at a global level. Spanning geographic boundaries, ubiquitous, and converting the geography of locale in spaces of flows (Castells, 2000), the Internet transfers information in copious volumes and in real time, creating what some have described as a fluid society (Hampton and Wellman, 2018).

The information society and networked individualism

Social scientists have used different metaphors to describe the information age: the post-industrial society, the information society, the network society, the cyber-society, and more. Although we acknowledge the different conceptual views, we differentiate the network society from the information age. The network society refers to a social system in which individuals, groups, organizations, and states show more flexibility in crossing boundaries, and individuals have greater awareness of the network configuration of their relationships (Castells, 1996; Van Dijk, 2005; Wellman, 2001; Hampton and Wellman, 2018). The information society denotes the growing tendency to involve computers in the maintenance of data records, information flows, knowledge systems, and communication channels. Naturally, the network society and the information age are closely connected terms. Both concepts describe the economic, political, and cultural changes, and their consequent social organization in a society, resulting from the production of information. It is a shift from production-oriented to service-based occupations, the manipulation of symbols, and a decrease in the percentage of the labor force involved in the production of tangible products. Most importantly, society is characterized by the emergence of "networked individualism," in which the likelihood of connectivity beyond the local group has increased dramatically (Wellman, 2001; Hampton and Wellman, 2018).

The notion of a network society is based on several social changes driven by technology. A central dimension of the change is the development of a new technological condition in which information technologies (including the Internet and mobile phones) facilitate the formation of new forms of social organization and social interaction over electronic networks. Information and communication technologies are not the reason for social change but they provide the infrastructure to make the change possible as they provide the means of communication necessary for the formation of new forms of production, management, organization, and globalization of economic activities. A further important dimension of the network society is the shift of the culture to symbolic communication and to organization primarily around an integrated electronic system of communication and entertainment. Media are becoming more and more diverse, with specific audiences making different choices, and causing fragmentation of the traditional means of mass communication. Hyperlinks to entertainment and news sites are critical for human culture, and the Internet is becoming the linchpin of the symbolic environment.

The result of these diverse changes is that the major functioning of society now relies on networks. The concept of networks is elaborated later in this chapter; in the meantime, we might look at networks as a form of social organization with certain qualities. They are flexible and adaptable, and electronic communications afford networks the capacity to decentralize and adapt the execution of tasks while coordinating purpose and decision-making.

This concept of networked individualism was established by sociologist Barry Wellman (2001). He depicts society as having moved from a form of social organization in which we belonged to and interacted within small, densely knit, socially homogeneous, social groups to a form in which we interact on an individual basis with other individuals, regardless of membership of social groups. Individuals are born into families, live in neighborhoods, and have jobs at workplaces. In the past, their social interaction was restricted to these social spheres, in which they tended to get together, become acquainted, and establish closer or more distant social ties. Now, the information society is transforming this type of organization and interaction into one in which networks are built across distance, group boundaries are permeable, interaction is with diverse others, links shift from network to network, and hierarchies are becoming flatter and more complex (Hampton and Wellman, 2018).

As the use of Instant Messaging (IM) and social networking sites exemplifies, rather than belonging to the same group, individuals in present-day society have their own personal networks through numerous social applications. Although complex social networks have always existed, recent technological developments have rendered their emergence as a dominant form of social organization and the paramount medium of global communication. Just as computer networks link machines, social networks link people. Moreover, computer networks and social networks work conjointly, the former linking people in the latter, while people bringing their offline situations to bear, when they use computer networks to communicate (Wellman et al., 1996).

The implication of networked individualism is that interpersonal relationships via computer-mediated communication are increasingly based on the specialized roles that people play. Such specialized

4 Information age, youth, social networks

relationships revolve around shared interests, common problems, short-time collaborations, and the need for information. Specialized social networks consist of like-minded people, and the Internet supports the development of groups and social connections which are based on shared interests and common lifestyles. Furthermore, people vary in the extent of involvement in different networks, participating actively in some, occasionally in others, and being silent lurkers in still others.

The capacity of the Internet to support the production and consumption of information cannot be gainsaid. Since its first introduction into homes, in many countries its most frequent use has been for communication. It offers delayed (asynchronous) communication applications, such as email and forums, as well as real-time (or synchronous) applications such as Instant Messaging and social networking sites. Internet communication is used to keep in touch with known individuals, to support existing relationships with co-workers, family, and friends, and to form new relationships. Youth are growing up in a multimedia and multi-communication environment. For many adolescents, the Internet is the main source of information and entertainment, and an important tool for communication. As youths tend to be the earliest adopters of this technology, their experience differs dramatically from that of their predecessors.

Public and academic discourse on the relationship between youth and ICT is ambivalent. Many commentators are enthusiastically utopian, maintaining that Internet applications provide children and adolescents with new opportunities for creativity and active learning (Tapscott, 1998; Prensky, 2001; Eshet-Alkalai, 2004; Meneses and Molino, 2010 Koltay, 2011;Teemed, 2019). Moreover, social policy emphasizes the development of skills such as computer literacy, because these skills are believed to be required for an increasing number of occupations. In this approach, which celebrates the emergence of the information age and the rise of the network society, the electronic media are seen as a means of empowerment, liberating children from social inequalities. At the same time, the Internet can have negative effects on teenagers. Because access can seldom be effectively regulated, youths risk exposure to inaccurate information and abusive content (Livingstone and Halper, 2007). Moreover, the Internet might be harmful to social and family life, as arguably time spent on computer activity comes at the expense of participation in family, social, leisure, and sports activities (Kaylan and Yelsma, 2000).

The debate on the social impact of ICT is particularly important for the study of adolescent life, because adolescence is a period of speedy biological, psychological, and social transformation, and of rapid expansion of social circles. In their peer group, in close association with friends

Information age, youth, social networks   5

and peers, adolescents develop life expectations, school aspirations, world-views, and behaviors (Turkle, 2011, 2015a; Miller, 2016; boyd, 2017).

Scholars from such diverse disciplines as cultural studies, psychology, sociology, and communication have studied the communication aspects of the Internet. In the early research we can identify the conceptual and methodological tensions that set the research agenda for subsequent years. In this Introduction we will refer briefly to only two of them, which are central to our conceptual argument; they are the interplay of technology and society with both the online and with the offline world.

Technological and social views

Communication using the Internet has been called computer-mediated communication (CMC) (Rice, 1980). The term underscores two features that were influential in shaping research agendas. First, the word "mediated" indicated a clear difference from interpersonal communication, in which individuals engage in symbolic interaction directly, without the use of technologies. Second, the features of the computer, the cultural artefact that is the mediator, were added to the concept and were assumed to shape the messages and interpersonal relations that it made possible. Technology, then, was assumed to constrain the options and meanings of the symbolic interaction between individuals. At the very start of the inquiry into the Internet and sociability, tension arose between two major perspectives: technological determinism and social shaping of technologies. It partially overlapped the tension between virtuality and offline reality, between generative and reflective approaches.

We distinguish between studies that regard the Internet as culture and those that regard the Internet as a cultural artefact (Hine, 2005). To study the Internet as culture means to regard it as a social space in its own right, and to explore the forms of communication, sociability, and identity produced in this social space and how they are sustained by the resources available in the online setting. From this perspective, the Internet has been referred to, not as a communication channel but as a place for being or dwelling, capable of sustaining complex social spaces. One's online sociability is conceived as different and even separate from one's offline identity. An individual was viewed as having a life online, usually separate from real life, as a parallel reality of the participating individuals. In this view, the virtual space is a coherent social space that exists entirely within computer space, wherein new rules and ways of being could emerge. Individuals operating in an online community may be geographically dispersed, experiencing different hours of the day in different locales, but they share the same virtual space and rules and

6 *Information age, youth, social networks*

have a common history. They can, therefore, treat their online interactions as real. In this view, online communication can exist in itself, completely separated from real life, and individuals can communicate at a distance, overcoming the fragmented character of offline life. Being online, individuals are not only released from the constraints of location but are also freed from the constraints of their offline personalities and social roles. Individuals can express online their real or inner selves, using the relative anonymity of the Internet to be the person they want to be, the individual whom they describe to others, experimenting with their identity and self (Bargh, McKenna, and Fitzsimons, 2002; boyd, 2017).

In this view, the relative anonymity of life on the screen gives individuals a chance to express often unexplored aspects of the self and offers the creation of a virtual persona. Cyberspace becomes a place to "act out" unresolved conflicts, to play and replay difficulties, to work on significant personal issues. Turkle (1996) summarizes this position: "We can use the virtual to reflect constructively on the real. Cyberspace opens the possibility for identity play, but it is very serious play." This approach has methodological implications. Conceiving of the Internet as an object of study means examining only the virtual persona, online communication, and online social norms, rules, and etiquette, without even considering the other direction, namely, how established social norms and values are reflected in the online world. In this case, the Internet has been hailed for the possibilities it is perceived to offer to its users to slough off the constraints of their material surroundings and bodies, enabling them to create and play with online identities. When photos or videos are not presented, cyberspace seems to provide an escape from social inequalities, such as racism or gender discrimination (Turkle, 1996). Similarly, from this perspective, Internet communication creates new forms of social relationships, in which participants are no longer bound by the need to meet people face-to-face but can expand their social arena by meeting others, located anywhere in the online universe, mind-to-mind. Virtual relationships are assumed to be more intimate, richer, and liberating than offline relationships, because they are based on genuine mutual interest rather than the coincidence of physical proximity. Cyberspace is described then as a zone of freedom, fluidity, and experimentation, insulated from the mundane realities of the offline material world (Bargh, McKenna, and Fitzsimons. 2002).

A completely different view obtains if one studies the Internet as a cultural artefact, an object immersed in a social context, considering how the technology is incorporated in individuals' everyday lives, and how it is used as a means of communication in an offline social world (Howard, Rainie, and Jones, 2002; Katz and Rice, 2002a, 2002b, 2007a,

Information age, youth, social networks 7

2007b; Mesch, 2012; Mesch, Quase-Han, and Talmud, 2012). Researchers who take this position regard the virtual as inauthentic, a reflection of the real, and shaped by real-life social conditions and dispositions. The disembodied identities of the virtual world are seen as superficial, and online forms of communication as fleeting, individualized, one-dimensional exchanges, in contrast to the more permanent and complex nature of human engagements in the offline world (McLauglin et al., 1995). ICT users are often characterized as so immersed in virtual interaction that they become detached from their offline social and physical surroundings, hence from their responsibilities in the real world (Kraut et al., 1998; Nie, Hillygus, and Erbring, 2002; Turkle, 2011, 2015a; Miller, 2016). Some commentators present a picture of children who are so absorbed in their online worlds that they reject the real one and distance themselves from offline social and familial relationships, withdrawing from the public outdoor space. This approach leads naturally to a probe of Internet patterns of use and activity as a deviant form of social behavior, a search for its pathological implications. This line of research developed such concepts as pervasive Internet use, and compulsive Internet use, to describe a small minority of individuals who spend long hours on the Internet searching for information and communicating online.

The technological deterministic view presents the Internet as an innovative force that exercises a profound influence on children and youth. Technology generates new patterns of expression, communication, and motivation. In describing this view, various terms have been used, ranging from "the net-generation", "the millennium generation," to "digital natives" (Tapscott, 1998; Prensky, 2001; boyd, 2017). These labels attempt to identify a large group of young adolescents who grew up at the time of Internet expansion and were exposed from early childhood to a media-rich environment; immersed in these technologies they use computers with the greatest of ease, playing online games, and constantly communicating with and connecting to their friends by electronic devices. These youths create and use digital spaces for social interaction, identity expression, and media production and consumption. Supporting this perspective, in the last decade, scholars of media consumption have described adolescents' lives as characterized by media privatization in a multimedia environment (Livingstone and Bovill, 2001; Mesch, 2012; boyd, 2017). The net-generation or digital natives are adolescents who, having grown up with the Internet and its uses, express different values, attitudes, and behaviors from those of their predecessors (Prensky, 2001; Mesch, 2012), even though they have also been socialized into Internet literacy (boyd, 2017). The net-generation is described as optimistic, team-oriented achievers who are skilled in technology. Immersion in

8 *Information age, youth, social networks*

this technology-rich culture influences teenagers' skills and interests in important ways. According to this view, they think and process information differently from their predecessors, actively experiment, and depend on information technologies to search for information and communicate with others. They are eager to acquire the skills needed to develop creative multimedia presentations and to become multimedia producers, not merely consumers (Tapscott, 1998; Prensky, 2001; boyd, 2017). Simply put, the Internet has created a new generation of young people, who possess sophisticated knowledge and skills with information technologies that express values that support learning by experience, the creation of a culture in a digital space, and who have particular learning and social preferences. Yet, this generation is not homogeneous in its social media use and digital skills and literacy.

Bolton and her associates (2013) attack the notion of calling current youth "digital natives." They claim that the latter concept describes only recent exposure to intensive social media applications (see also boyd, 2017). More specifically, they rightfully criticize most of the previous research as principally

> [(a) it focuses] on the United States and/or (at most) one other country, ignoring other regions with large and fast-growing Gen Y populations, where social-media use and its determinants may differ significantly; (b) tends to study students whose behaviors may change over their life cycle stages; (c) relies on self-reports by different age groups to infer Gen Y's social media use; and (d) does not examine the drivers and outcomes of social-media use.
>
> (Bolton et al., 2013)

Nonetheless, there is considerable intergenerational variation in youth social media use, arising from societal factors (including economic, cultural, technological, and political/legal factors), and from individual features (Bolton et al. 2013).

More to the point, the notion of a net-generation or "digital natives" is consistent with a deterministic view of the effect of technology on society. Technological determinism views technology as an independent force that drives social change (Bimber, 2000; boyd, 2017). According to this view, technology itself exercises a causal influence on social practices, and technological change induces changes in social organization and culture, regardless of the change's social desirability.

This view is highly controversial, as it is difficult to assume that information and communication technologies are a force that homogenizes young people into a single entity with unique characteristics (Herring,

Information age, youth, social networks 9

2007; Valkenburg and Peter, 2013; Valkenburg and Taylor-Piotrowski, 2017). Technology is an inherent part of society; it is created by social actors. Approaching technology as a social construction, it is important to note that social groups differ in the extent of access, skills, and meanings they associate with technology. The same technology can have different meanings for different social groups of users. Technologies can and do have a social impact, but they are simultaneously social products that embody power relationships and social goals and structures (Smith, 1985). Technological changes are a process and do not have a single direction. Understanding the place of the Internet in the life of young individuals requires avoiding a purely technological interpretation and recognizing the social embeddedness of the technology and variable outcomes (Sassen, 2002; Mesch and Talmud, 2007a, 2007b, 2007c). The Internet can be constitutive of new cultural features of young people's social life but these can also reproduce older conditions. A purely technological approach ignores the material and cultural conditions within and through which these technologies operate. Digital spaces, such as social networking sites, blogs, and clip and photo sharing, are owned by commercial companies that target youth and try to shape their consumption patterns. At the same time, by using these spaces, youth become empowered, and they assume an important role in society as co-producers of Internet content and reach out with their innovative presentations to large and global audiences.

A more accurate and subtle approach is to envisage the Internet not as generating a new world, but as reflecting some existing conditions of society. The Internet is a space of activity, but its function is limited to supplementing existing means and, in some cases, displacing them (Hampton and Wellman, 2001, 2018; Baym et al., 2004). Rational considerations, such as the interaction of time, distance, and cost, are at the heart of decisions to use the Internet instead of other channels. Existing characteristics of the relationships are instrumental and central in determining which channels to use and when. Strong ties make use of all the channels, weak ties use only some of them (Haythornthwaite, 2002; Mesch and Talmud, 2006a, 2006b). The emphasis in this view is on the actor: the integration of the Internet into existing relationships reflects the actor's rational choices in maintaining existing social ties (Scholz et al., 2020).

The two perspectives differ as to whether the development of online worlds is a positive or negative influence, but they share the tendency to regard the offline world and the virtual as not only different but also as discrete. This understanding of the relationship between online and offline has been increasingly subject to criticism. For example, the ability

10   *Information age, youth, social networks*

to access online spaces presupposes certain offline material resources—at least a computer and the electricity to run it. In additional, physical or material access is also linked to digital and computer literacy, information skills, and motivation (Van Dijk, 2005; Drori, 2006; Correa, 2014, 2016; Van Deursen and Van Dijk, 2014a, 2014b; Correa et al., 2015; boyd, 2017; Jenkins and Sun, 2019).

In this book, we attempt to see how online and offline worlds are connected, and we focus on adolescents, the group most involved in Internet use, to show how online spaces are used and interpreted in the context of young people's everyday offline lives, and the extent to which the Internet as an arena of social interaction reflects, but can also modify, individuals' social involvement in personal relationships.

Adolescence and social ties

Adolescent attraction to friendship, its formation, and its quality have received much sociological attention (Kandel, 1978; Hallinan et al., 1988; Crosnoe, 2000; Moody, 2001; boyd, 2017; Valkenburg and Peter, 2013; Valkenburg and Taylor-Pioterkiwski, 2017). Adolescence is a period characterized by rapid developmental changes. As children enter their teenage years, they interact less with their parents, while peer relationships expand and assume greater importance (Giordano, 2003). Peers act as emotional confidants, provide advice and guidance, and serve as models of behavior and attitudes (Crosnoe, Cavanagh, and Elder, 2003; Brooks, 2015; Kim, 2017). Studies show a significant relationship between the quality of one's friends and one's well-being. Adolescents who lack attachment to peers are more likely to report psychological distress and to even harbor thoughts of suicide (Beraman and Moody, 2004). Although parents continue to influence behaviors and decisions, the time that adolescents spend with peers expands, and peers become their most important reference group (Hartup, 1997).

The combination of societal change and expansion in the use of ICTs—especially in user-friendly social applications on smartphones—challenges us to grasp if the nature of adolescence has changed (Turkel, 2011, 2015a). In an early review, Larson and Verma (1999) argued that adolescents face a world in which daily forms of social life are changing, with direct implications for their own lives. Daily interactions are likely to occur less and less in the context of stable, small-scale, culturally homogeneous and tightly knit communities, and more and more in transitory, culturally heterogeneous, negotiated, and sometimes more impersonal relationships. There is a variety of social reasons for this process. Families are shrinking as the average number of children per woman has fallen in most Western countries. In the short term, lower levels of fertility mean that adolescents have fewer siblings; in the long term, it implies fewer uncles, aunts, and far fewer cousins, nieces, and nephews, that is, a much smaller extended family. Other contexts of interpersonal life are also affected by change, as schools, work, and friendships tend to separate adolescents from adults. Adolescents tend to spend more time and more years in school, and to engage in extracurricular activities, than in the past. As families shrink in size, adolescents turn increasingly to peers for social support. These trends mean that peer relationships acquire greater importance in adolescents' preparation for adulthood. The Internet further enlarges the adolescents' world of peer interactions and opens new communication paths with people outside their immediate community, across barriers of distance, ethnicity, age, and gender, and with the advent of computerized translation programs, even of language.

Youniss and Smollar (1985) extensively studied the meaning of friendship in adolescence, and found that relationships with peers and parents usually do not compete but serve wholly different functions. Peers are generally more accepting than parents, who are necessarily more future-oriented and concerned more with the potentially negative consequences of the children's behavior. The elevated level of acceptance in the peer context, and the tendency to focus on the present, help explain the higher levels of self-disclosure and mutual trust that often develop as a basic characteristic of adolescent peer ties. Adolescent friendships serve also as an academic resource; in one study, adolescents whose friends liked school did well in school themselves, and had fewer academic problems than did those whose friends were less academically oriented (Crosnoe et al., 2003; Kim, 2017).

Internet use by adolescents has increased enormously in recent years, and studies show that adolescents use the medium mainly for social purposes (Lenhart, Rainie, and Oliver, 2001; Gross et al., 2002; Lenhart et al., 2015; Miller, 2016; boyd, 2017; Smith and Anderson, 2018). They use social apps more than adults to communicate after school, exchange gossip and information about homework, and obtain social support. Online relationships are already an integral part of adolescent culture and social life. Studies confirmed these relationships and reported that 14 percent of US teenagers have formed close online friendships (Wolak et al., 2003; Miller, 2016; Smith and Anderson, 2018). Relationship formation and maintenance are one of the most appealing aspects of Internet use for young people, given that forming relationships is a developmental imperative of adolescence and adolescents are closely involved with the technology.

Sociological studies on adolescent friendship (attraction, formation, and quality) have relied mostly on the proximity-similarity hypothesis

12 *Information age, youth, social networks*

(Kandel, 1978; Shrum, Cheek, and Hunter, 1988). According to this perspective, homophily in social relationships results from the combination of proximity, which provides opportunities for frequent and mutual exposure, and shared social status, which creates attraction between individuals who share the same social experience and context. People's daily activities are socially structured, creating an array of opportunities that tend to bring individuals into frequent contact. When people who share social status meet, social attraction and relationship formation are likely to occur because a given social status is associated with sharing similar life experiences and similar needs for information, communication, activities, and support (Suitor, Pillemer, and Keeton, 1995; boyd, 2017; Kim, 2017). Studies on adolescent friendships have typically relied on data from school samples, disregarding other contexts of friendship formation (see, e.g., Kandel, 1978; Schrum et al., 1988; Mesch and Talmud, 2006a, 2006b, 2007a, 2007b, 2007c). This approach has several serious limitations. First, using the proximity-similarity hypothesis with school samples makes it impossible to disentangle the effects of proximity from those of similarity (Aboud and Mendelson, 1996). To ask respondents to name friends at school only (as most studies have done) is to ask for friends who are already in their proximity and therefore similar. This approach omits from the study friends who are not in proximity, do not attend the same school, and those who were met online. Second, the fundamental argument of the proximity-similarity hypothesis is that the quality of friendship between similar friends is higher than between less similar ones. Studies based on school samples cannot verify this hypothesis because they have not compared the quality of friendship in different social contexts of friendship formation.

Furthermore, recent studies have shown that adolescents make new friends not only in their neighborhood and at school but also online. Occasionally, online friendships trigger face-to-face meetings (Gross, Juvonen, and Gable, 2002; Wolak, Mitchell, and Finkelhor, 2003). There is some evidence that these relationships can become intimate and provide social support (Gross et al., 2002; McKenna, Green, and Gleason, 2002; DeAndrea et al., 2012). But most of these studies derive their data from samples of Internet users, which precludes comparisons between the quality of online and face-to-face relationships.

The Internet and family tensions

These developments have several implications for adolescents and their families. Families of adolescents need to adjust and adapt their relationships to accommodate the increasingly maturing adolescent. This is especially true in

Information age, youth, social networks   13

the information age, which breeds new areas of tension. Changes in parent–child relations are influenced by adolescents' growing desire to increase their sense of autonomy and individuation. As they grow up, adolescents become less satisfied with their parents' authority over their personal lives and activities, and more willing to disagree openly with them, which can lead to heightened conflict (Youniss and Smollar, 1996). Many contentious exchanges concern parents' regulation of adolescents' everyday lives, such as curfew rules, friendship relations, and personal activities such as use of Internet, cell phones, and TV (Smetana, 1988; Collins and Russel, 1991). In the past, adolescents were exposed to friends at school and in the neighborhood, places where parents exerted great influence and control. Housing is determined by the parents' social standing; when they choose a residential environment, they make a long-term decision on the composition of their young and adolescent children's peer group. The Internet introduces an element of tension in this area, as adolescents can diversify their social networks beyond their school and neighborhood, thereby weakening their parents' ability to control their associations.

Families are social systems characterized by a hierarchy of authority. The computer can change this hierarchy, as the adolescent, a frequent user, becomes the family expert upon whom other family members rely for technical advice and guidance (Watt and White, 1994; Kiesler et al., 2000). Adolescents increase their resources vis-à-vis their parents and enhance their power within the family. Furthermore, as adolescents search for autonomy, parental controls over their activities steadily diminish. Studies have shown that although parents report supervising the sites their children visit, children usually report that their parents do not control their computer activities (Lenhart et al., 2001, 2015; Livingstone and Bovill, 2001).

During adolescence children's and parents' expectations of each other change, and gaps in these expectations can cause family conflict (Steinberg and Silk, 2002). Children may expect adolescence to be a time of greater freedom, and parents may expect adolescents to self-regulate their behavior so that social and leisure activities do not interfere with school activities (Collins and Russel, 1991). Parents are aware that computers can enhance academic performance. Studies found that parents appreciated the new educational resources that the Internet provided for their children, but worried about the erosion of standards (reading short articles instead of books) and the credibility of online information (Subrahmanyam et al., 2001), and expressed concern that the Internet may distract children from other activities.

Studies exploring family interactions on media issues report that parents expect adolescents to self-regulate their Internet use and to make attempts to restrict the time spent on computer-related activities

14 *Information age, youth, social networks*

so as not to interfere with school work and socializing (Pasquier, 2001; Livingstone and Bovill, 2001). Parents may perceive frequent Internet use as a violation of their expectations, and it may become a source of intergenerational conflict. We maintain therefore that the diffusion of communication technologies can change the process of adolescent social association and intergenerational relationships. Additionally, there are evidence that adolescents using social apps are more involved in their community than non-users (Loader, Vromen, and Xenos, 2014). Lee (2020) has recently examined how millennials' use of social network sites is associated with volunteering. Analyzing the 2013 data of the Minnesota Adolescent Community Cohort Study, he found a curvilinear relationship between social network sites' usage and volunteering. More precisely, Lee uncovered a positive association between a moderate level of Facebook use and volunteering, although heavy users were not more likely to volunteer than nonusers. In other words, moderate online adolescent networks seem to contribute to positive community engagement (Box 1.1).

Box 1.1 Potential effects of information and communication technologies on families with teenagers

- Adolescents' diversification of social networks beyond their school and neighborhood, thereby weakening their parents' ability to control their associations.
- Challenging the family hierarchy, as the adolescent, a frequent user, becomes the family expert upon whom other family members rely for technical advice and guidance.
- Parental supervision and monitoring of web sites challenge adolescents' autonomy.
- Expectation gaps as parents expect computers are used to enhance academic performance and adolescents' expect computers to enhance their social life.

Social networks

Social networks offer a theory and method for the study of patterns of relationships and interactions among social actors. While other perspectives focus on the actors' social characteristics, such as age, gender, socio-economic status, and personality, the focus of social networks is on

Information age, youth, social networks   15

the properties of their interactions, such as their nature, content, intensity and frequency (Kadushin, 2004; Haythornwaite, 2005). Social network methods have been employed to study organizational behavior, interorganizational relations, citation patterns, virtual communities, and other domains (Wasserman and Faust, 1995; Monge and Contractor, 2003; Kadushin, 2004).

The social network perspective centers on the exchanges (or the lack of exchanges) between two actors who form a pair. A social network relation denotes the type of exchange or interaction occurring in any pair in a system of actors. A pair who maintain an exchange or interaction are said to have a common tie that links them (Garton et al., 1999). Across a set of actors, ties accumulate and create social networks. Such networks reveal the flow of resources (information, sociability, communication, goods, etc.) between actors and how sets of actors are connected to each other. The chief distinction between a network approach and other approaches is the focus on exchanges and interaction between actors, not on the individual characteristics of the actors engaged in the exchange of resources. Social network analysts seek to describe networks of social relations, their prominent patterns, and the flow of information or resources through them, and to learn what affects the characteristics of social networks and what effect social networks have on people, organizations, and communities. Social network analysis is used to describe the network and to explain how involvement in a particular network helps to explain the attitudes and behavior of its members. Social network analysis is very helpful in explaining how information and other resources flow through direct and indirect ties, how people acquire resources, and how individuals are associated with other network members.

Any study of social networks seeks out several of their central characteristics. Social networks differ in *network size*, that is, the number of social actors constituting the network. Large social networks provide more resources, as the individual can depend on more people to access social support, sociability, and advice. Additionally, larger social networks tend to have more heterogeneity in their members' social characteristics and resources. The estimation of network size is often difficult, because it requires defining boundaries around individuals' networks, which can dynamically vary according to a person's everyday life. Recent studies suggest the existence of a cognitive constraint on the size of social networks, perhaps because the number or volume of neocortical neurons limits an organism's information processing capacity, and hence the number of social relationships that an individual can monitor simultaneously (Hill and Dunbar, 2003). Since the size of the human neo-cortex is known, the relationship between the group size and neo-cortex size can

16 *Information age, youth, social networks*

be used to predict the cognitive group size for humans. Dunbar (1993) used this approach to predict that humans should live in social groups of approximately 150 individuals. The same limitation seems to be working on the size of online social networks. Dunbar's findings created interest in the possibility that social networking sites might increase the size of human social groups. There is some evidence that the average number of friends in a Facebook network is 120, and that women tend to have somewhat more than men. But the range is large, and some people have networks numbering more than 500. The number of people as active ties on an individual's friend list is smaller. An average man responds to the posting of only seven of those friends by leaving comments. An average woman is slightly more sociable, responding to ten (*The Economist*, 2009). A recent study sample of 6,000 adolescents' MySpace pages found that the median number of ties a teenager has in MySpace is 60. Girls have more listed ties than boys with a median of 103 ties (Pfeil, Arjan, and Panayiotis, 2009). These results suggest that network size both online and offline is lower but close to Dunbar's number of 150 ties. In the early stages of Internet use, there was concern that it was time-consuming, and that it might reduce the size of individuals' offline social networks, implying a social displacement effect (Kraut et al., 1998). This issue is explored in Chapter 2.

Homophily is a well-established and central concept in social network analysis, and it describes the characteristics of the social network members. It indicates that contact and social interaction are more likely to occur with similar individuals. The notion implies a similarity attraction expectation: people are more likely to interact with others with whom they share similar traits, interests, and life experiences (Wasserman and Faust, 1995; McPherson, Smith-Lovin, and Cook, 2002; Monge and Contractor, 2003; Kadushin, 2004).

Homophily seems to be the result of a structure of opportunities for interaction emerging from the social structuring of activities in society. Similar individuals tend to reside in the same neighborhoods, to work in the same organizations, and participate in the same activities (Feld, 1981). This aspect of homophily might be challenged, as individuals use information and communication technologies to maintain ties, but also to seek new ones, based on shared concerns, interests, hobbies, and social support (Pearson, Steglich, and Snjiders, 2006) and shared interests may bring into contact individuals who differ in their social background (Mesch and Talmud, 2007a).

Another important concept concerned with the amount and type of network exchanges is multiplexity. The more numerous the exchanges in a tie, the more multiplex it is. Multiplex ties are not specific or limited

Information age, youth, social networks 17

to a single type of resource exchange but encompass the exchange of various kinds of social support, information, and sociability. They are usually more intimate, voluntary, supportive, and durable than unidimensional ties, and are maintained through more communication channels. Online social networks apparently tend to be less multiplex than offline social networks. Online communication fosters specialization as social ties are created around a shared specific interest or topic, and this specialization constrains the variation in the resources being exchanged.

A related issue is media multiplexity, a concept developed out of recognition that individuals communicate through a range of channels (Wasserman and Faust, 1995; Monge and Contractor, 2003; Kadushin, 2004; Haythornwaite, 2005). The social network approach can be used to see where relations and ties cross media lines: which kinds of groups maintain ties via multiple media, and which communicate only by means of a single medium. For example, an online community might coordinate a meeting by email, exchange information in the online community, and meet face-to-face. Individuals who belong to the same social network communicate using face-to-face meetings, phone and cell-phone conversations, SMS, and Internet communication. With the introduction of new information technologies, and the flourishing of ubiquitous social apps, communication with acquaintances, co-workers, family members, and friends has undoubtedly become diversified, making the study of social networks difficult and complex. Today the study of social networks in our society requires us to ask ourselves who is talking to whom about what, and via which media. The closer individuals are to one another, the more means of communication are seemingly used, indicating that studying networks online does not always reflect an individual's real network (Mesch and Talmud, 2006a, 2006b).

Centrality refers to the identification of the users or individuals at the center of the network, that is, the network members who have the most connections to others (degree centrality), or members who are tied to network segments not otherwise connected (betweenness centrality). In the latter case, this is the member whose departure might cause the collapse or disappearance of the network. The notion of centrality is important for many Internet applications whose adoption and existence depend on network members who are recruited to join the application. For example, Instant Messaging requires that individuals start using the application, and invite others with whom they interact frequently to use it. If one member is at the center and decides to move to another application, the entire network will very likely disappear from such an application. The cumulative effect is an application that once was highly used

18 *Information age, youth, social networks*

and is no longer in the market as it has lost its members; the network links people, but often people link networks.

Density is a key structural dimension of social networks that measures the extent to which members of social networks know one another and their exchanges are reciprocal. More specifically, it measures the proportion of actual ties to all possible ties. Network density increases with transitivity in social relations. Given that member A knows member B and member B knows member C, if the conditional probability that member A also knows member C (or vice versa, assuming network symmetry) is high, then transitivity is prevalent (Wasserman and Faust, 1995). High density typically occurs in cohesive groups, and it is more likely to be pronounced in small communities.

Finally, an important concept is *tie strength*. A tie's strength is usually assessed by a combination of factors, such as perceived closeness, intimacy, and trust (Granovetter, 1973). Weaker ties are evinced in more casual relationships and in sparser exchanges; they typify relationships of those who enjoy fewer kinds of support. Weak ties are important in getting general information, accessing distant and non-similar contacts, and obtaining information that one's close ties do not possess. Strong ties exist in relationships on a high level of intimacy and trust, involving more self-disclosure, shared activities, emotional as well as instrumental exchanges, and long-term interaction (Marsden and Campbell, 1984). From this definition it can be argued that strong ties are the ones we develop with family, close friends, and co-workers, that is, with people of the same social circle and who are similar in social terms. Their exchanges are frequent, the resources exchanged are of multiple types (emotional and instrumental), and they have a high level of intimacy, self-disclosure, and reciprocity in exchanges. People with strong ties have a powerful motivation to share their resources.

Weak ties are characteristics of acquaintances and casual or secondary contacts, and are deemed to develop between individuals who differ socially and belong to different social circles; their interaction is infrequent and primarily instrumental. They are organized around a common interest or need. One interesting aspect of weak ties is that because those who evince them belong to different social circles, they can become a resource for information that is not known to the actor and his or her close social network.

Social diversification

This approach attempts to link Internet use, social interactions and the individual's social circles and resources (Table 1.1). Theoretically, when

Information age, youth, social networks 19

Table 1.1 Structural characteristics of social networks

Structural characteristic	Definition
Network size	The number of social actors who constitute a network
Homophily	The degree of social similarity within the network
Resource multiplexity	The variety of resource types which are exchanged within the network
Media multiplexity	Variation in the quantity of media used to maintain social ties in the network
Centrality	Identification of individuals at the center of the network
Density	Measures the extent to which members of social networks know one another
Tie strength	A tie's strength is usually assessed by a combination of factors such as perceived closeness, intimacy, duration, commitment, and trust
Reciprocity	The extent to which communication from one member to another is replied

used for communication purposes, the Internet seems to be a global communication device, bringing together individuals who share needs and interests in different locations without time limitations. Hardly any scholarly attention has been paid to the way the Internet is associated with the geographic reach of personal ties, social heterogeneity, and the ways in which ICT affects adolescents' mix of social interactions and social relationships.

From a more socio-structural perspective, social network analysts have also tended to see matters this way. They have argued that virtual communities can be viewed as social networks, linking individuals from different neighborhoods, cities, and countries (Wellman et al., 1996; Wellman, 2001; Kadushin, 2004; Miller, 2016; Hampton and Wellman, 2018). Systematic differences may be expected to exist between individuals who meet friends online and offline. The likelihood of online friendship formation will presumably be higher for adolescents who report low self-esteem and who also lack social closeness to face-to-face friends. Because people need intimacy and companionship, the Internet provides a new space to meet others and create close relationships.

Information and communication technologies are conceived as agents of change in society because they support the rapid creation, diffusion, and accessibility of information, the formation of social networks, and the accumulation of social capital. Their extensive use for communication purposes and their integration with our daily life might lead to a

20 *Information age, youth, social networks*

change in the structure of the social networks, exposing people to non-similar others, overcoming the limitations of proximity, age, and gender. This presumed impact is particularly relevant to adolescents, who are confined in more local, cohesive social ties than adults. This exposure to individuals with similar interests but different social background leads to a diversification of the social network, facilitating access to resources, information, and knowledge, and is a potential means for the reduction of social inequalities.

At the center of the diversification approach is a conceptualization of the Internet and mobile devices as a space of activity and social interaction. The Internet is not only about communication with existing ties. Certainly, many individuals and organizations use the Internet as another channel of communication with existing ties, but the Internet's innovation is precisely to provide opportunities for activities that induce social interaction, furnishing a space for exposure to new social ties. Here the social use represents more than a communication channel; often it is a space of social activity. People playing interactive games online do more than that: as in any game, the players form groups, interaction is recurrent, and names and phone numbers are exchanged. Forums are used for advice, social support, and information search, creating opportunities for social interaction and involvement. It is not uncommon that users who are acquainted introduce others to their social network.

Societies are characterized by varying levels of social segregation. In societies that reward individuals differentially according to income, prestige, ethnicity, and power, stratification systems result in a differential ability of individuals to gain access to jobs and residential locations. As a result, individual social associations tend to be with people of similar social characteristics such as age, gender, marital status, ethnicity, religion, and nationality. Studies on the formation, development, maintenance, and dissolution of close social relationships have emphasized the importance of network homophily. Social similarity in the social network may also arise as a result of the opportunity structure for interaction, which emerges from the social structuring of activities in society. Feld (1981) used the concept of *foci of activity*, defining them as "social, psychological, legal or physical objects around which joint activities are organized." Whether they are formal (school) or informal (regular hangouts), large (neighborhood) or small (household), foci of activity systematically constrain choices of friends. From this perspective, association with others is the result of a two-step process: foci of activity place individuals in proximity (for example, they provide opportunities for frequent meetings), which causes individuals to reveal themselves to each other. According to Feld (1981), whatever the basis of their initial association with a focus, it may be difficult, costly, and time-consuming not to associate with certain individuals who share the same foci. For all these reasons, individuals' association with particular foci of activity may have unintended social consequences for them. Specifically, people tend to choose their friends from the set of people available through these foci. The Internet as a focus of activity becomes an institutional arrangement that brings individuals together in repeated interactions around the focal activities.

Consequently, an important motivation for individuals to form online relationships is to diversify their social network and identify other individuals who share their interests, concerns, or problems, but who are not part of their social circle. Online social formation is thus not a general need, as not all individuals are involved in this activity; nor is it the result of insufficient relationships with family or friends but merely the need to find other individuals with similar interests, not available in the social network because of its deterministic similarity. Diversification of social ties, rather than a need for company and lack of social skills, motivates online relationship formation (Lin, 2005).

Network diversification can be linked to social capital, a concept that has been used to explain the actual and potential effects of online social interaction on society. Among several accepted definitions and operationalizations, social capital is generally understood as network ties that provide mutual support, shared language, shared norms, social trust, expansive reach of social ties, and a sense of mutual obligation from which people can derive value (Huysman and Wulf, 2004). It is perceived as a by-product of social relations and as benefiting group members. Social capital has been linked to positive social outcomes such as low crime rates, better health, better educational achievement, and higher income.

The definition emphasizes the central role of the size, structure, composition, and trust in social networks (Wasserman and Faust, 1995; Monge and Contractor, 2003; Kadushin, 2004). According to these qualities, networks provide differential access to resources that include opportunities, skills, information, social support, and sociability. Social capital—and one of its components, social networks—are structural concepts that refer not to dyadic interactions but to the characteristics of the groups in which people are embedded. Central to social capital is that it is made up of networks, norms of reciprocity, and trust, which enable participants to act together more effectively to pursue shared objectives. The concept of trust refers to being able to rely on known individuals, but also on unknown individuals. So trust is a property of intimate relationships, but also refers to a generalized trust in other community members.

Putnam (2000) argued that active membership in community and in voluntary groups is decreasing, causing a decrease in social capital.

22 *Information age, youth, social networks*

Membership in voluntary associations and activities provides opportunities for gathering, social networking, developing networks and norms, which deepen trust in society. This author cites the increased penetration of television into households as a central factor explaining the decrease in social capital. This reference to the negative effect of media impels scholars to investigate how involvement in online activities influences social networks, and ultimately social capital, in society.

An interesting issue is how a person's online and offline relationships affect social capital. This is important, if we think of the Internet as supporting information exchange and interpersonal communication, linking individuals already involved in the same social circle, supporting past friendships and family ties that have become less active due to geographic mobility, and creating new acquaintances, thus expanding the social circle by bridging different social groups. The focus should be on social characteristics and media simultaneously, to understand which social groups benefit from online social ties, which do not, and how these benefits or deficits are translated into social life. A good place to start exploring of these issues is the close social environment of young people, namely, the family.

The effect of ICTs on adolescents' social ties, as well as the impact of sociological and psychological factors on the uses and implications of ICTs, can be summarized as in Table 1.2.

The two polar perspectives, technological determinism and social constructivism, are situated at the two extremes (presuming that only one effect of either social or technological factors is dominant). These extreme perspectives were quite common in the first studies of ICT. By contrast, most contemporary theories take into account both technological and social systems in shaping ICT structure and users' conduct. The theories in cells (1) and (2) assume high technological impact on the

Table 1.2 Theories of ICT, according to forms of embeddedness

Dimension		Social context	
	Effect	*Strong*	*Weak*
Technological	Strong	(1) Media richness Social affordance Net generation Online diversification	(2) Technological determinism (i.e. lack of social cues)
	Weak	(3) Social constructivism Social capital	(4) Networked individualism Relationship reconfiguration

Information age, youth, social networks   23

use of ICT, while the perspectives marked in cells (3) and (4) attribute a weak impact, if any, of technological impacts on the use and structure of online social ties (Katz and Rice, 2002a; Haythornthwaite, 2005; Hampton and Wellman, 2018).

Likewise, the theories in cells (1) and (3) attribute a strong impact of social factors on the use and implications of ICT. Media richness theory, for example, takes into account the technological characteristics in relaying complex information among users, while also accounting for the human capacity to discern complex social communication.

The theories in cell (1) implicitly assume a strong impact of social embeddedness on ICT as well as the undeniable qualities of ICT in fostering the expansion of adolescents' social relations. The last cell (4) does assume some impact of both technological and social factors on online social factors, yet these two factors are not considered very strong. Networked individualism and relationship reconfiguration (treated at length in Chapter 6) constitute key elements of the information age for people's choices of relational quality and communication, and for their construction of social networks. Certainly, sociological variables affect adolescents' choices, but they can choose communication and friendship ties with far fewer constraints than before the diffusion and the domestication of ICTs in classrooms, families, and households. Young people's ability to choose among many ties, to form, maintain, and expand their social networks, and to widen flows of communication with close friends has become possible only with the emergence and broad applicability of ICTs.

Summary

In this chapter, we reviewed technological and social views of the ICT regarding the presumed association of technology and social relationships. We surveyed the literature on the spread of the information society, and the emergence of the network society which is accompanied by a new manner of social awareness and relational management: networked individualism. As adolescence is a sensitive and critical developmental life stage, we briefly described how adolescents' involvement with Internet activity is embedded in family tension. Further, we explained how youth and adolescents are using their social ties, using concepts drawn from social network theory. Finally, we explained how the structural nature of social networks and the attributes of social ties create online social diversification.

2 The Internet at home

Introduction

It is a widespread belief that the Internet causes family tensions. In this chapter we describe the impact of the adoption of the Internet in families with adolescents. The discussion rests on the concept of family boundaries and family cohesion which accords well with the diversification approach we developed in Chapter 1, capturing the nature of changes in the family system and peer relations. Following the conceptual consideration, we review research findings on the implications of the Internet at home for parent–adolescent relationships. In the final part of this chapter, we treat family adjustment, discussing the concept of family mediation and the different strategies that parents use to control family boundaries.

The rise in the use of information and communication technologies, including social networks platforms, in society has stimulated research on how these new technologies are associated with everyday life in general and family life specifically. Scholars have studied the relationship of new information and communication technologies and the extent of community involvement and participation (Hampton, 2016; Mesch and Talmud, 2010), and interpersonal relations, sociability, and social capital (Nie, Hillygus, and Erbing, 2002; McPherson, Smith-Lovin, and Brashears, 2006; Vriens and Van Ingen, 2018). Despite this large body of research on the ways in which communities, organizations, and individuals adapt to new communication and information technologies, the existing research literature on the impact of computer technologies on the family is relatively limited (Watt and White, 1994; Hughes and Hans, 2001; Mesch 2006; see Carvalho, Francisco, and Relvas, 2015, for a comprehensive review). This is quite surprising, as the incorporation of computer technologies into the home is a complex process in which the consumer plays an active role, involving multifaceted decision-making processes in determining modes of selection, acceptance, and familiarization of ICT (Silverstone

The Internet at home   25

and Haddon, 1996). During this "domestication process." "new technologies and services, by definition to a significant degree unfamiliar, and therefore both exciting but possibly also threatening and perplexing, are brought (or not) under control by and on behalf of domestic users" (Silverstone and Haddon, 1996: 60). In fact, the notion of domestication implies a two-way process: the family needs to adjust to technologies, and this, in turn, affects family interaction patterns. In this chapter, we focus on the potential effects of ICTs on the family and on the ways in which families cope with the new technology (Hertlein, 2012).

The family system and ICT

Here we draw on the conceptual framework developed by Watt and White (1994), who take a family development and human ecology approach to the study of the effects of ICTs on the family. These effects are assumed to depend on family functioning and communication that ultimately affect family patterns, boundaries, and cohesion (Carvalho et al., 2015). All these processes might differ according to the family's developmental stage (Watt and White 1994), as the following examples show. The communication aspect of the Internet and social media can support the process of mate selection, where individuals who have never met before can establish a close and intimate relationship; during pregnancy the couple can rely on online information and online forums to acquire health-related information and advice; at the stage of early preschool children, participation in a community bulletin board may provide the family with help in babysitting and finding activities for children (Mesch and Levanon, 2003); and in the post-parenting age, when adult children have left home, computers may facilitate family communication as they provide a new channel for family members to communicate and share experiences through email, Instant Messaging, or SNS (social networking sites). Of particular interest is the use of popular smartphone applications (i.e., WhatsApp) for extended family communication. Extended families refers to families, consisting of family members representing two or more generations who may live in the same or different households (Rudi et al., 2015). Family WhatsApp groups offer a particular channel to maintain and nurture stronger family ties whether near or afar, providing both synchronous and asynchronous modes of communication, supporting being in touch with the family, despite busy individual daily agendas and timetables. These affordances of closed WhatsApp chat groups resonate well with the particularities of contemporary extended families, which tend to be geographically dispersed, less hierarchical, and change their composition over time. More to the point, these affordances have made WhatsApp a

26   *The Internet at home*

very fit medium for one-to-group communication, and allow constant family connectivity.

A study that investigated the use of WhatsApp in Finland, Italy, and Slovenia, found that WhatsApp is considered to facilitate family interaction across generations. The success of WhatsApp in the extended family context is accounted for by two main factors: first, the possibility of reaching the whole family at once; and, second, its capacity to promote short message communication and sharing of pictures, short movies, and voice messages. While utilizing various communicative modalities of WhatsApp (text and voice messages, photos, videos), family members take into account others' preferences and communication skills. The use of the application increases the frequency of being connected across generations and distance, supporting the identity of the extended family and the close ties with uncles and grandparents (Taipale and Farinosi, 2018).

Interesting enough as technology evolves and new applications are being used, there is a more equalizing role in family systems. A study on the use of WhatsApp for intergenerational family relationships reported that it seems that WhatsApp provides a functional platform for facilitating intergenerational communication, especially between young people and their late-middle-aged parents and grandparents, as it allows the whole family to be reached at once. As parents have begun sending photos, video clips, and voice messages, it can even be argued that WhatsApp is marking a shift away from the straightforward division between "texting teenagers" and their "talking parents," and facilitating in a closed family group more equal communication as each generation can make use of the skills it feels most comfortable with (Taipale and Farinosi, 2018). In family WhatsApp communication, social bonding via multiple modalities, such as short text messages, photos, and video clips, often appears as a superior form of communication to the exchange of messages with a high information value. In dyadic family relations, WhatsApp's many modalities permits the choice of the most desired and most suitable mode of communication for every family member individually.

However, the picture is not always clear-cut, when it comes to parent–child use of ICT for family communication. Studies that investigated family communication preferences of parents and children report the difficulties of cell phones and text messages communication when children are outside the home. It seems that parents prefer to use cell phones to check with their children when they are outside the home. This communication is initiated by parents with the aim of soliciting information about their child's whereabouts, activities, and peers. One interesting finding is the mismatch of preferences of parents and children. While the parents express a clear preference for a cell phone voice communication, youth reported avoiding voice calls and their preference is to communicate with their parents through text messaging. Youth felt that parents excessively use cell phone conversations to monitor their activities, for that reason, they prefer text messaging, as those messages tend to be shorter and less intrusive (Racz, Johnson, Bradshaw, and Cheng, 2017). Youth express concerns regarding parental intrusiveness through Facebook. Several participants indicated that they have accepted requests to be "friends" with their parents, but linked this request with their concerns that parents have done this to control their activities and content of their Facebook profile pages (Racz, Johnson, Bradshaw, and Cheng, 2017).

A second example has to do with the friending and unfriending of parents on social networking sites. In recent years, both youth and adults have been increasingly using social networking sites (SNS). For example, in the age group 50–64, 56 percent report having a profile on Facebook (Dugan and Brenner, 2013). The widespread adoption of SNS in this age category has resulted in parents connecting with their children as "friends" online (Madden, Cortesi, Gasser, Lenhart, and Duggan, 2013). This new form of connection between parents and children has prompted researchers to investigate the motivation for friending, the extent to which the parent–child connection influences children's perceptions of parental invasions of their privacy (Guerrero and Affifi, 2013), and the behavioral outcomes for teens of connecting with their parents such as relational aggression and internalizing of behavior (Coyne, Padilla-Walker, Day, Harper, and Stockdale, 2014). Some studies have shown that in requesting to friend their children, parents are motivated more by concerns about their children's online activities rather than using SNS as a family communication channel (Ruppel, Tricia, and Burke, 2015). In addition, many of studies on the effect of parent–child connections on SNS have tended to focus on college students (cf. Juhaňák, 2019). Parents learn about their children's activities in two ways: from parental controls and by voluntary disclosures from their children. Parental monitoring or control refers to the extent of knowledge that parents have about what their children are doing, or with whom they are associating. It includes parental solicitation, asking their children's friends and other adults about their children's activities, and parents imposing rules and restriction on their children's activities and associations (Smetana, 1988; Stavrinides, Nikiforou, and Georgiou, 2015; Wang, Zhao, and Shadbolt, 2019). Monitoring online activities involves checking the websites their children visit; using software to block, filter, or monitor their children's activities and restricting the amount of time that youth use the Internet (Sasson and Mesch, 2014, 2016, 2017; Wang, Zhao, and Shadbolt, 2019).

28 The Internet at home

An increasing percentage of adolescents report that at least one of their parents has befriended them on SNSs. This connection implies that some of the adolescents' online behavior is open to parental scrutiny (boyd et al., 2011). More important, it should be understood that the presence of a parent as a connection of his or her child on an SNS is a new form of child disclosure and parental control, and in some form is reshaping and expanding the norms of parental monitoring and youth autonomy. In contrast to monitoring, child disclosure refers to the children providing information to their parents about their online activities and social interactions freely and willingly (Mesch, 2018b). Acceptance of the request to be a "friend" provides the parents the opportunity to observe their children's activities on the SNS, including their posted pictures, their written comments on their wall, and the reactions of others' posted comments. In addition, it provides the parents with the opportunity to learn who their children's online friends are and to see the type of content to which they are exposed.

A pertinent conceptual framework, highlighting the effect of ICT on family ties, is human ecology theory. Watt and White (1994) employ this theory, which perceives human development as taking place within the context of relationships. According to this perspective, the family is a social system with permeable borders, and technology is conceived as a major source of change. Technological innovations enter the family, creating changes in norms and social roles. A simple example is the need to accommodate the computer and to find space for the machine. While parents usually prefer to place media in the public spaces of the household, adolescents would rather locate it in their bedroom (Horst, 2008). A second example that we have just presented is the way parent–children friending on social networks' platforms changes the dimension of parental monitoring and children's disclosure of online and offline behaviors (Sasson and Mesch, 2014). The bedroom has a special meaning for adolescents as a place where they can conduct private activities. In that sense, arranging their room according to their needs, consuming their preferred media, and decorating the room with symbols of youth culture are exercises in autonomy.

Nevertheless, the direct observation of the children's online behavior might have disadvantages and become a source of tension between parents and young people seeking autonomy (West, Lewis, and Currie, 2009; Kanter, Afifi, and Robbins, 2012). Adolescence is a period in which social relationships outside the family expand and include the peer group. An important developmental task in adolescence is the gradual attainment of autonomy from direct parental control of the teenagers' social behavior (Kerr, Stattin, and Burk, 2010). Social interactions with peers provide a forum or space for learning and refining the socio-emotional skills needed during relationships. Adolescents whose parents befriend them may perceive a reduction in their sense of control over their online activities and even an invasion of their private information. They may even feel a need to censor what they write in an attempt to shield information from their parents (Kanter et al., 2012). Thus, there are arguments on both sides regarding the benefits and disadvantages of attempts to protect children. In a recent study, Mesch (2018b), conducting secondary analysis of parent-child data from the US, found significant differences between parents who befriend their children, and the ones who do not. Parents who are friends with their children on a SNS tend to be found among parents of younger children, among married parents more than single parents, among parents with lower education, and children who befriend their parents are found among children who have a public profile on the SNS.

New information is converted into new functions, and one possible result is specialization as children sometimes acquire computer skills rapidly and take on the role of advisors and aids to other family members. This specialization involves changes in the nature of the relationships in the family subsystem, as knowledge is often reflected in doing tasks for the parents and at the same time monopolizing computer time.

According to the family developmental-ecological approach, the family is a relatively closed social system and the Internet is a technology that has "opened a hole in the fence of the family" (Daly, 1996: 82). This conceptualization of the family emphasizes the importance of family boundaries as reflected in the need for privacy and family time as a functional requirement for the effective operation of the family system (Berardo, 1998). The boundaries between the family and the external world are important and necessary to preserve the parental role of socialization, and the nuclear family provides clear-cut, often rigid, boundaries between public and private life and between children and adults (Elkind, 1994). Strong family relationships evolve through an awareness of boundaries between family members and the rest of the world. In their lives together, parents and children negotiate ideas about how and why they are similar to and different from each other, and from other families and people (Berardo, 1998).

Following the developmental-ecological approach rather than discussing the family in general, we now focus on one stage of the family life-cycle: families with adolescents. In this stage, parents' and adolescents' relationships center on issues of family boundaries, parental authority, adolescent autonomy, and expansion of the adolescents' social circles (Fuligni, 1998; Smetana, 1988).

30 *The Internet at home*

The developmental-ecological approach is consistent with the diversification approach taken in this book. ICTs are conceived as an agent of change in society because they support the rapid creation, diffusion, and access to information and the formation and maintenance of social networks (Rogers, 1995; DiMaggio et al., 2001; Lin, 2001; Centola, 2015). At the center of the diversification approach is a conceptualization of the Internet as a space of activity and social interaction. One innovative aspect of the Internet is to provide opportunities for activities that induce social interaction. The Internet provides a space for playing online games, presenting a public identity through the creation of a public profile in a social networking site, accessing information, connecting with new acquaintances, maintaining family and friendship relationships, and meeting new individuals. Through participation in interactive games, groups are formed, interaction is recurrent, and names and phone numbers are exchanged. Teenagers' social network sites are used for sharing information, providing and receiving advice, social support, and creating opportunities for social interaction and involvement. It is not uncommon for teens who know each other to introduce friends or family members to other friends and family members, creating opportunities for social interaction with new acquaintances. Moreover, the introduction of new media in smartphones has intensified the usage of adolescents in texting and sharing contents with their peers, potentially displacing time spent with family members.

Family boundaries and information

The introduction of ICTs into the home creates tensions in the perception of the family boundaries, both external and internal. As to the former, ICTs hold the promise of moving many activities (such as working, learning, and shopping) that were dispersed by industrial society back into the home (Tapscott, 1998: 251). The boundary between work and family has become blurred as people increasingly work from home or are asked to be available through mobile devices at home for work (Silverstone and Haddon, 1996; Valcour and Hunter, 2005).

While this allows the family more time together, there is a danger that work activities will interfere with family time (Chesley, 2005). The Internet and cell phones provide the opportunity of continuous contact with work when one is at home, and with family when one is at work. This technological affordance has been linked to the blurring of boundaries between work and home which is assumed to increase the stress on family relations. A study in Australia tested the extent that the use of ICTs was perceived as affecting the work–family life balance. It found

The Internet at home 31

that the use of cell phones affected the perception of spillover of family life into work time but not that of spillover of work activities into family life (Wajcman, Bittman, and Brown, 2008).

Since the early studies, mobile communication has become more integrated into the everyday life of individuals, families, and workers. It is interesting to see how this integration might change the early studies over time. Recent studies indicate that indeed this result is apparently dependent on the extent of the integration of cell phone mobile technologies into the individual everyday life. Those who have a high level of integration and more frequent work-related smartphone use during off-job time are associated with better family role performance through reduced work–family conflict. For those with a low level of integration of technology into their everyday activities, smartphone use may have an impact on work–family conflict and family role performance. These findings suggest that for integrators, smartphone use during off-job time may be useful to simultaneously meet both work demands and family demands, which has the potential to reduce work–family conflict and enhance family role performance (Derks et al., 2016).

An additional tension with implications for family boundaries is that ICT use exposes adolescents to greater amounts of information, covering any topic, anytime, anywhere. Multicommunication and perpetual connectivity have led to a communication with a multitude of weak and strong ties, and disclosure of personal and intimate information that can be shared worldwide. This can lead to situations of loss of family control in virtual interactions, and subsequent family conflicts: the disconnection between verbal and non-verbal signals can result in misunderstanding or family members in the same house becoming isolated from each other instead of establishing personal connections (Carvalho and Relvas, 2015).

ICT has the potential to modify the permeability of family boundaries due to the change in flow of information. The family gains unrestricted access to a diversity of information blending the external world with the family environment. Boundaries between the family and the environment and the external world are relevant and necessary, but are being blurred. Also through the use of the boundary metaphor, communication privacy management theory illustrates the way people manage their privacy, personally and in their relationships.

For the most part, this information is very important as it supports schoolwork and homework. Yet, a central concern for parents is that adolescents are more exposed today to negative content as well, and the impact of this exposure might be serious for a number of reasons. First, adolescents are the most frequent users of the Internet and mobile communication for both information search and communication purposes.

32   *The Internet at home*

Second, adolescence is a developmental period characterized by identity formation. In the creation of this identity, youth search for answers to existential problems, and in doing so they might be exposed to wrongful information or information that is at odds with the family's values. Third, adolescence is a period of expansion of the peer group and high involvement in social relationships, which might expose the youth to other risks such as harassment and online bullying, a topic that will be expanded in Chapter 7.

As for unwanted content, a major worry arising from the increase of Internet access at home has become adolescents' exposure to pornographic content. The ease of access and the abundance of pornographic content on the Internet tend to increase anxiety about the harmful influence of Internet pornography on minors. Pornography is perceived as more accessible to minors through the Internet than in its traditional forms (Greenfield, 2004). Pornography is the term most often used for sexually explicit content that is primarily intended to arouse audiences sexually (Malamuth and Impett, 2001).

A recent review of the literature has shown that from the large number of studies reviewed a picture emerges that explains adolescents' exposure to pornography as a combination of both personality and family characteristics (Peter and Valkenburg, 2016). Adolescents who used pornography more frequently were male, at a more advanced pubertal stage, sensation seekers, and had weak or troubled family relations. Less commitment to the family (Mesch, 2009), poor family functioning in general, and specifically less mutuality in family functioning (Shek and Ma, 2014) were all associated with a stronger use of pornography. The same was true for a poor emotional bond with the caregiver and a caregiver who used coercive discipline. In addition, family conflict and poor family communication were related to more pornography use on the Internet and in traditional media, albeit mediated by less positive youth development (Ma and Shek, 2013).

The literature suggests a number of negative effects of frequent and long-term exposure to this material (Peter and Valkenburg, 2016). First, it leads to more liberal sexual attitudes and greater belief that peers are sexually active, which increases the likelihood of first intercourse at an early age (Flood, 2007). Second, adolescents exposed to sexual behaviors outside cultural norms may develop a distorted view of sex as unrelated to love, affection, and intimacy, and a desire for emotionally uncommitted sexual involvement (Byrne and Osland, 2000). Third, youth exposed to pornography may develop attitudes supportive of the "rape myth," which ascribe responsibility for sexual assault to the female victim (Flood, 2007; Seto, Maric, and Barbaree, 2001). Studies on the extent of youth exposure to pornography have focused on "chance" or unwanted Internet exposure to pornographic material (Greenfield, 2004; Livingstone and Bober, 2005). Chance exposure is the receipt of pornographic material by email and pop-ups, and reaching sites with pornographic content fortuitously in the course of a search for material for homework. An implicit assumption is that the wide availability of X-rated material on the Internet and through commercials results in involuntary exposure to this content (Greenfield, 2004). Results of these studies show that exposure by chance is frequent with between 10–30 percent of youth reporting it (Wolack et al., 2003).

Another risk is exposure to online hate content (websites), inciting violence against, separation from, defamation of, deception about, or hostility toward others based on race, religion, ethnicity, gender, or sexual orientation. The web is a unique medium that facilitates the dissemination of hate messages in a variety of forms, from cartoons and jokes to pseudo-educational narratives, and the use of multimedia. Frequent exposure to hate might result in the adoption of stereotypes, attitudes supporting racism, lack of empathy for minorities, aggressive behavior, and involvement in hate crimes. From the research literature it appears that despite the wide availability of hate sites, only 20 percent of adolescents report having been exposed to content that advocates hatred of minorities. Of those who were exposed, more than a third (36 percent) reacted by ignoring the site and its content. Another third of them had informed a friend or an adult about the site (MNET, 2001).

An additional concern for parents is that youngsters using the Web might convey information about themselves and their families to marketers, enabling them to create detailed profiles of a family's lifestyle (Turow and Nir, 2000). Accurate or not, such portraits can influence how marketers treat family members; for example, what discounts to offer them, what materials to send them, how much to communicate with them, and even whether to deal with them at all.

Parental concerns are reinforced when certain technological characteristics of the Internet are considered. The Internet has been portrayed as conducive to deviant behavior because of its use in isolation from others, as opposed to consumption of other media, which are found in the presence and even with the collaboration of others. The relative anonymity of the medium may promote activities that an individual does not usually engage in when he/she is part of a group, where members tend to conform to culturally accepted behavior (Pardum, L'Engle, and Brown, 2005).

In sum, Internet use for the search of information presents a challenge to family boundaries as it increases the unsupervised exposure of adolescents to a wide variety of content. Much of this content is important, for

34   *The Internet at home*

Table 2.1 Summary of Internet effects on external family boundaries

Blurring of family's external boundaries	Weakening of parental control of information that family members have access to, and of access by external agencies to family information	Blurring of the boundary between work and family life. Work interferes with family activities such as meals together, conversations, and games. Family life interferes with work activities.
		Time displacement from family activities to individual-centered Internet activities
		Youth access to Internet information including violent, hate and pornographic content
		Providing information on family consumption patterns to commercial sites

example, in supporting homework and searching for answers to existential issues. Yet this increased exposure might blur family boundaries, creating tensions (Table 2.1). The convergence of telecommunications, the Internet, and new social media has lowered the thresholds of technological domestication and raised the challenges of family boundary maintenance. Families deal with these tensions and try to adjust to the new challenges that Internet access poses by using technological and social devices to mediate adolescents' exposure. Later on in this chapter we will present the strategies used by families to exert control over family borders and to restrict access to unwanted information by youth.

The Internet and family time

Family cohesion is defined as the "emotional bonding that family members have toward one another" (Olson, Russell, and Sprenkle, 1983: 60). This means a positive involvement of parents with their children, as reflected in shared activities, supportive behavior, and affection. The beneficial implications of family cohesion for children's behavior and development enjoy strong support in the social sciences. Adolescents who report being close to their parents show higher achievements at school, fewer episodes of truancy and school dropout, and fewer cases of seeking medical care for emotional or behavioral problems (Amato and Rivera, 1999).

Family time can be seen as a central dimension of both family cohesion and family boundary construction and preservation. If we think of families as social systems having a collective identity, that identity is the result of shared recollections of togetherness created as family members spend time together in shared meals, games, and chatting (Daly, 1996). In Western societies many families struggle with the concept of family time. In the dual career family, in which the boundaries of work and home are blurred, family time is sometimes the sharing of space and time that arises from the intersection of busy lives (Daly, 1996).

Although the ideal of private family time continues to be salient as a cultural ideal, a variety of forces impede the realization of this goal. With the proliferation of technology at home, families seem to be at the crossroads of two different tracks: one that provides them with many opportunities for shared activity within the home and another that easily distracts them into the solitary world of technology that demands their individual attention (Wajcman et al., 2008; Derks et al., 2016). Studies have shown that the time a family spends together in activities such as recreation are positively related to family cohesion (Orthner and Mancini, 1991). An early large-scale study in the US on Internet use in families with adolescents found that members of all the families explicitly stated how much they valued spending time together. Many families scheduled time to watch TV shows, movies, and videos together. That is, parents and adolescents conceived the shared consumption of media as facilitating communication and bonding (Horst, 2008). A small but growing proportion of the families with adolescents increased family time, with parents engaging in the co-production of media together with their teenage children.

In this way, those adolescents working with the support of parents learn new skills of multimedia production; From the parents' side, they described these activities as becoming more involved in their children's interests and culture (Horst, 2008). Shared activities are depicted as forces, contributing to clarifying and strengthening family boundaries because they create opportunities for interaction, communication, and memories that contribute to the perception of the identity and uniqueness of one's family (Hofferth and Sandberg, 2001; Zabrieskie and McCormick, 2001).

A second explanation is time displacement, as it has been argued that Internet use is negatively associated with family time. The main argument is that time spent on one activity cannot be spent on another (Nie et al., 2002). Internet use is a time-consuming activity, and in families that are connected to the Internet, high frequency of use might be negatively

36 *The Internet at home*

associated with family time and positively associated with family conflict. In fact, parents and adolescents have worried that Internet use might have a negative effect on family communication and closeness (Turow and Nir, 2000; Jackson et al., 2003). This concern received limited verification, mainly from studies conducted at the early stages of diffusion of the technology into the home. A study based on family time diaries found that Internet use at home was negatively related to time spent with family. Furthermore, the reduction in family time was higher for the average Internet user than for the average TV watcher (Nie et al., 2002). The perception that the amount of daily Internet use might affect family time is expressed by both parents and adolescents. A study in the US of a sample of youth and parents found that 29 percent of parents believed that online time interfered with family time, while only 16 percent of teens believed so (Rosen et al., 2008). Another study conducted among a large sample of adolescents reported that Internet use did not help them improve their relationships with their parents, and that the Internet consumed time they would have spent with their families (Lenhart, Rainie, and Lewis, 2001).

Williams and Merten (2009) in two studies explored the use of several technologies for adolescents and their parents in order to verify the impact of these technologies on the family connection and parent–child dynamics. On the one hand, ICT is perceived by parents as facilitating family closeness and increasing the quality of communication. On the other hand, the large variety of ICT channels, and the dramatic increase in usage frequency arguably seem to be related to a reduction in family time and intimacy between family members, leading to the isolation of those who live in the same house.

Some research focuses on the reduction of time spent as a family. One interesting approach is to define family time as active versus passive time. In passive family time, the family does not actively do anything specific, but is just being there, while communication time includes only the active family time. Using the two measures of time, Lee and Chae (2007) found, against the common popular belief, that the total time that families spend on Internet use is associated with a decrease in family time, but not in active communication time. The decrease is due to the online activity performed by children.

A typical approach to alleviate the effects of the technology use, in particular, smartphones, on family time has been the creation of rules of technology usage. This approach is also known as "restrictive mediation" (see end of the chapter). A study on the family rules, that included separate reports of children and parents, identified two general types of rules: contextual rules and activity rules (Hiniker, Schoenebeck, and Kientz, 2016). Activity rules refer to rules created by parents that include the right of parents to check children's phone activity, forbid the production or distribution of sexually explicit media, and request the child to be polite in its interactions. Contextual rules indicate when and where is allowed the use of technology and include rules that forbid the use at night, with fixed time limits of use. The study investigated rule compliance and found that the type of rule affects the ability of the children to follow the rule. Children were significantly more likely to follow rules about activity constraints than about context constraint. Thus, children reported that it was easier to comply with rules that restrict them to particular technology activities than rules that prohibit them from using technology at all, even for short periods of time (such as during a family meal). When asking parents on the difficulties in enforcing the rules, adults agreed with the children and reported that they have to put much more effort enforcing context constraints than activity constraints and that children are less likely to comply with such rules. Parents reported that there is no difference between them and the children in the awareness of family expectations of context constraints compared to activity rules. Yet the inability of children to disconnect themselves from technology in certain contexts is a source of tension in families (Hiniker et al., 2016; Wang, Zhao, and Shadbolt, 2019).

A second change is a change in the hierarchy of authority, as technology might change this hierarchy because of the children becoming the technological gurus. Carvalho et al. (2016) draw attention to the fact that the tasks of adolescence, such as negotiation of autonomy and independence became a central issue of teen technology interactions. The empirical evidence appears to point to an enhancement of the development of technological abilities by young people which tends to increase the digital gap between generations and to deflect parental authority, by questioning the rules and values that they try to transmit.

However, before reaching a conclusion, we should keep in mind that time spent with parents decreases as the youngster becomes older. This is the result of social development: the older the adolescent, the more likely he or she is to spend more time with peers than with parents. Therefore, studies need to control for age. Such a study was conducted among a representative sample of Israeli adolescents, investigating how the amount of daily Internet use by adolescents was related to family time and cohesion. The relation was found to be negative. This result was statistically signficant even after controlling for types of Internet use, age, and number of siblings (Mesch, 2006).

While these studies provide evidence for a relationship between Internet use and a reduction in family time, they treat the Internet as a unified technology. Youth differ in the extent they use the Internet

38   *The Internet at home*

for communication, information search, and entertainment, and different uses probably have different effects on family time. Studies on the association between different types of youth Internet use and family time found evidence that Internet use decreased the amount of time youth spent with their families. Notably, different youth activities had different effects. Playing online games decreased both the total time spent with the family and the time communicating with family members. Using the Internet for communication with friends resulted in a small decrease in family time. However, using it for educational purposes, such as searching for homework or doing homework, did not affect family time (Lee and Chae, 2007).

Despite this evidence of a negative effect of youth Internet use on family time, the overall picture is more complex because of generational effects. At the early stages of family ICT domestication, parents and children faced a generational divide, a gap in technology skills, where children were more likely to possess better skills than their parents. Today many more young parents have acquired the skills needed to use the Internet in complex activities. This trend is reflected in a number of studies that suggest that rather than isolating children from their parents, the Internet has become a shared household activity (Kaiser Family Foundation, 2003). However, as another study shows, the extent that parents share time consuming and producing media with adolescents depends on parents' education and computer skills. Parents with less education and low computer skills are more likely to perceive the Internet as a force that isolates them from their children (Horst, 2008).

In sum, most of the empirical evidence on the association between Internet use and family time shows a reduction in the time parents and youth spend together (Rosen et al., 2008; Mesch, 2006; Lenhart, Rainie, and Lewis, 2001). This evidence remains firm even when youth age is controlled, indicating the existence of an Internet effect on family time. Recent studies indicate that Internet use by youth for social and entertainment purposes has a more pronounced effect than its use for information search and homework (Lee and Chae, 2007).

ICTs and parent–adolescent conflict

Family time is negatively associated with family conflict. Cross-sectional and longitudinal studies have shown that low levels of family time were associated with higher levels of conflict (Fallon and Bowles, 1997; Dubas and Gerris, 2002). Apparently, families that share time in common activities enjoy a higher quality of communication which facilitates discussion of disagreements before they become open conflicts.

The Internet at home   39

There is some concern that Internet access in the household may negatively affect patterns of interaction between parents and children, increasing intergenerational conflicts and weakening family cohesion (Watt and White, 1994; Lenhart et al., 2001).

Families are social systems characterized by a hierarchy of authority. The introduction of the computer has the potential to change that hierarchy as the adolescent becomes the family expert on whom other family members rely for technical advice and guidance (Watt and White, 1994). Under these conditions the adolescent increases his/her resources relative to the parents, and also his/her ability to dominate the family sphere. A study of computer help-seeking among 93 US families found that teenagers were more likely than parents to help others in the family. Adolescents became the experts, and when parents needed help they had to rely on information and advice from them (Kiesler et al., 2000; Carvalho, Francisco, and Relvas, 2015). Similarly, in the UK, traditional adult–child relations appear to be reversed in many households because children are more technologically competent than their parents (Holloway and Valentine, 2003). Children, thus, were able to define to a much greater degree than family members the meaning and uses of the computer and Internet in the home (Sutherland et al., 2003; Huisman, Edwards, and Catapano, 2012). Through time it appears that parents, instead of increasing their skills and extending their power to control technology, have come to struggle with the situation. A recent large-scale survey of pre-adolescents and adolescents found that in many households the Web had become work for the school-aged as parents assigned them "cyberchores." The study found that 38 percent of youth helped parents to share photos and send emails to relatives online, and 36 percent helped with parental information searches. Regarding the reasons, almost half of the teen respondents (47 percent) said they performed "cyberchores" because their parents lacked online skills; 29 percent stated that they did so because their parents did not have time to do these jobs themselves (Kidsonline@home, 2007).

Adolescence is a time when families need to adjust and adapt their relationships to accommodate the increasingly maturing adolescent. Many of their exchanges concern parents' regulation of adolescents' everyday lives, such as curfew rules, friendship relations, and personal activities such as phone and TV use (Collins and Russel, 1991). Studies on adolescents show that as they become older, they submit ever less to parental authority over aspects of their personal lives. At the same time they demand more and more autonomy and show greater readiness to disagree openly with their parents (Fuligni, 1998). Parents attempt to guide

40   *The Internet at home*

the use of the Internet by creating rules on time use, websites permitted, disclosure of personal information, and context of use of mobile technologies (Hiniker et al., 2016). Definition of rules and their enforcement appear inconsistent.

As previously mentioned, parents are likely to report that there is no difference between them and the children in the awareness of family expectations regarding activity rules of social network use such as frequency of technology use, social behavior on social network sites and refraining from disclosure of personal information online. Yet the inability of children to disconnect themselves from technology in certain contexts is a source of tension of families (Hiniker et al., 2016).

Supporting this view, there is empirical evidence that parents and adolescents perceive the rules differently. An early large-scale study of families and media showed that while parents were able to articulate the rules, children forgot to mention them or stated that their parents mentioned rules but these were open to negotiation. Parental discourse about rules very likely reflects their intentions more than actual deeds (Horst, 2008). A study of 1,124 adolescents and their parents in Singapore found discrepancies between parents' and children's reports. For example, parents reported sitting with the adolescents while they were on the Internet more often than the children did; and parents reported checking bookmarks or browser history more often than adolescents did. Parents tended to over-report the frequency of control and monitoring they exerted (Liau, Khoo, and Ang, 2008). The pattern of communication existing in the family may be an explanation for the gaps found in the perception of rules regulating the use of the Internet. In families in which parents and adolescents perceived their communication as open, empathetic, encouraging, and trusting, their reports regarding family rules on the use of media were consistent (Cottrell, Branstetter, Cottrell, Rishet, and Stanton, 2007).

Of particular importance are the domains of parent–adolescent disagreement over authority and autonomy. In one study, adolescents and parents were found to agree that parents had legitimate authority over moral issues (adolescent actions that could be harmful to others or violate mutual trust), prudential issues (smoking and drinking behavior), and friendship issues (seeing friends that parents do not like). As for personal issues, such as regulation of TV time, regulation of phone calls, and choosing clothes, adolescents regarded these as less legitimately subject to parental jurisdiction, and obedience less obligatory, than other issues (Smetana and Asquith, 1994). Furthermore, the frequency and intensity of parents' and adolescents' conflicts over personal issues proved relatively high (Smetana and Asquith, 1994).

The Internet at home 41

During adolescence, children's and parents' expectations of each other change, and gaps in these expectations can cause family conflict. Children may expect adolescence to be a time of greater freedom, and parents may expect adolescents to self-regulate their behavior, so that social and leisure activities do not interfere with school activities (Collins and Russel, 1991). Parents are aware that computers can serve as a tool to enhance academic performance. For example, word processing programs that correct spelling and provide a thesaurus can enhance language abilities. A study found that parents appreciated the new educational resources that the Internet provided to their children, yet they worried about the erosion of standards (reading short articles instead of books) and the credibility of online information (Subrahmanyam et al., 2000), and expressed concern that the Internet might distract children from other activities.

Studies exploring family interaction on media issues report that parents expected adolescents to self-regulate Internet use and to make efforts to restrict the time used in computer-related activities so that this would not interfere with school work and socializing (Pasquier, 2001; Livingstone and Bovill, 2001). Parents may perceive frequent Internet use as a violation of their expectations, and it may become a source of intergenerational conflicts.

The introduction of computers into the family has the potential to create new conflicts over authority and autonomy. Parents' concern may impel them to formulate rules on the amount of Internet use. Adolescents perceive rules as interference in personal matters and an attempt to reduce their aspirations for increased autonomy (Smetana, 1988). Computer use requires knowledge and skills, and children acquire them before their parents. The balance of family power may change as the adolescent becomes the person in the family to whom others turn for technical help. Studies have shown that when this is the case, adolescents monopolize the machine and restrict the computer use of other family members (Watt and White, 1994; Kiesler et al., 2000).

Another source of conflict is the development of expectation gaps between parents and youth. Parents seem to view the Internet as a positive new force in children's lives and surveys in different countries report that the main reason families buy computers and connect their children to the Internet at home is for educational purposes (Turow and Nir, 2000; Lenhart et al., 2001; Livingstone and Bober, 2004). Many parents believe that the Internet can help their children to do better at school, do better research for homework, and help them learn worthwhile things (Livingstone and Bober, 2004). But not all teens use the Internet in the same way. While some spend most of their Internet time searching for information, acquiring skills, and researching for homework, others mostly use it for social purposes (email, instant messaging, and

42 *The Internet at home*

participation in chat rooms) and entertainment purposes (playing games online) (Livingstone and Bober, 2004; Lenhart, Madden, Rankin, and Smith, 2007). It is plausible to assume that when youth use the Internet for social and entertainment purposes, parental expectations contradict the actual use, aggravating conflict between adolescents and parents. Conversely, using the Internet for learning and education purposes, a use highly valued by parents and consistent with parental expectations, will be negatively associated with family conflict (Mesch, 2003). Parents are concerned with the possibility that Internet activities will distract the children from school activities. Parents restrict the time they can play games and enter social network sites before schoolwork and household chores are completed (Horst, 2008).

At this point, the central questions are to what extent do these conflicts exist? And how do they compare with other prevalent conflicts in adolescence? Mesch (2007), using a representative sample of the Israeli youth population, investigated perceptions of adolescents' conflicts with their parents. He aimed at conflicts over mundane issues such as household chores and homework, and the association of Internet use with the frequency of the various types of argument. In particular, the study found that the frequency of perceived conflicts over the Internet and computers was higher than that of conflicts over school-related issues and equal to that of disagreements over household chores. The most salient finding of the multivariate analysis was that computer and Internet use exerted a generalized effect on perception of conflicts with parents. Adolescents with online friends reported a higher frequency of conflicts with parents over household chores than adolescents without online friends. The amount of Internet use was positively associated with the perception of frequent arguments over school-related issues. Finally, perception of conflicts with parents proved to be associated with older age. Older adolescents reported conflicts over household chores, school-related issues, and computer and Internet use less frequently than did younger adolescents. After identifying the association between Internet use and frequency of perceived adolescent–parent arguments, the final question of the study was whether these arguments had consequences for the young people's perception of family closeness.

The most salient result of the multivariate analysis is that arguments over the Internet and computer use have a statistically significant negative effect on family closeness (Table 2.2). Arguments over household chores and school-related issues do not undermine the relations between parents and children, while computer and Internet use does. As expected, family time is negatively related to family closeness. In sum, this study indicated that only arguments over the Internet have a negative effect on family cohesion.

The Internet at home 43

Table 2.2 Summary of Internet effects on internal family boundaries

Internal border	Effects on parents' and children's expectations and family hierarchy	Adolescents become technology experts and exercise control over computer time and location
		Parents create media rules and adolescents tend to break them
		Parents expect children to improve school performance and teens use the computer for social purposes
		Parents expect self-regulation and adolescents expect more autonomy in the use of the Internet

Family adjustment and the Internet

As we have shown in this chapter, the entry of the Internet into the home affects various spheres of family functioning. The family becomes exposed to large amounts of information (both positive and negative) that circulates inside and outside the home. Youth become exposed to new acquaintances and parental control over their friends declines. Family time and cohesion might be reduced. At the same time the family as a system attempts to adjust to the technology. One way to adjust is to incorporate the Internet as both a shared activity and a channel of communication. Is the Internet used as a shared family activity, in which children and parents use the technology together? A study conducted in a Toronto suburb investigated the extent that the Internet was used together with the respondent's spouse and children. The numbers of hours per week that was used with spouse was found to depend on the average hours a week that the respondent used the Internet. Heavy users spent 2.8 hours using the Internet with their spouses, and light users spent 1.2 hours doing so. As to using the Internet with children, the results are similar, and for individuals using the Internet more than 8 hours a week, on average 3.2 hours were spent using it together with the children (Kennedy and Wellman, 2007). In a study in the US with a representative sample of the Internet population, 54 percent of the parents reported going online with another person a few times a week. Half of them (27 percent) indicated that they go online with their children (Kennedy, Smith, Wells, and Wellman, 2008).

44 The Internet at home

An additional adjustment mechanism is the adoption of the Internet for family communication. We investigated the extent that the Internet is used in Israel for communication between spouses and between parents and children, taking a representative sample of the population of the country. We found that the cell phone had been rapidly adopted as an important channel of mediated communication between parents and between parents and children. Spouses and parents heavily rely on cell phones. Sixty-three percent of the married respondents called their partner by cell phone every day; and similarly, 51 percent of those with children aged 12–18 called them every day. Email proved much less common: only 4 percent of respondents sent an email to their spouse every day, and 1.7 percent sent an email to their children every day. Correspondingly, mobile phone calls in Canada are also the leading channel of mediated communication between spouses, and between parents and children (Kennedy and Wellman, 2007). In the US, 47 percent of couples with children who have Internet access communicate daily with their partner by cell phone, and only 8 percent sends an email daily. This is parallel to parental use: 42 percent of the couples with children 7–17 years old communicate daily by cell phone and only 3 percent send an email (Kennedy, Smith, Wells, and Wellman, 2008). A study in the UK found that 13 percent of cell phone text messages were sent to the spouse and 3 percent to family members. Gender differences were found in the use of text messages. Messages between men were shorter than those between women, and text messages from men were longer when they text women. Women write longer messages on average than men (Yates and Lockley, 2008). In Australia, a recent study found that a third of all cell phone calls were made to family members. Cell phones were used for micro-coordination of family activities, the greatest number of calls being made to get information on the time of the children's arrival home (Wajcman, Bittman, and Brown, 2008; Wajcman et al., 2010).

These studies in different countries yield a consistent picture, indicating that for families with children, their ICT and mobile phone usage is linked to the ways this new technology is integrated into their shared family activities, and fewer use the Internet for family communication. For the vast majority of families, mobile phones have been better integrated into family communication. As a shared activity, the Internet has been integrated by about a third of the families, indicating that this is certainly one form of adjusting family activities to Internet. As a family channel of communication, the Internet is well behind the cell phone, and is difficult to say if it will be integrated at all as a daily channel of mediated communication.

Parental mediation

Since the beginning of research on children's television watching, scholars have investigated the ways that potential negative effects of the media can be reduced. One important approach has been to investigate how the family regulates and mediates these potential ill-effects. Parental mediation means some form of effort by parents to do the following:

- explain media content and guide children and teens in the interpretation of its content and its relationship to the real world;
- reduce access and prevent exposure to unwanted content, and reduce interference of media consumption with educational, extracurricular, or family activities.

Parental mediation is a concept that has been extensively studied in relation to children and youth exposure to television programs. Bybee, Robinson, and Turrow (1982) studied parental media mediation and identified three dimensions:

1. Social co-viewing
2. Restrictive mediation
3. Strategic and non-strategic mediation

Social co-viewing

Social co-viewing refers to the occasions when parents and children consume media content together, sharing the experience (Valkenburg, 1999). Co-viewing may be an interactive activity, when parents and children discuss media content, or a passive activity, when all parties sit silently together in the same room, eyes focused on the screen. Through co-viewing, parents can monitor the content that youth are exposed to, and intervene if undesirable content is online. In this way co-viewing allows parents to discuss offensive content if they are so inclined. In the case of the Internet, active co-viewing can be described at the extent that youth and parents jointly use the Internet for shared activities, including playing online games, searching for information and planning vacations. In a slightly different sense, the concept describes family differences arising from the location of the computer. It is plausible to assume that when the computer is located in a family public area, its use by youngsters will be more controlled than when it is installed in youth's room (Livingstone et al., 2007).

46   *The Internet at home*

Restrictive mediation

Restrictive mediation is the formulation of rules for media consumption by young people. Families establish rules of computer time and the types of content, exerting control over what is watched. The use of rules to control viewing known as restrictive mediation can have important effects on children. A recurrent problem with investigation of rules is the extent of agreement on their existence. Various studies have reported that measures of restrictive parental mediation are not reliable, because parents and children offer conflicting reports about computer and Internet rules (Livingstone, 2007; Livingstone and Helsper, 2007). Moreover, parents tend to report their existence more than their children; parents' responses most probably reflect social desirability effects. In the specific case of the Internet, two types of restrictive mediation have been used. One is the imposition of rules to limit the amount of time and the types of websites that parents allow. The other is installation in the computer of technological devices that restrict the web pages that can be accessed and software that informs parents of the web pages visited by their children (Eastin, Greenberg, and Hofschire, 2006; Sasson and Mesch, 2014, 2016, 2017). Yet research indicates that restrictive mediation is not always effective. More specifically, it seems that its effectiveness decreases with age (Valkenberg and Piotrowski, 2017: Chapter 14).

Strategic and non-strategic mediation

Strategic and non-strategic mediation means making deliberate judgments about media content (strategic) or casual comments about media in general (non-strategic) (Eastin et al., 2006). In this case, parents discuss different websites with children, show them techniques to check the reliability of the information given by a website, discuss the process involved in information creation and the relationship of the content to the real world, and are actively involved in their children's use of the Internet.

Studies are starting to provide evidence on the extent that parental mediation is used to regulate children's and youngsters' exposure to the Internet. Regarding co-viewing, there is some empirical evidence that this is an effective technique. A study of youth in Korea found that parental recommendation of websites and co-viewing were positively related to educational online activities. That is, the more parents recommended websites for their children and the more they used the Internet together, the more frequently children searched the Internet for educational material for homework and played educational games (Lee and Chae, 2007). A recent study of teens who had profiles on social networking sites found that parenting style and mediation affected adolescent Internet behavior. Teenage children of parents who set limits and monitored online activities were less likely to disclose information in MySpace (Rosen, 2007).

There is a sense that parental mediation has intensified over time. A study of teens and parents in the US found that most parents of teenagers who go online set time limits on their Internet activities. While in 2000, only 41 percent of parents had installed filtering software on home computers, in 2005, the figure was 54 percent. In both years, 2000 and 2005, the same percentage of parents (62 percent) reported checking the websites that their children visited. In 2006, 69 percent of parents reported having rules about how much time the child can spend online, 85 percent had rules on the kinds of personal information the child could share, and 85 percent had rules on the kind of websites that their children may or may not visit (Lenhart et al., 2007). Similar findings are reported in a study in Canada. Comparing findings for 2001 and 2005, the survey found that in 2005 the percentage of parents reporting rules was higher for all rules, indicating an increase over time in parental awareness of the need to monitor and set rules on their youngsters' online behavior. This study also investigated the effect of the rules, comparing online behavior of youth from homes with and without rules. The findings indicate that teens from the former were less likely to visit non-permitted sites than youth from the latter. Furthermore, the amount of time spent by youth online depended on the existence of a rule. Children of grades 10–11 from families without any rules spent an average of 3.8 hours a day online; the figure for youth from families with rules was 2.5 hours (Media Awareness Network, 2005).

The type of parental strategy used depends on the parenting style, of which four have been singled out: authoritarian, authoritative, permissive, and neglectful. Authoritarian parents place a high level of demands on their children and a low level of warmth, and restrict autonomy. Authoritative parents monitor and impart clear rules for their children's behavior, but provide a high level of warmth and allow for autonomy. Permissive parents are low in demands on their children, are responsive to their needs, and provide high levels of autonomy. Permissive parents are non-traditional and lenient, and allow considerable self-regulation and avoid confrontation (Eastin et al., 2006). Authoritative parents use evaluative and restrictive mediation techniques more than authoritarian and neglectful parents. Blocking of sites was practiced by authoritarian, authoritative, and permissive parents. Parental mediation was associated with age, and the older the child, the less it was applied (Eastin et al., 2006). More evidence of a link between parenting style and media use comes from a US study of parents and teens. The study focused on youth who participated in social

48   *The Internet at home*

networking sites, and investigated the influence of parental styles on their online behavior. Authoritative parents proved the most likely to view their teens' social networking page, followed by authoritarian and permissive parents. Authoritative and authoritarian parents were more likely to set limits on computer behavior (Rosen, 2007). Thus, the link between parenting style and parents' rule-setting and monitoring seems to be strong; but other factors are at work as well. Wang, Bianchi, and Raley (2005) investigated the correlates of parental rules (Sasson and Mesch, 2014, 2016, 2017). A multivariate analysis was conducted on Internet rules, checking websites and monitoring software. Teens' age was found a highly significant predictor of Internet rules and monitoring software. Parents subjected older teens less often to time limits on Internet use, and were also less likely to place monitoring software on the computer. Parents' age and gender were associated with whether they checked the websites their teens visited. Older parents were less likely to check websites than younger ones, and fathers were more likely to check than mothers. Parents' education proved a significant predictor of monitoring software but not of rules. In sum, fathers, younger parents, parents who use the Internet with their children, and parents of younger teens engage in a higher level of parental monitoring (Wang, Bianchi, and Raley, 2005; see also Wang, Zhao, and Shadbolt, 2019).

Summary

In this chapter we described the process of Internet domestication. More specifically, we took a developmental-ecological approach, which conceptualizes the effect that children's and adolescents' exposure to Internet content might have on family boundaries. The effect of integration of the Internet is diverse: its increases young people's exposure to helpful content, but also to unwanted content. The latter includes non-reliable information, pornography, and hatred, which are expected to influence the youth's view of the world. Concern about content is particularly important because adolescence is a developmental stage when teens search for information that provides answers to mundane issues in which youth express interest.

After concluding that the Internet influences the permeability of the family system, our discussion went on to inquire into the extent that the technology affects internal family borders. In the second part of the chapter we turned to the effects of the Internet on parent–adolescent relations, focusing on three central dimensions: youth–parent conflict, family time, and family cohesion.

Family time is important for the development of family cohesion. It tends to dwindle after children enter adolescence, as they spend less of it with parents and more with peers (Smetana, 1988). We presented evidence that even after controlling for age, daily Internet use by youngsters has a moderately negative effect on family time. This association requires further investigation, as the results might represent a period effect. When technologies are innovative, they need time to be learnt, and this learning time may temporarily be at the expense of time of social interaction. When the technology has become integrated, the time needed for its use decreases and its effect on family time might diminish.

Likewise, the empirical evidence presented seems to indicate that Internet use is associated with an increase in conflict between parents and youngsters. This is indicated not only by studies on the sole effect of the Internet, but it is also covered by features in studies on conflict associated with Internet use, as well as other developmental conflicts between parents and youth, for instance, over school grades and household chores. Still, it is unclear from the studies what the sources of these conflicts are. There is some evidence that they may be related to the relations created online: one study showed the level of conflict to be higher for youth who reported having online friends. Such friends constitute an additional challenge to family boundaries, as parents generally exert some control over the type of friends their children have. For teens who use the Internet for relationship formation, this usage might be a source of conflict with their parents, as it threatens family boundaries, providing additional peer support and influence. Other sources of conflict have not been explicitly exposed yet. Future studies on the ways in which family communication rules are produced, as well as their violation, along with adolescents' exposure to content that is forbidden by parents are areas that require more research.

The last part of the chapter was devoted to family adjustment to the Internet, reviewing a new and growing area, namely, the application to the Internet of the concept of parental mediation, previously widely used in television studies. The concept seems relevant to the study of family efforts to adjust to and to adopt the Internet, but it seems more appropriate for the Internet's informative aspect.

More theoretical and empirical work is needed to be done before it can be transferred from television studies to Internet research especially regarding ICT use by social networks and other applications for relationship formation and maintenance. This particular social use of the Internet is the focus of Chapter 3, wherein the question of whether the Internet has an effect on youngsters' sociability is explored in detail.

3 Sociability and Internet use

Introduction

The aim of this chapter is to investigate the association between Internet use and adolescents' sociability. We take a multidimensional approach, examining how adolescents' Internet use is connected to various dimensions of sociability. Furthermore, we delve into the different aspects of the displacement hypothesis, to prepare the ground in Chapter 4 for scrutinizing the motivations for online friendship formation.

In the last decade, scholars of media consumption have described adolescents' lives as being characterized by media privatization in a multimedia environment (Livingstone et al., 2001). In Western societies young people's cultural consumption includes a large number of media artefacts such as television sets, VCRs, landline and cell phones, play stations, compact disc players, MP3 players, and computers. An important observation is that over time households tend to acquire more than one media item and privatize media consumption. Adolescents appropriate the media, and more and more media tools move from the public spaces of the household to private places—from the living room to the bedrooms; they pile up in the teenager's room. In various Western countries, children's and youngsters' bedrooms contain many of the devices listed above; this is privatization of media and it entails more and more indoor activity. These processes give rise to expectations and concerns.

The wide exposure of adolescents to these media seems to be a central cultural characteristic of a new generation, the "Net-generation," youths who have access to new information and communication technologies and are eager to acquire the skills needed to develop creative multimedia presentations and to become multimedia producers and not merely consumers (Tapscott, 1998; Prensky, 2001). Referring specifically to computers and Internet access and use, scholars have indicated that children will master language and math skills through them. For example,

Sociability and Internet use 51

word processing software with automatic error correction and grammar structure suggestions can be construed as learning tools that with practice help children and adolescents to acquire better writing skills. Software can be used to improve mathematical skills by helping the teenager in a field in which it is necessary to practice a great deal.

However, the potential negative effects of media privatization and the bedroom culture have sparked public concern. The rapid adoption by youth of numerous media artefacts raises the question of how teens manage their already busy social life. In the public and scholarly discourse, the existence of a risk has been mooted: intensive use of new media leads to "time displacement" and "activity displacement" (Lee and Kuo, 2002; Lee and Leung, 2008). Put simply, it is argued that the use of computers and the Internet requires time, which is passed at the expense of time adolescents spend with parents and peers (Kraut et al., 1998; Nie et al., 2002; Lee and Leung, 2008). Moreover, when adolescents immerse themselves in new multimedia environments, they retreat from sports and other leisure and extracurricular activities (participation in games with peers and attending meetings), which are critical for the development of their physical and social skills (Sanders et al., 2000). Public health concerns have been voiced that excessive computer use is conducive to Internet addiction and weight gain (Subrahmanyam et al., 2000; Kautiainen et al., 2005).

The displacement argument has drawn two types of criticism (Gershuny, 2003; Robinson, 2008). One is that Internet use is not necessarily at the expense of other activities. This position rejects the idea that time is a given. The Internet facilitates information search, communication, game playing, file downloading, and other activities, and thus provides a technological infrastructure for a more efficient way of conducting these activities. It is not at the expense of other activities, because technology can decrease the time required to coordinate social activities with peers and friends or for research activities for homework. According to this view, adolescents use these communication tools primarily to reinforce existing relationships, both with friends and romantic partners. More and more they are integrating these tools into their "offline" worlds, using, for example, social networking sites to get more information about new entrants into their offline world. Note that adolescents' online interactions with strangers, while not as common now as during the early years of the Internet, may have benefits, such as relieving social anxiety. Electronic communication may also be reinforcing peer communication at the expense of communication with parents, who may not be knowledgeable enough about their children's online activities (Subrahmanyam and Greenfield, 2008). The second criticism rejects the assumption that Internet use is a solitary

52   *Sociability and Internet use*

activity, conducted alone and without the involvement of others. In fact, according to this view most Internet use is social. Rather than isolating the user, the Internet facilitates interpersonal contact, so that users may actually be more socially involved than others not online. The arguments presented in this chapter have been explored partially among adult populations, and no conclusive knowledge exists about how they apply to adolescents. Furthermore, as adolescence is a crucial period in the development of social skills, any isolating effects should be taken more seriously in respect of youth. Finally, empirical findings on time and activity displacement are considered in the context of multitasking, that is, the simultaneous use of different communication channels and media.

After reviewing the most important arguments in the literature, this chapter presents in detail the available findings on the link between Internet use and sociability. The focus is on the association of Internet use with the consumption of other media, involvement in social activities, and time with peers.

The displacement hypothesis

The origin of the displacement hypothesis can be traced to the early days of television. Its main features are presented in Table 3.1. Once acquired, this medium seems to impose high demand on children's already busy schedules, and the question arose concerning how they find room for its active consumption. Regarding the Internet, at the early stages of its adoption by households it was asked if the introduction of this new medium into users' busy schedules would cause a reduction in time spent

Table 3.1 Prediction of the Internet displacement principles

Displacement principle	Definition
Functional similarity	Internet use results in less newspaper reading, less listening to radio programs, and less time watching television
Marginal fringe activities	Internet use reduce the time spent on organized activities, such as participation in extra-curricular activities and sports.
Physical and social proximity	Internet use reduces the time spent in face-to-face and phone interpersonal communication. Replaces time used in family activities.
Transformation	Old media change and adapt to Internet competition.

Sociability and Internet use 53

on other activities, social relations, and community involvement (Kraut et al., 1998; Nie et al., 2002; Kayany and Yelsma, 2000).

The notion of displacement is simple; it assumes that a new medium such as the Internet requires time, which is taken at the expense of other activities important for adolescents' social and cognitive development. In this type of analysis, a central assumption was a zero-sum relationship among the various activities.

The view was that youth and children are in a conflict situation and make decisions that result in the displacement of other activities in order to free up enough time to accommodate media consumption (Neuman, 1991).

Study of the displacement hypothesis calls for some methodological considerations. Measures of time in each activity are usually gained through individual reports. Self-report is not always reliable because of difficulties recalling how much time has been invested in each activity per day. Second, as the number of media increases and some media become integrated in a single tool, not all media activities are measured; the risk arises of some being left out. Then it is hard to know if there is displacement of, or an increase in time spent, and where the displaced time goes and where the extra time comes from.

Principles of displacement

The displacement hypothesis assumes that the type of media and activities likely to be displaced depend on several principles. According to the principle of functional similarity, youngsters will be more likely to desert media that appear to satisfy the same needs as the Internet but less effectively. Television and Internet serve an entertainment function, so by this principle Internet use might reduce the time used to watch television, read newspapers and books, listen to the radio, etc.

A second principle concerns marginal fringe activities: more casual and unstructured activities are more likely to be displaced than organized and structured ones. Unstructured activities lack specific time boundaries and have an undefined character other than spending spare time. According to this principle, Internet use may displace free play, going out with friends to hangouts, casual visiting, and time spent relaxing.

The third principle is transformation, namely, established media will come to be used in a more specialized way. With the entry of a new medium, the old medium will adapt by transforming and changing its content so as not to compete but to avoid competition. According to this principle, television will provide different content, not found on the Internet or not competing with it.

54 *Sociability and Internet use*

The last principle concerns physical and social proximity: activities will be displaced if they share the same physical space and provide less satisfaction than the Internet. According to this principle, housework chores are done in the same space where the Internet is located, but the latter provide less psychological satisfaction and will be displaced in favor of Internet use. After presenting the definition of the principles we now turn to a more detailed account of them.

Functional similarity

The study of the effect of Internet use on media consumption is important. The Internet is in itself a multimedia environment that provides access to a large variation of content. It differs from other media in that it provides access to information, news, diverse types of entertainment (music, movies, radio, games, etc.). Learning the Internet's possible effect on the use of other media requires studies in which more than one Internet use is compared with a large number of alternatives. But before we can reach any conclusions, we must distinguish early studies from late ones. Early results might have been affected by the new medium's novelty and innovation, with increased attention to these, but as time passes and the media become increasingly incorporated into the daily life of youth, the displacement effects might come back to the point of departure. Another temporal consideration is the development of the Internet itself. Not all its features were available at first, but they came into use over time.

Early studies found some indication of a media displacement effect. A study that compared adults and adolescents for self-reported use of Internet on television viewing, newspaper reading, telephone use, and family conversations found evidence of functional displacement. Time spent watching TV was found to be less for Internet users; also, scores of adults and children showed a significant difference. Children reported higher displacement effects than adults on TV viewing and phone conversations. The extent of displacement in youth was related to their Internet daily use: heavy users tended more to report displacement (Kayany and Yelsma, 2000). While this effect was also reported in other early studies (Nie et al., 2002), the kind of displacement might be more pronounced when the relative importance of each medium for individuals is taken into account. Data on respondents' rating of the importance to them of watching TV, reading newspapers, and using online media in searching for information and entertainment will most likely show stronger effects among users who in the first place rated the use of traditional media low and the use of the Internet high.

Sociability and Internet use 55

A serious limitation of the studies outlined above is their cross-sectional design. This design provides information on media use and infers displacement from comparison of group behavior. Longitudinal studies allow inference of differences in media use for the same individuals through time. In a well-designed longitudinal study, 1,251 high school students were surveyed in 1999 and 2000 for the extent of their Internet use and six other activities: television viewing, newspaper reading, radio listening, participation in sports and physical exercise, interaction with family, and socializing with friends. Increased Internet use proved associated with decrease in television viewing only. Also, changes in how these respondents perceived the importance of Internet use predicted changes in how they perceived the importance of television, newspapers, and radio as information sources. As the youngsters' perception of the Internet as an important medium increased, they reported a decrease in the importance they attached to TV and newspapers but not to radio (Lee and Kuo, 2002). With the steadily greater integration of the Internet in adolescents' daily life, and the addition of more options for activities online, we may be witnessing an effect other than displacement, namely, substitution. Ever more news sources are becoming available online, from newspapers to web portals and blogs constantly updated, as well as music clips, radio stations, and television channels. So youth might refrain from reading newspapers or watching television, preferring to conduct these same activities online rather than search for new ones. In that case, the Internet does not displace the other media but provides a new channel to media consumption online. This so-called substitution effect differs from displacement. Relatively few studies have expanded the displacement framework for the substitution one. A recent study that assessed displacement and substitution effects provides preliminary support for this claim. The more time users spent online for news and information the less they were found to spend on reading newspapers; the more time they spent online for entertainment the less they spent watching television (Lee and Leung, 2008) (Table 3.2). These preliminary results indicate the need for more investigations of this possibility.

Regarding the principle of marginal fringe, unstructured activities are more likely to be displaced than structured activities. Internet use is more likely to displace free play and going out with friends. One of the most persistent themes in the literature is the possibly narrower social world of adolescent Internet users than that of non-users. We now take a close look at the adolescents' participation in peer, leisure, and sports activities, asking whether adolescents who use the Internet are more or less likely to be involved in leisure and sports activities. To the extent that the Internet is an isolating activity, we expect to find differences between adolescents

56 *Sociability and Internet use*

Table 3.2 Examples of displacement and substitution effects

Displacement	*Substitution*
Internet use reduces the frequency of reading newspapers and books	Newspapers and books are read online
Internet use reduces the frequency of face-to-face meetings with friends	Communication with friends after school hours is carried out through Instant Messaging and social networking sites
Internet use reduces the frequency of meeting friends to play games	Video games are played regularly with friends online
Internet use reduces the use of encyclopedias and books for doing homework	Homework is done conducting online search for relevant materials for school

who do and do not use the medium in the type and amount of participation in social gatherings, sports, and evening courses.

Finally, we relate the study of social involvement and association to a quantitative dimension of friendship, and ask if adolescents who do and do not use the Internet differ in the size of their social network of close friends. After presenting the results we discuss again the extent of social participation/isolation, taking into account the contexts of adolescent involvement: peers and friends.

Participation in activities and the social development of adolescents

The development of a child from infancy to adulthood requires involvement in different social and leisure activities with others. These activities provide contexts for learning and opportunities for engagement with others (Larson and Verma, 1999; Hansen et al., 2003; Valkenburg and Taylor Pioterkiwski, 2017). Each context engages participants in a set of behaviors and rules and results in learning social skills and a body of knowledge. Activities such as play and conversation provide opportunities for developing social and emotional skills. The quantity of time spent on these activities serves as an indication of the exposure to different social experiences, with more time leading to greater absorption of the skills and knowledge of that context (Hofferth and Sandberg, 2001).

Children learn not only in formal settings such as schools. For early adolescents, play is an integral part of learning social norms and

Sociability and Internet use   57

behavior as well as school material. During play, children develop initiative, self-regulation, and social skills (Larson and Verma, 1999). Some activities are unstructured, such as playing cards, board games, and unspecified indoors and outdoor play, including computer games. Others are structured activities, such as sports programs and participation in youth groups and organizations (Pellegrini and Smith, 1998). Activities of this type are expected to promote children's academic achievement and social behavior. Activities are a central component of friendships. Youniss and Smollar (1985) found that in their close relationships, male and female adolescents enjoy activities that take them out of their homes and allow them to interact with each other independently of parental involvement or observation. These include going to movies, parties, concerts, and sports events, or just driving around or hanging out together. The nature of the activity does not seem important; what matters is that friends are together and out of the home, implying both distance from parents and association with peers. Some differences can be found between males and females. Males prefer doing things together, whereas females enjoy mostly talking together. When close friends talk, the topic is more likely to involve personal issues and problems if the friends are female than if they are male. This does not imply that friendships between adolescent males lack personal or intimate communication, but that this aspect is more characteristic of close friendships between females.

The developmental importance of participation in extracurricular and leisure activities with others for adolescents' social and academic development has been demonstrated, and the extent that Internet use interferes with this development is a central issue to be explored, which we do in the next sections of the chapter.

Finally, there are issues of personality, as individuals who report low self-esteem may be more involved in Internet use to compensate for their social anxiety (Kraut et al., 1998; Nie et al., 2002). In our study, we explored this possibility. Respondents were asked to indicate how important it was for them to spend time with their friends, how important it was to have close friends, and how important it was to have friends always willing to listen to them. Responses were given on a 4-point Likert scale from "Not important at all" to "Very important." Users and non-users showed no significant differences in the extent of pro-social attitudes, and the findings do not support the argument that Internet users are less socially oriented than non-users. Youngsters without access to the Internet in both 2001 and 2004 did not report having more or less interest in having friends than those who used the Internet.

58   *Sociability and Internet use*

The Internet and activity displacement

With the increase in Internet use by adolescents, a concern exist that Internet use may be at the expense of other social, sports, and scholastic activities. Some studies have shown that adolescents who used computers were more overweight than non-users (Attewell et al., 2003; Hughes and Hans, 2001; Attewell and Battle, 1999). Nie et al. (2002) formulated the hypothesis of activity displacement based on studies of the influence of media in the household and suggested that given time limitations, time used on the Internet is at the expense of face-to-face interaction and social participation. This argument maintains that Internet activity requires time and is conducted in solitude. Therefore, individuals connected to the Internet, particularly frequent users, will presumably report a high degree of lack of involvement in sports, leisure, and social activities conducted outside the household. The basic assumption of this model is that time spent on one activity cannot be spent on another (Nie et al., 2002). The Internet is time-consuming, and children who stay online for long spells are liable to be affected in their involvement in peer-related activities. The balance between the acquisition of Internet skills for participating in the information society and more traditional activities is an important area of discourse among academics and practitioners who research adolescents and their parents.

In our study of Israeli adolescents, we asked them to indicate the frequency of their participation in 13 activities. Answers were provided on a 5-point scale: every day, two or three times a week, one to three times a month, several times a year, not at all. By means of a principal components factor analytic technique and varimax rotation, the 13 activities were found to represent three dimensions. One was *social activities*, that is, activities usually conducted in the presence of other friends. These included going to a party at a friend's house, to discos, to the movies, to arcades and to concerts, and cruising with other friends. The second dimension was *extracurricular and sports activities*, such as taking evening courses, participating in a youth movement, and participating in sports activities. These questions were asked in two separate studies for adolescents who report using and not using the Internet, for the years 2001 and 2004. The findings were consistent, and showed that adolescents who used the Internet were more, not less, involved in most activities social in nature and conducted in the presence of others than adolescents not connected to the Internet. In both 2001 and 2004, this was the case regarding going to discos, going to the movies, and walking about with friends in the neighborhood; likewise in both years regarding extracurricular and sports activities.

Sociability and Internet use 59

But it is premature to conclude that Internet use is associated with more, not less, participation in social activities as the differences between Internet users and non-users may be due to other causes. For example, participation in some social activities, particularly extra-curricular, requires an outgoing personality or close involvement in a social network, but also the ability to pay the costs of consumption. We should explore the association of Internet use with participation in social activities after controlling for family income and parental education as proxy measures of socio-economic status. This control is important to eliminate the possibility of self-selection, meaning that at this point in the history of Internet access middle-class groups may be over-represented in its user population. Other important considerations are how close adolescents feel themselves to their parents. There are theoretical arguments that when adolescents do not feel close, and do not receive sufficient parental support, they tend to go to their friends, spend time with them, and substitute peer support for the lack of parental support.

Bearing all the above in mind, in our study of Israeli adolescents we conducted a multivariate analysis in which we tested three models for the association of Internet use with the three dimensions of adolescent activities defined above. The multivariate analysis controls for other characteristics, beyond Internet use, that might affect involvement in social and extracurricular activities and the consumption of other types of media. We found that Internet use was positively associated with participation in social activities in both years. Participation in social activities was associated with other variables as well, and the effect of these was higher than that of Internet use. Males were more likely to participate in socially organized activities than females. Socio-economic status also seemed an important factor, and participation in these activities was less frequent as mother's education was lower. As expected, in both years, individuals who reported positive attitudes toward their friends showed more frequent participation in social activities. Adolescents who reported having had friends for years, and who felt close to their friends, were more involved in social activities. The same multivariate analysis was conducted regarding frequency of participation in extra-curricular activities, which proved related to developmental factors as well. In both years, participation frequency in these activities was higher among younger than among older adolescents, and again males tended to participate in extra-curricular activities more than females. Taken together, the most consistent finding of the different models was the absence of any evidence for the time displacement hypothesis. Indeed, Internet users formed a group of adolescents more likely to participate in social and extra-curricular activities than non-users.

60 *Sociability and Internet use*

Similar results were obtained in two separate surveys in the USA. The Pew Internet and American Life project conducted two studies of teens and their parents (in 2004 and 2006) that afford us an additional opportunity to compare changes in teenage Internet activity over time. In both surveys young Internet users were asked to indicate the extent of their participation in four extracurricular activities: a school club such as drama or language, a school sports program, other extracurricular activity like bands, and a club or sports program not affiliated with school, such as a church youth group. The two years 2004 and 2006 evinced much stability. For example, regarding a school club, 35 percent of young Internet users reported participating in both years; 50 percent reported participating in a school sports program; 41 percent reported participating in other extracurricular activity; 56 percent reported participating in a club or sports program not affiliated with their school.

Time displacement

The "activity displacement" hypothesis has a temporal component as well. An adolescent's involvement in social activities may not be affected merely by his/her being connected to the net; the amount of time he/she invests in each session may be detrimental to participation in normative adolescent activities. Accordingly, we tested for the effect of the frequency of Internet use on young users' participation in all activities. Again, frequency of use was found not statistically significant, and results of the regression analysis supported the earlier descriptive findings: involvement in social activities and extracurricular activities was positively associated with Internet use. Thus, even controlling for developmental factors such as age, socio-economic status, and closeness of family and friends, Internet use is not an activity that isolates individuals but contributes to their engagement in social activities. As Gershuny (2003) argues, the Internet has probably become an efficient coordination tool, resulting not in isolation but in expanded relations with others as it facilitates the coordination of mutual activities and reduces the cost of arranging meetings. Moreover, Internet use had no effect on the use of the old media, and Internet users did not differ from non-users in their use of radio, TV, and books.

The Internet and time with peers

Another concern of parents, teachers, and the public is that the Internet may distract children from other developmentally important activities, such as spending time with friends, and that computers may have an isolating effect on children (Subrahmanyam, Kraut, Greenfield, and Gross,

2001; Lenhart et al., 2001). Consideration of the presumed anti-social or asocial nature of computers has led some to conclude that regardless of the instrumental benefits, excessive preoccupation with computers may pose a risk especially to children's social relationships.

Adolescence is a period characterized by developmental changes in the social and physical realms. As children enter their teenage years, they interact less with their parents, and peer relationships take on greater importance (Steinberg and Silk, 2002; Giordano, 2003). Peers act as emotional confidants, provide advice and guidance to others, and serve as models of behavior and attitudes. But evidence suggests that parents continue to influence their children's behaviors and decisions well into their teens in important ways (Collins, Maccoby, Steinberg, Hetherington, and Bornstein, 2000). But whereas in childhood parents were the main source of social relationship, during adolescence, parents represent only one circle, and peers form another important component (Giordano, 2003; Crosnoe et al., 2003; Crosnoe, 2000). Furthermore, early adolescents attach greater importance to acceptance by peers than by parents, and increasingly turn to their peers for advice and comfort, distancing themselves from their parents.

In our research conducted in Israel, we asked adolescents three questions to ascertain their subjective perception of time spent with peers and alone. The questions probed a typical week in the school year and asked how many evenings adolescents spent with their family, friends, and alone. Responses ranged from 0–7 and are summarized in Figure 3.1.

The results show that in both 2001 and 2004 Internet users reported spending fewer evenings with their parents than non-users. In 2001,

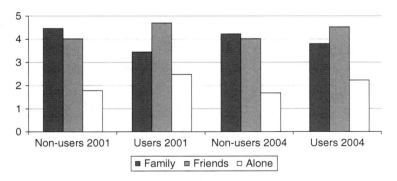

Figure 3.1 Time spent with family, friends, and alone by early Internet users and non-users

62 *Sociability and Internet use*

non-users spent on average 4.46 evenings a week talking and playing with parents, whereas Internet users spent only 3.42 evenings a week doing so. The results for 2004 were similar, as non-users spent on average 4.24 evenings with their parents, and Internet users spent only 3.8 evenings with them. Internet users, however, reported spending more evenings with their friends than non-users in both 2001 and in 2004. In 2001, Internet users reported spending more evenings alone (2.48) than non-users (1.80). All the differences are statistically significant.

Figure 3.1 shows that Internet users spent less time with their parents but more with their friends and alone than non-users. Spending less time with parents and more time with friends may be associated not only with Internet use but with a developmental process that is common in adolescence. We expected gender differences as well, as females may spend more time with their parents and less with friends and alone than males. We tested this possibility but found that the differences in evening spent with parents, friends, and alone did not differ by gender. We also checked each age category separately and found Internet users of all ages tended to spend less time with parents and more time with friends and alone than non-users.

The results presented in Figure 3.1 may reflect the effects of other factors as well. To control these, we conducted a multivariate analysis and explored the extent to which Internet use in general was associated with the amount of time spent with family, friends, and alone. As to time spent with friends, in this area of sociability Internet users and non-users evinced no statistically significant difference in either year. Positive attitudes toward friendship and participation in social activities were the most important predictors of time spent with friends. Regarding the number of evenings spent alone, Internet users reported spending more time alone than non-users, but only in 2001.

The results suggest that overall Internet use has a minor association with the time that adolescents spend with their friends and alone. On the positive side, Internet users are not isolated from their friends, as Internet use has no effect on time spent with friends. Internet use slightly decreases the time spent with family and slightly increases the time being spent alone. We conducted the same analysis for Internet users alone to find out whether frequency of daily use was associated with time spent with friends and time spent alone. Frequency of daily use was found not to affect in any way time spent with friends and time spent alone. Consistent with our previous findings, we concluded that having an Internet connection and frequency of its use were not related to time spent friends and time spent alone, indicating again the absence of evidence for an Internet isolation hypothesis. This finding is consistent with

Sociability and Internet use 63

the results of a recent study in the USA that concluded that online communication has become a central aspect of adolescents' social life. The use of Instant Messaging and Social Network sites to maintain and expand school relationships is widespread among youth. The Internet and cell phones are friendship-driven technologies that provide continuous contact with friends, social support, and the coordination of dyadic and group activities conducted both online and face-to-face (boyd, 2008).

Internet use and network size

A final consideration in respect of potential isolation through Internet use is the size of the network of friends. The number of close friends is only a quantitative measure of social support, not of its content or of the adolescent's ability to mobilize these ties for companionship, support, and resources; but it is nevertheless an additional dimension of the social circle. Individuals may differ in the size of their social circle, and even a reduced size can provide companionship and social support, thus, the smaller the size of their circle, the higher the likelihood that individuals will perceive themselves as less able to mobilize friends for companionship and support. Assuming that individuals have multiple responsibilities, simple arithmetic suggests that a teenager who has only two close friends will face the possibility of these friends being busy more frequently than a teenager who has three friends.

We investigated the association of Internet use with number of close friends. Adolescents were asked to name up to six close friends, and provide information about their age, gender, place of residence, place where they met, and length of time they had known each other as friends. On average, each adolescent reported having five friends (standard deviation, SD 1.472). Of the sample, 6.3 percent reported having two friends or fewer, and 77 percent reported having between four and six close friends. Comparison of adolescent Internet users and non-users for the average number of their friends elicited no statistically significant difference.

Network size does vary with age (the older the adolescent, the larger the number of friends reported), but again the results point to the importance and relevance of developmental factors. Age proved related to frequency of Internet use, and also to the size of the social network. But age was not related to differences in each age category in the number of friends as reported by Internet users and non-users. Nor were any gender differences found.

We did find an important difference by nationality. When we inspected separately the size of the social network of Israeli Arabs and Jews, we found that only among the Jewish population were there differences

64 *Sociability and Internet use*

in the number of friends based on Internet use. On average, Jewish adolescents who did not access the Internet reported 4.7 friends (SD 1.49), and adolescents who did access it reported on average 5.1 friends (SD 1.40). The difference is not substantial but it is statistically significant and indicates that, among the Jewish population, Internet use is associated with more social involvement, not less.

One explanation for this finding has to do with the higher rate of technological penetration among Jewish adolescents in Israel, which means that is very likely that being connected to the Internet is important for being socially involved. Adolescents connected to the Internet used it mainly for social purposes, to facilitate the maintenance of friendship even after school hours. The high rate of Internet penetration among Jewish adolescents may make it mandatory to be connected in order to be "in" and maintain good relationships at school. In Arab society, the rate of penetration is relatively low, and being connected to the Internet does not increase the size of the circle of friends because friendships are maintained primarily face-to-face or by traditional channels of communication.

Displacement or multitasking?

The idea of displacement is simple, yet as we have shown in this chapter, there is little empirical evidence for its very existence or for the existence of real negative effects on adolescents' social involvement. Alternative explanations for this state of affairs are possible, and a natural candidate is multitasking. With the extensive use of computers, multitasking has become part of the way teens manage a busy life. Media multitasking can be defined as engaging in more than one media activity at a time, by switching constantly back and forth between such diverse activities as email, IM, web search, and text messaging friends (Foehr, 2006). In a comprehensive study on multitasking in the USA, teenagers were asked how often, when principally using any one of four media (reading newspapers, watching TV, using computers and video games), they concurrently used other media. About a quarter replied that they multitasked most of the time, about half said they did so from time to time, and only 20 percent said they never did. A central finding of that study was that multitasking was not common when the primary medium being used was TV. Not surprisingly, multitasking was very common when the computer was primarily in use, as the other activities were computer-related. When using email, 83 percent of the respondents reported conducting other media activity simultaneously. When using Instant Messaging or searching websites, 75 percent reported doing so simultaneously with consumption of other media. When used for computer games, the computer was very likely used for Instant Messaging and phone conversations too. Its use for Instant Messaging was probably concomitant with searching web sites, emailing, and watching TV. When used for sending emails, the popular secondary activities were found to be eating, watching TV, and other computer activities. Finally, when searching for websites, the most popular secondary activity was conducting Instant Messaging conversations.

This preliminary study provides some important insights that can guide future exploration of the displacement hypothesis. First, it renders evidence of the primary role of television and of teenagers' reluctance to conduct other activities when watching TV programs. It also attests that computer use is associated with conducting other computer-related activities at the same time. A web search was often combined with Instant Messaging, chatting, and emailing. This finding indicates that using the Internet does not displace other activities such as homework, entertainment, and social involvement. The difference is that is these activities are conducted simultaneously, sometimes providing content for friends' exchange.

Future studies on the effects of the Internet or other new media on media use and social involvement should include measures of displacement, but also of multitasking.

Early studies on the effect of the Internet in adolescence focused on both the potential costs and potential benefits of Internet use. Some studies exposed the potentially positive effects of the Internet and of computers based on the ability of these technologies to foster young people's academic and intellectual development, increasing their language and analytical skills (Tapscott, 1998), and to furnish the tools adolescents need to shift from being passive consumers of the media to active producers of multimedia presentations, blogging, and musical composition. Others were more concerned with the potential effects on a central aspect of adolescence, namely, participation in social activities and social networks; they expressed concern that Internet use may lead to social isolation or a decrease in individuals' involvement in social activities and social networks.

The major argument for potentially negative effects was the displacement hypothesis, which suggests that Internet use is at the expense of other areas of social involvement. In this chapter we disaggregated the different components of the argument and tested them one by one. We showed that the displacement argument is not one unified concept but has been formulated differently by different authors. Some have argued for a displacement of activities, suggesting that the Internet is an activity that requires time and therefore may reduce time left for participating in social and leisure activities.

66 *Sociability and Internet use*

Testing this argument, we found that adolescents who used the Internet were more, not less, involved in most activities that are social in nature and are conducted in the presence of others. For example, in both 2001 and 2004, Internet users reported on average a higher frequency of participation in social activities, such as going to discos and movies, and strolling with friends through the neighborhood. In both years too, Internet users reported a higher frequency of participation in evening classes outside school and in sports activities. Our findings accordingly disprove the argument that Internet use is detrimental to participation in extra-school activities and show that Internet users are more active in these activities than are non-users.

Another explanation for the displacement hypothesis suggests that time used for Internet activities reduces time spent with parents and friends, and as the use of computers and the Internet is suspected of being a solitary activity, conducted in isolation from others, it might be time spent alone. This argument is important because the significant others during adolescence are parents and friends. We put this argument to the test, using our surveys of adolescents in Israel. Initially we found mixed support. Without controlling for other relevant variables, the descriptive findings show a decrease in Internet users' time spent with parents and an increase in time spent with friends. But we suspected that this shift in emphasis may be the result of a developmental process unassociated with Internet use, so we conducted a multivariate analysis, again on data for 2001 and 2004. The results suggest a minor effect of Internet use, and that only in 2001, when a relatively small percentage of the adolescent population had access to the medium. By 2004, more than two-thirds of adolescents had access to the Internet, and this effect had disappeared. The effect of age, a measure of maturation during adolescence, was consistent and larger, indicating its greater importance. There was also clear evidence that spending time with friends is related to structural opportunities for this. Adolescents who reported participating in social activities and extracurricular activities also reported spending more time with friends. Therefore, our analysis does not support the time displacement hypothesis.

Lack of evidence of any isolating effect of the Internet is important to our central argument. The main concern of this book is the motivation for online relationship formation and the structure of adolescents' social networks in the information age. In Chapter 1, we put forward the argument that online friendship formation may not be associated with social isolation and lack of social skills, but with a need for diversification and expansion of social networks. As adolescents are characterized by high similarity to their friends and the lack of geographic mobility to meet others, we suggest that the need to diversify and expand social networks, not isolation, drives online friendship formation, and we have shown that Internet users do not represent a socially isolated group of the adolescent population.

Media convergence: more channels in play

Our argument is that the Internet is being incorporated into adolescents' everyday life and is becoming part of the web of their responsibilities and social involvements. From this perspective, Internet use is not at the expense of other activities or of time spent with family and peers, but is incorporated into them and represents an additional space of activity. This incorporation indeed diversifies their activities, their sources of information and guidance, and their social relationships.

The transformation of the Internet from (mainly desktop) computer-mediated communication into a novel, more integrated, technology of smartphones, tablets, and social devices, has had dramatic, both quantitative and qualitative, influences on the relations between youth sociability and the digital world. Quantitatively, the convergence of the new media has intensified the frequency, duration, intensity, engagement, and time spent in social media usage. Qualitatively, it has significantly contributed to the emergence of parallel, new modes of communication channels between youth and adolescents' friends and peers, but also between parents and children. From an analytical point of view, it is important to conceptualize the blurring of boundaries between telecommunications, mass media, and social media, as the crucial meaning of media convergence. The result of the convergence of telecommunications and broadcasting is more than just the sum of its parts. It has created a "convergence culture." The net result of media convergence is then variously described as multimedia, TIME (telecommunications, information technologies, media, entertainment), or cross-media, emphasizing its overlapping media character (Latzer, 2013).

Most significantly, the convergence of the new media into a loosely intraoperative platform, its relative harmonization, and its user-friendliness across platforms, have considerably impacted the inclusion of new generation of users—older ones, who could now extensively text and talk over VoiceIP with friends and relatives. In other words, the interoperability and ubiquity of web applications such as Facebook, WhatsApp and Messenger, WeChat, Skype, Google Talk, etc., have blurred in the minds of ICT users the boundaries between oral communication, text messaging, and even video broadcasting. Additionally, it has made ICT less costly than ever and easier to use. More to the point, it seems that it has played a key role in

68   *Sociability and Internet use*

intensifying communication frequency between friends and classmates, but especially between parents and their children. Research has indicated that social media convergence has modified modes and intensity of family conflicts over ICT use—as shown in Chapter 2. More pertinently, the rising use of educational media over convergent media devices at school and home has the potential to facilitate more nuanced communication using the ICT. More specifically, the new integrated media contain positive social affordances such as: immediate reactivity, customizability, and social facilitation (Christakis, 2014; Valkenburg and Taylor Piotrowski, 2017: Chapter 14).

More to this point, theoretically, ICT use can be treated as an "elastic activity," depending on current needs and constraints (Vilhelmson, Thulin, and Elldér, 2017). Social affordances of the new media are raising the possibility of flexible media time-use, multitasking, while emphasizing the relevance of adopting a wider, bidirectional, and interactive understanding of the relationships between ICT use and alternative time uses.

Moreover, the increasing incorporation of ICT into smartphone relational patterns has been intensively more extant, as the new media technology have become more unified, mixing different communication channels, hence blurring the boundaries between content, gaming, messaging, and social networking (Treem et al., 2016).

Summary

In this chapter, we have outlined the link between online activities, sociability, and adolescents' developmental stage. More specifically, we securitized common hypotheses, discussing the manners in which possible displacement effects or—alternatively—multitasking activities shape the relations between online activity and adolescents' sociability. Additionally, we linked online adolescents' sociability and media convergence, and the continuously confusing confines between online activities, especially in smartphones' usage. It seems that the commonly accessible web and smartphone applications are involved with adolescents' online engagement and sociability, but not necessarily at the expense of adolescent's other offline sociability. Adolescents' online and offline sociability tends to relatively overlap. In fact, as we will show in Chapter 4, online usage enables adolescents to expand their social ties.

4 Online relationship formation

Introduction

As stated in Chapter 3, online sociability is an integral part of young people's digital literacy and cultural consumption of technological artefacts. The ability of the Internet to facilitate online contact, especially with geographically remote people, has caught the popular imagination and the empirical attention of researchers studying online relationship formation. The main consequence of adolescents' online engagement is the expansion of their social ties. However, this expansion is random. It is confined by social regularities governing the ways in which humans interact, online or offline, thus making the formation patterns of online social ties predictable by social analysts.

Studies on the use of ICT by youth apprise us of the active role that youth play in online activity, and that the parents' and the adolescents' views regarding ICT do not always converge. Parents indicate that the computer is bought and connected to the Internet, reflecting their willingness to provide a tool to improve their children's academic performance, to provide access to information needed for school work, to adapt to the school requirement of typed assignments, and to link the teens to the information society. By contrast, teens experience the Internet as a tool for social purpose and play (Lenhart et al., 2001; Livingstone and Bober, 2004; Cohen, Lamish, and Schejter, 2008). Boase and Wellman (2006) argue that in contrast to the popular image of the Internet as a trigger and facilitator of new relationships, "only a relatively small proportion of internet users have ever met someone new online."

Adolescents play an active role in their communicative conduct. Consequently, their primary uses of the Internet do not always match their parents' expectations and wishes. Adolescents are most likely to use the Internet to communicate with others for social and gaming purposes, and in some cases to reach out and communicate with others not of their

70 Online relationship formation

proximate or immediate social circle at school or in their neighborhood. Moreover, adolescents learn to utilize computer-mediated communication as an additional form of social environment, developing digital literacy, and making new contacts over the Internet. Online relationships nowadays appear to be an integral part of youth culture (Helsper, 2008a). The technological features of ICT smooth barriers of communication, yet they cannot completely remove the effects of social constraints on social interaction. The odds of forming new relations are higher among those socially similar, geographically close, and having at least one friend in common ("transitive relations") (Kadushin, 2004). Forming online relationships might be one of the most appealing aspects of Internet use to young people, given that forming relationships is an important developmental task of adolescence, and in this task youth are limited in their choices by geographical constraints.

Understanding the process involves studying motivations impelling youth to form relationships online, their choice of communication channels and content, the effect of online ties on young people's existing ties and social life, and the quality of online associations. In this chapter, we tackle these topics.

The notion of online relationship formation requires conceptual clarification. Most research has not clearly defined what is meant by online ties. It was largely conducted to elucidate the effects of channel characteristics on interpersonal communication, emphasizing the lack of social presence, lack of richness, and lack of clues in Internet communication (Sproul and Kissler, 1986), and it sought the conditions under which this communication is non-personal or becomes hyper-personal (Walther, 1996). Another direction has been research to understand channel choice across distances and to inquire whether one online communication supplements or replaces the use of other channels of communication among kin and friends. These studies show that Internet use is associated with more and not less communication, and that the more individuals contact by phone and face-to-face, the more they contact using email (Chen et al., 2002); it is suggested that connectivity increases local and long-distance communication (Hampton and Wellman, 2002). Most of this research reflects the conduct of online communication but makes no major attempt to define the nature of the online relationship. Lack of conceptual clarity may lead to contradictory findings.

Prior to the information age, adolescents' social choices were severely restricted by time and place. Their lack of geographical mobility and their belonging to an age group expected to go to school structurally reduced their social circle to friends who were in the neighborhood, at school, and at extracurricular activities. Proximity was a central social constraint for

Online relationship formation 71

relationship formation. Living in the same neighborhood and attending the same school entailed a high level of social similarity.

Internet and mobile access and communication have produced a number of changes in social communication patterns. Relationship formation has been expanded from geographical spaces of interaction (the neighborhood, the school) to digital spaces (social networks applications). Friendships that in the past were based on social groups with clear boundaries and social expectations of mutual interaction changed to personalized peer-diverse and dispersed personalized peer networks that lack clear boundaries and norms of social behavior. Channels of interpersonal communication are multiplex, including in addition to face-to-face and phone, mobile applications and diverse platforms of social media.

As a result, the limits of interpersonal communication have been blurred and include:

- perpetual contact with the social network anywhere and anytime;
- communication is personalized, relying on ego-networks rather than social groups;
- contents are not exclusive and can be forwarded without the owner's knowledge;
- activities are coordinated through social media.

These major changes in the patterns, frequency, content, and quality in interpersonal friendship formation, maintenance, and communication have been noted by a large number of studies that focus on different aspects of this major social change. In this chapter we focus on one important aspect, namely, the similarities, differences, and overlaps between online and offline social relationships.

With the growing popularity and ubiquity of social media, the public and, to some extent, also research were concerned with the increasing growth of online relationships and the concern that these are replacing more high quality offline relationships. Studies conducted in the early 1990s found that adolescents in western countries were reporting that they meet individuals and maintained interpersonal communication with others whom they had met online at the same time as they met with friends face-to-face. Online/offline relationships were at that time defined according to the space of interaction that the respondents indicated was where they meet their friends. Online relationships were the ones that were formed in forums, chat rooms, gaming, and messenger. Offline relationships were usually defined as the ones that were initiated in the neighborhood, school, or any other face-to-face space of social interaction.

72 *Online relationship formation*

It is important to recognize that a comparison between the two kinds of relationships designated as online and offline may imply either that they are mutually exclusive or opposed to each other. Yet over time is clear that interpersonal relationships are created, developed, and sustained through integrated online and offline interaction. The entire range of offline relationships, from family through school and work to social relations in the wider neighborhood, may also be present online in a manner that is rarely separated out from one's offline life. The popular perception of online relationships as relationships that can be contrasted with a "real world"—inhabited by one's real or more authentic offline relationships— seems therefore simplistic and misleading. This corresponds to an earlier critique of the concept of the "virtual," a term prominent during the early years of Internet use. In short, our study treats social media in much the same way that everyone treats the landline telephone, never described today as a separate "online/on-phone" facet of life. It is, however, essential for us as researchers to recognize that whatever misgivings we may feel as academics about this dualistic terminology, it remains a primary mode by which people around the world understand and experience digital media.

Because of this perception that online life can be contrasted to offline life, we start this chapter with a summary of the perspectives that explain online relationships formation.

"The rich get richer hypothesis" proposes that individuals with higher extroversion, who are more more comfortable in social situations or have already social resources would be more likely to use social media for online relationship formation, extending their social networks and enhancing the quality of their friendships (Kraut et al., 2002). According to this hypothesis, individuals who are extroverted and already have strong social skills would do better in sharing their views and asking for help online, thereby attaining additional social support and higher life satisfaction through cyberspace (Khan et al., 2016).

Conversely, "the poor get poorer hypothesis" argues that individuals who are introverted have higher levels of social anxiety, and have poorer social skills and confidence would be more likely to use the Internet to escape from and avoid problems in real life, and this could lead to negative outcomes.

Studies present some interesting evidence on the association of personality characteristics and online relationship formation. The first HomeNet study was a longitudinal investigation of 93 non-representative families in the Pittsburgh area. They were provided with computers and an Internet connection free of charge for three years. The study found extroversion was negatively related to frequency of Internet use; introverts were more likely to be frequent Internet users (Kraut et al., 1998). Internet effects

Online relationship formation 73

proved to differ according to personality characteristics, in particular, extroversion/introversion. The authors found support for "the rich get richer hypothesis": extroverts reported more Internet use and creating more online relationships. Introverts who used the Internet extensively reported less social involvement. In sum, Internet use was associated with better outcomes for extroverts and worse outcomes for introverts. In particular, extroverts who used the Internet more reported increased well-being, including low levels of loneliness. In contrast, introverts who were heavy Internet users showed a decline in their well-being (Kraut et al., 2002). The HomeNet study was based on the dystopian assumption (see Preface) that the Internet exerts negative effects on the individual's well-being, partly because of another assumption that time invested in the Internet is non-social time, diverted from other sources of sociability.

Others who subscribe to these perspectives have investigated the link between personal attributes and online activities, such as sensation-seeking and Internet dependence (Lin and Tsai, 2002). The social needs outlook has found much corroboration in social psychology. A study in Holland with a sample of 687 adolescents investigated personality characteristics and the perception of online communication. Socially anxious and lonely adolescents were found to value online communication more strongly. Youngsters with these personality characteristics perceived the Internet as providing them with more opportunities to reflect and control the messages they sent, and they perceived online communication as deeper and more reciprocal than face-to-face communication (Peter and Valkenburg, 2006). Similarly, in Germany, Wolfradt and Doll (2001) investigated the relation between extroversion/introversion and three Internet uses (information, entertainment, and interpersonal communication) among 122 adolescent Internet users. The social needs hypothesis was mainly supported by specific personality traits, such as neuroticism, which was proved to be positively associated with the entertainment motive and with the interpersonal communication motive; extroversion was positively associated with the communication motive only. Wolfradt and Doll (2001) argued accordingly that personality traits predict corresponding types of Internet activities. All in all, existing knowledge indicates that personality characteristics are influential in the use and choice of this medium for relationship formation. Online communication is an important means for socially anxious, introverted, and lonely adolescents to overcome their inhibitions in face-to-face settings. The Internet not only offers such young people a new venue to fulfill the need for association and involvement in a social circle, it also compensates for their lack of social skills and ultimately may help them to gain self-confidence, to be enjoyed later in face-to-face interactions.

74 *Online relationship formation*

The association between online communication and relational closeness is particularly interesting. Using a large sample of Dutch youth aged 12–17 years, Valkenburg and Peter (2007a) investigated whether online communication stimulated or reduced closeness to friends, and whether intimate disclosure of personal information online affected their closeness to online ties. These authors found that only 30 percent of the adolescents perceived online communication as effective in disclosing personal information. Furthermore, online communication with others whom they met online proved to have a negative effect on the perceived closeness to friends (Valkenburg and Peter, 2007a).

The social compensation hypothesis

On the contrary, the social compensation hypothesis proposes that individuals with higher levels of social anxiety or lower levels of social support, use social media to create online relationships to compensate for their lack of social ties, as social anxiety is a barrier for the creation of offline relationships (Van Ingen and Wright, 2016). According to this hypothesis, the relative anonymity of social media and the process of self-disclosure online provide individuals with a more comfortable social situation due to a perceived lower risk for self-disclosure because of the lack of nonverbal cues (Schouten et al., 2007). Furthermore, the Internet may provide more opportunities for some people to gain social support, explore their self-identities and social identities, and improve their social skills, as well as a greater opportunity to use online coping resources (Van Ingen and Wright, 2016). Additionally, Ellison et al. (2007) proposed that online activities were beneficial for individuals to form weak ties in social networking, which would be very useful for those with lower self-esteem to improve their social capital but would be harmful for those with higher self-esteem since it would reduce their opportunities to maintain their strong offline ties. In other words, "the poor get richer" and "the rich get poorer."

Social diversification

As discussed, most of the previous perspectives focus on personality characteristics as motivations for online relationship formation. The social diversification perspective relies on social network and social capital assumptions to explain variations in these motivation for disadvantaged groups in society.

The social diversification hypothesis deals specifically with differences in the use of communication and information technologies among racial

Online relationship formation 75

and ethnic minorities (Mesch and Talmud, 2010; Gonzales, McCrory, Calarco, and Lynch, 2018). Relying on the literature demonstrating the stratification of multicultural societies along ethnic and social class lines, the social diversification hypothesis argues that network-based social closure affects the ability to obtain social capital and is more likely to benefit the dominant group's members (Mesch et al., 2012). According to this perspective, social media platforms might support the expansion of social relationships, including improving access to information, knowledge, and skills that are unavailable locally, and provide opportunities for the diversification of social relationships (Mesch and Talmud, 2010). As Mazur and Kozarian (2010) found in their study of older adolescents, despite the partial overlap of online and offline ties, online communication tends to diversify the structure of peer networks and expose youngsters to others who share their interests, regardless of their age, gender, or location. In that sense, the social diversification hypothesis argues that social media provides a platform for overcoming the existing segregation in society. Therefore, this perspective maintains that disadvantaged groups will have greater incentives to use Facebook to expand their social circle and overcome existing physical and social barriers to information and association. At the same time, majority groups will use the Internet to keep their existing relationships and maintain the closure of the network. In addition, they will be less likely than disadvantaged minorities to use Facebook to expand their social ties.

The social diversification perspective emphasizes the potential of social media platforms for empowering disadvantaged groups through affiliation with weak ties (Mazur and Kozarian, 2010). Indeed, a study of the online practices of young adolescents in a large rural area in California, planning for their vocational future, determined that the youngsters relied on computer-mediated communication and the establishment of contacts with weak ties to access information unavailable to them locally (Robinson, 2011). Similarly, the use of social media has been associated with the diversification of core networks of discussion (Hampton, Sessions, and Her, 2011). A study of a large sample of college students established that access to the Internet was still higher among White students than among Latinos and African Americans. However, when it comes to the use of social media platforms for content creation (blogs, video clips), a social capital-enhancing activity, Blacks and Hispanics reported a higher average of online content creation than Whites, even after controlling for socio-economic status, gender, and age, as well as Internet experience and psychological predictors (Correa and Jeong, 2011).

For young adolescents, SNSs may provide an opportunity to expand the size and composition of their social networks. Indeed, a study of

76 *Online relationship formation*

Internet use in a representative sample of Greek and Turkish youth in Cyprus suggests the existence of a reverse digital divide, as the more disadvantaged community engaged more often in Internet use for self-expression and association with weak ties (Milioni, Doudaki, and Demertzis, 2014). Mesch (2018a) conducted a test of this hypothesis and investigated the role of race and ethnicity in the self-reported strength of the social ties of young adolescents on Facebook. Based on the social diversification hypothesis, which argues that in multicultural societies, race and ethnicity are key factors that shape the nature of associations, we investigated whether there are ethnic and racial differences in the size and strength of the ties of adolescent Facebook users and the role of the strength of these ties in several positive outcomes. Using data from the US Teens' Social Media and Privacy Survey conducted by the Pew Research Center's Internet and American Life Project among 802 teens aged 12–17, we found no differences in the total number of ties that adolescents from different ethnic and racial groups reported. However, African Americans reported a significantly higher number of online weak ties, while White Americans had a significantly higher number of online strong ties. The results are consistent with the social diversification hypothesis.

Online ties and the structure of youth social networks

A prominent theme in the public discourse regarding social networks, reflected in the tone of many scholastic studies, is the claim that creating online social ties reduces the number of offline friends. Studies have warned that excessive Internet use may isolate adolescents from their friends. Available data indicate that the size of a social network is not affected by online relationship formation. A temporary decrease may be expected as more energy and time are invested in the creation of online ties; but over time, as online associations become integrated, the size of the network even slightly increases as new associations are added and old ones kept (Valkenburg and Peter, 2007b). In that sense, the effect of online relationship formation seems not to differ from the effect of cell phones. Igarashi, Takai, and Yoshida (2005), analyzing text messages over cell phones in Japan, found general support for the claim that mobile phones can change social networks among young people by increasing the number of possible contacts and promoting selective relationship formation. Mobile phones increase the frequency of communication, and allow opportunities for expanding interpersonal relationships.

The effect of expansion of social networks seem more pronounced on extroverts than on introverts, and varies according to attachment style, but overall, online relationship formation enlarges the social network for the

Online relationship formation 77

majority of adolescents who choose to become involved in this activity (Mesch and Talmud, 2010).

Associating with similar people is another social network dimension influenced by online relationship formation. One of the most significant and consistent findings reported in the literature is that social relationships are characterized by social similarity, or homophily. Studies on the formation of close social relationships have emphasized the importance of social similarity in friendship and attraction in intimate social relationships. Similarity molds network ties, resulting in relatively homogeneous social networks in terms of socio-demographic, behavioral, and interpersonal characteristics. This tendency of individuals to associate with others who are similar to them has important social consequences. For example, similar individuals exchange information that suits their personal characteristics, preferences, and social style. Contacting similar individuals, however, limits personal social horizons, thus restricting the exposure to different others, thereby reproducing social stereotypes.

Studies found that adolescents who created online social ties also reported a higher heterogeneity of their social network by age, gender, and location. In an early study, Mesch and Talmud compared youngsters with online friends and with face-to-face friends for the respective average age difference between those friends and themselves (Mesch and Talmud, 2010). The former reported that their online friends were on average older than themselves; the latter did not report this. The difference was small, online friends being on average one year and a half older. Accordingly, to a certain extent, online friendship formation breaks through the barriers of age-grade segregation which is imposed by the social structure of schools.

An important dimension to consider is the perceived closeness of youth to their online ties, and its possible effect on their perceived closeness to their face-to-face ties. Online relationship formation is a dynamic process, and accordingly calls for longitudinal studies. The perception of being less close to online friends seems to depend on the developmental stage of the relationship. Online ties are relatively newer than face-to-face ties, and are based on narrower shared interests. Furthermore, it takes time to develop relationships. Hence, more investigation is required to examine the process of changing the perceived online ties' strength. Still, there is no evidence that youth are exchanging close offline friendships for distant and narrower ones. Online ties, then, do not seem to replace but to supplement face-to-face connections.

Studies comparing the percentage of friends of the opposite sex, as reported by youth with and without online friends, found less sex segregation for the former than for the latter (Mesch and Talmud, 2006a,

78 *Online relationship formation*

2006b). More to the point, adolescents whose friends were similar in age, ethnic background, and place of residence were more likely to report forming friendships online (Mesch and Talmud, 2006a, 2006b).

Another component of the shared opportunity for mutual exposure is residential proximity. Proximity facilitates the likelihood of friendship formation and communication by increasing the probability that individuals will meet and interact. Proximity is of particular importance for adolescents limited in their geographic mobility as they must rely on public transport, which is not always reliable. For adolescents who are restricted in their physical mobility, and for whom the main arenas of social interaction are the school, the neighborhood, and extracurricular activities, the Internet represents a new focus of common activities. Adolescents connect to the Internet, chat, and exchange emails with friends, with friends of friends, and with unknown individuals. In these activities they encounter a new space that facilitates joint activities and social interaction. For adults, as well as for a large majority of adolescents, the Internet is an innovative place for social interaction, different from the phone and television.

Quality of offline and online ties

One of the key features of friendships is their quality. The quality of friendships refers to the experienced closeness, trust, and understanding between friends. Several studies have investigated and compared the quality of online versus offline friendships (Mesch and Talmud, 2006a, 2006b). These studies have consistently demonstrated that online friendships are perceived to be lower in quality than offline friendships (Mesch and Talmud, 2006a). Furthermore, although the quality of both online and offline friendships increased over time, the quality of online friendships improved significantly more than offline relationships. Specifically, they discovered when online friendships lasted for more than a year, their quality became comparable to offline friendships.

The association between online communication and relational closeness is particularly interesting. Using a large sample of Dutch youth aged 12–17 years, Valkenburg and Peter (2007a) investigated whether online communication stimulated or reduced closeness to friends, and whether intimate disclosure of personal information online affected their closeness to online ties. These authors found that only 30 percent of the adolescents perceived online communication as effective in disclosing personal information. Furthermore, online communication with others whom they met online proved to have a negative effect on the perceived closeness to friends (Valkenburg and Peter, 2007a). A possible explanation

Online relationship formation 79

for the perception of relational closeness of online ties is provided by an Israeli study with a large representative sample of adolescents, in which this perception was found to result from the length of communication. In fact, online ties are acquainted for less time than face-to-face ties, so they are still at the phase of relationship development and are therefore perceived to be of lesser depth and breadth (Mesch and Talmud, 2006b). Yet as time goes by, and as the topics of conversation expand from a small number of shared interests to a wider range, the perceived distance to online contacts is assumed to decrease.

Recent research

In the early days of ICT, the main distinction made was between online and offline ties. The definition of these ties was based on the origin of the relationship that often shaped the communication channels and the communication content. With the increase in Internet access, the proliferation of online platforms of communication (including social network sites, Instant Messaging, WhatsApp), the distinction became more difficult and today it is more reasonable to capture the social world of young and adults as being composed of online, offline, and mixed mode friendships. By mixed mode friendships, we mean the integration of online and offline ties and their interaction in our lives. Thus mixed mode friendships are the ones that originate online and extend to offline settings.

The notion of online relationship formation requires conceptual clarification. Most research has not clearly defined what is meant by online ties. It was largely conducted to elucidate the effects of channel characteristics on interpersonal communication, emphasizing the lack of social presence, lack of richness, and lack of clues in Internet communication and it sought the conditions under which this communication is non-personal or becomes hyper-personal (Walther, 1996). By contrast, in our view, the definition of online and face-to-face ties has to do more with the origin of the relationship and not with the mode of communication. This is a more pertinent perspective as social media has undergone significant convergence and has changed the domestication of ICT and youth sociability via digital social media (see Chapter 3). Youth communicate with close school friends using Instant Messaging, email, social networks sites, and school forums. In this case, someone can have friends whom one meets every day at school, yet conducts most of their communication online. Our interest lies mainly in the differences between online and face-to-face ties origination, so that our definition is that online ties refer to individuals who were first met online by means of applications, such as email, Instant Messaging, SNSs, chat rooms, or online

80   *Online relationship formation*

game groups. According to our definition, then, a face-to-face friend is someone whom one met in person, in a setting such as school, the neighborhood, or other extracurricular activity (Mesch and Talmud, 2010).

How do online, offline, and mixed-mode friendships differ? Antheunis, Valkenburg and Peter (2012) conducted a study in which they compared the quality of online, offline, and mixed-mode friendships and the relative contribution of proximity, perceived similarity to the quality of friendship. The study was based on data gathered from a large sample of members of a Dutch social networking site (n = 2,188). An important finding is that differences in quality between online and offline friendships were found and remained significant over time, but those between mixed-mode and offline friendships disappeared. As already mentioned in the literature, the migration of a connection from being a person met online to one met face-to-face and voice-phone is an important step that increases the closeness between them. For that reason, mixed mode relationships tend to be more similar over time than solely face-to-face and only online ties.

The first question is the extent to which proximity and perceived similarity differ among online, mixed-mode, and offline friendships. The study found significant differences in the level of proximity between the types of friendship, the actual distance between offline friends is the lowest, followed by mixed-mode and online friends. As to perceived similarity between online, mixed-mode, and offline friendships. there is a significant difference in perceived similarity between the online and mixed-mode friendships, and between online and offline friendships. Perceived similarity was the highest in mixed-mode friendships and offline friendships, and lowest in online friendships (Antheunis et al., 2012).

In accordance with earlier studies, they found that respondents perceived offline friendships to be of higher quality than online friendships. However, the study also found that mixed-mode friendships, which are also formed online but then also migrate to offline communication modalities (i.e., telephone, face-to-face communication), were rated similar in quality as offline friendships. Thus, it is not important whether a friendship is formed online or offline, but rather, it is more important that newly formed friendships also migrate to cue-richer communication modalities, such as telephone and face-to-face contact friendships (Antheunis et al., 2012).

The study found that the quality of all three types of friendship improved as the friendship developed over time. The quality of online friendships remained significantly lower than that of offline friendships, even after two years. According to those authors:

Online relationship formation   81

- *Proximity.* They in fact found that offline friends lived closer to each other than mixed-mode and online friends. This suggests that in online and mixed-mode friendships, actual geographic proximity is less important to becoming friends.
- *Similarity.* they found that the level of perceived similarity was lower in online friendships compared to mixed-mode and offline friendships. They did find, however, that the effect of similarity on the quality of friendship was higher for online friendships than for mixed-mode and offline friendships. These results indicate that though the level of similarity is low in online friendships, similarity is a more important determinant of friendship quality in online friendships than in the other two categories of friendships (Antheunis et al., 2012).

Virtual interactions and online spaces are, in fact, additional sites of interaction in which youth can explore their identities, belonging, and sense of themselves (Stern, 2004). As they get older, their Internet literacy as well as their tendency to share personal information seem to grow, though with limited understanding of the risks involved (Livingstone, 2008). Still, perceptions regarding the risk involved in online relations have been modified: while in 2003 distrust in online ties was associated with geographical proximity between persons, the link between mistrust of the Internet to geographical proximity had disappeared between 2003 to 2006 (Dutton and Shepherd, 2003; Helsper, 2008b). Additionally, young people report a growing dependency on the Internet for activities ranging from managing their daily lives to building and maintaining online social interaction. The embeddedness of ICT in social structure creates a dual nature of communicative space, where both adolescents' offline and online domains serve as facilitators of communicative action in key life experiences (McMillan and Morrison, 2006). Over time, enthusiasm for meeting strangers on the Internet wanes, and reports of boredom surface, even among children (Livingstone and Bober, 2004).

In the context of the "fear of strangers," it is important to note the process of movement from online to face-to-face relationships. After the young people became acquainted online, and discovered common interests and topics of discussion, sometimes they would exchange emails, often using IM, then they communicate by phone, and finally in few cases they arranged to meet face-to-face in a public place. This is cautious progress, moving from online meeting as strangers, followed by a rise in the frequency of communication and in the number of its channels. The goal of these successive moves is the establishment of trust, resulting from progressive disclosure of personal information (Mesch and Talmud, 2007a).

82 *Online relationship formation*

Furthermore, the concept of the stranger is not always adequate to describe relationship formation online. Frequently, online communication and mobile communication are a way to introduce mutual friends to each other (Wolack et al., 2003). This happens when a new friend is introduced to an existing group or when an adolescent suggests to another friend that he or she meet a new person who has the same interests or the same personal problems.

Interpersonal lives and the computer and mobile activities of early adolescents reflexively amplify each other. Contemporary moral development is less about mastering distinctly right and wrong answers, and more about negotiating different social contexts. Additionally, even in a CMC environment, interpersonal and even intimate clues can be possible (Walther, 1996). There is evidence that the number of personal relationships occurring via the Internet is increasing as more people gain access to it (Underwood and Findlay, 2004; Lawson and Leck, 2006). What adolescents do after school hours, through the windows of their computer screens, has become an integral and important part of their individual and social identity formation and of their moral development (Bradley, 2005).

Valentine and Holloway (2002) found a rich variety of adolescents' strategies to reconfigure their personal activities between offline and online spaces. The study found four ways in which adolescents, aged 11–16, incorporated their offline worlds and their online spaces: (1) by direct (re)presentations of their offline identities and activities; (2) by the production of alternative identities also contingent on their offline identities; (3) by the reproduction online of offline class and gender divides; and (4) by reducing the ways in which everyday material realities limit the scope of their online activities. These authors also identified three different processes whereby adolescents incorporate online space into their offline worlds: (1) online activities maintain and develop both distant and local offline relationships; (2) information gathered online is incorporated into offline activities; and (3) online friendships are incorporated into or reconfigure offline social networks and position within networks (Valentine and Holloway, 2002).[1]

Notwithstanding important, adolescents' conduct offline seems similar to their conduct online. Their ways of social coping online and offline are markedly associated. Seepersad (2004) found a strong relationship between avoidant coping strategies offline and Internet use for entertainment. Moreover, adolescents who considered communication the most important use of the Internet also contended with loneliness through expression of emotion and social coping. Results suggest that online and offline coping behaviors are strongly related, especially if they are avoidant

Online relationship formation 83

(Seepersad, 2004). Many positive and negative developmental behaviors, such as dating, smoking, formation of musical tastes and frictional violence, are transferred via adolescents' peer social networks (Neal, 2007).

Adolescent friendships, networked individuals, and the information society

For some young users, the Internet is becoming another location to meet and socialize, and relations created there tend to migrate to other settings too (Wolak et al., 2003; Mesch and Levanon, 2003). As young people become less controlled by traditional social authorities, they can overstep their geographical limits and their local groups' boundaries, using electronic communication technologies (Wellman, 2001).

The Internet is typically used by adolescents as an additional space of activity and social interaction, which often complements rather than replaces offline spaces of social communication, activity, and gathering. Networked publics provide an additional virtual context for youth to develop social norms in negotiation with their peers, forming social ties, maintaining friendship networks, and accruing information and entertainment items and devices from remote environments. The adolescent is a sophisticated "networked individual," who negotiates a wider range of messages and identities using multiple means of computer-mediated, mobile, and face-to-face channels of communication.

Adolescents' online activity and subculture are unique. This distinctiveness stems from both an age effect and a generational effect. The age effect refers to the influence of life-stage characteristics on adolescents' social conduct and network structure. The generational (or cohort) effect refers to the cultural change adolescents are exposed to in their formative years. Nowadays computer and Internet literacy, online communication, smartphone and hyper-textual literacy are skillfully mastered. Social networks sites are unique artefacts that allow early adolescents to share and discuss ideas and feelings, ask and answer each other's questions, or showcase projects, all of which promote a pro-social attitude. If in the past the formation of the youth culture was limited to neighborhood hangouts, now spaces and channels of interaction are expanded, allowing individuals to find peers to share interests, hobbies, and feelings conditional upon having access and skills.

Expansion of weak ties via online social networks compensates, in particular, youth with deprived life outcomes. A study of social networks sites has suggested a close association between the use of Facebook and social capital, the firmest relationship being with "bridging" social capital. In addition, Facebook usage was found to interact with measures of

84 *Online relationship formation*

psychological well-being, suggesting that it might provide greater benefits for users experiencing low self-esteem and low life satisfaction (Ellison, Steinfield, and Lampe, 2007).

Typically, adolescents' offline networks are denser and much more age- and sex-homogeneous than those of adults. Typically, adults also have more options to form new social ties, drawn from more diversified social foci of activity, than adolescents. Peer-group pressure on adolescents is more likely to encourage dense social ties, comprising of closely knit, transitive relations (in which a person's friends know his or her third parties as well), which tend to be geographically proximate as well.

In our view, the digital communication space reflects the social structure, its access and use are dependent on the social stratification process. Individuals bring to their online participation the diverse social status that they occupy and their social norms of behavior. Yet, at the same time online communication exerts some transformative effects on adolescents' behavior and friendship formation. Conceptualizing the Internet as foci of activity, we argue that technology is embedded in social structure. Digital platforms are another sphere of social interaction and action, where social agents play digital games, and exchange information, give and gain social support, and other instrumental and expressive resources. Thus, digital platforms are conceived as a social arena of shared and integrated activities. Hence, the social context molds relationship formation, not merely individual motivations and preferences. Technological features impact the use of digital platforms as well, by reducing costs, proximity considerations, and scope of choice among various channels of synchronous and asynchronous communication devices. Digital social interaction embeds certain properties from adolescents' offline social networks as well as from the digital environment; these act as social contextual facilitators, relevant to online sociability. These properties are in fact social affordance devices, bringing individuals together for purposes that create opportunities for social interaction, and introducing individuals to one another.

A comprehensive survey of 1,303 adolescents in Seoul, Singapore, and Taipei found that the Internet users among them differed in their Internet connectedness patterns in the nature of their social environments, in their family social status, and in other environmental factors (Jung, Lin, and Cheong, 2005). Most notably, the rate of Internet adoption by peers was an important factor explaining social media use. As the proportion of friends using the Internet increased, the more likely was the user to find technical support and to broaden and intensify online communication, thus increasing the likelihood of connecting through digital spaces. Considering that online activities are more likely to be shared among

Online relationship formation 85

peers, the high rate of participation in these activities suggests a strong effect of peer groups in the likelihood of conducting communication is digital spaces (Jung, Lin and Cheong, 2005).

Effects of online relationship formation on social networks

The last part of this chapter is dedicated to understanding some of the potential effects of online relationship formation on young people's social circle. Table 4.1 presents the different perspectives on online relationship formation.

An important dimension of social networks, and one at the center of many studies, is the extent that its use reduces, enlarges, or does not change the number of friends. Studies have warned that excessive use of digital spaces may isolate adolescents from their friends. As we saw in Chapter 3, the available data indicate that the size of a social network is not negatively affected by online relationship formation. A temporary decrease may be expected as more energy and time are invested in

Table 4.1 Perspectives on online relationship formation

Disciplinary origin	Perspective	Implications
Psychology	Motivation theory	Correlation between personality traits and communication needs and gratification
	Social needs	Either the expansion of social ties, or the compensation for face-to-face relationship scarcity
	Sensation seeking Intimacy theory	Compensation for anxiety, isolation, or stimuli
Social structural	Dual embeddedness	Reconfiguration of communication strategies; coping in virtual space is similar to offline life
	Social affordance	Information spreads rapidly in CMC, but neither universally nor homogeneously
	Social network analysis	Homophily and transitivity drive relationship formation, but online relations are larger in size, weaker, and more sparse

86   *Online relationship formation*

the creation of online ties; but over time, as online associations become integrated, the size of the network even slightly increases as new associations are added and old ones kept (Mesch and Talmud, 2006a; Valkenburg and Peter, 2007b). In that sense, the effect of online relationship formation seems not to differ from the effect of cell phones. Igarashi, Takai, and Yoshida (2005), analyzing text messages over cellular phones in Japan, found general support for the claim that mobile phones can change social networks among young people by increasing the number of possible contacts and promoting selective relationship formation. Mobile phones increase the frequency of communication, and allow opportunities for expanding interpersonal relationships.

The effect of expansion of social networks seem more pronounced on extroverts than on introverts, and varies according to attachment style, but, overall, online relationship formation enlarges the social network for the majority of adolescents who choose to become involved in this activity (Buote et al., 2009; Hamburger and Ben-Artzi, 2000).

Associating with similar people is another social network dimension influenced by online relationship formation. One of the most significant and consistent findings reported in the literature is that social relationships are characterized by social similarity, or homophily. Studies on the formation of close social relationships have emphasized the importance of social similarity in friendship and attraction in intimate social relationships. Similarity molds network ties and results in homogeneous social networks in terms of socio-demographic, behavioral, and interpersonal characteristics. This tendency of individuals to associate with others who are similar to them has important social consequences. For example, similar individuals exchange information that suits their personal characteristics and social style. By mutual influence or by association, they reject social links and information coming from others who differ from them in social attributes, attitudes, or values. Contact with similar individuals limits one's personal social horizons, restricting exposure to different others, thereby reproducing social stereotypes.

Perceiving oneself as being less close to online friends seems to depend on the developmental stage of the relationship. Online ties are relatively newer than face-to-face ties, and are based on narrow shared interests. Relationships take time to develop and the process of moving from being perceived as less close requires more investigation. Regarding their effect on existing ties, there is no evidence that youth are exchanging close friendships for distant and narrow ones. Online ties, then, seem not to replace but to supplement face-to-face connections.

Online relationship formation 87

A highly consistent finding in the literature is that school years are characterized by gender-based segregation. There is evidence that the extent of segregation decreases over the years, in particular from middle school to high school, but it remains relatively high even at the end of high school (Shrum, Cheek, and Hunter, 1988). Studies have shown that in adolescence there is a "sex cleavage" in friendship relations (Cotterell, 1996). In our study, we compared the percentage of friends of the opposite sex as reported by youth with and without online friends. We found less sex segregation for the former than for the latter (Mesch and Talmud, 2006a). Adolescents whose friends were similar in age, ethnic background, and place of residence were more likely to report forming friendships online (Mesch and Talmud, 2006a).

Summary

In this chapter we have discussed how online spaces are used in the context of relationship formation and the creation of friendship ties by means of ICT. We have emphasized the role of online communication as providing an alternative and also a complementary space for relationship formation, given the specific restrictions that youth face. These constraints are mainly geographic, constituting a contextual barrier that motivates some adolescents to turn to the Internet in seeking others who share their specific interests or differ in their racial/ethnic background and social characteristics. Heterogeneity in adolescents' social networks, occurring more often when the origin of the friendship is online, has developmental implications that require further investigation. For example, Stanton-Salazar and Spina (2005) found that non-romantic, cross-gender online relationships between adolescents proved an important source of social support. They afforded emotional support, particularly for the males. If the Internet reduces friendship gender segregation for young adolescents, this in the future may have an impact on the process of dating and first-time sexual relationships. Another potential effect is in the early exposure to individuals of diverse ethnic and racial groups and of varying political views. If this is confirmed in future research, digital spaces are very likely to become a central agent of socialization, which has to be integrated into our understanding of youth socialization.

The existing division in research between the "virtual" and the "real" does not of course accurately capture the lived social experiences and identity negotiations of adolescents in their socialization process, nor their belonging to peer groups, nor does it encompass the complexity in which offline and online spaces are mutually embedded.

88 *Online relationship formation*

The emergence of ICT into adolescents' identity management, personal communities, and friendship formation seems to have changed the character of "private" and "public" spaces, constituted by adolescents' activities on and around the screen. In Chapter 5, we connect elements of offline and online interactions regarding the maintenance and expansion of social ties, and the diversification of social networks through ICT.

Note

1 For a general theory considering the reconfiguration of ICT communication, see Walther (1996).

5 ICT and existing social ties

Introduction

Online communication can be intimate, personal, or non-personal. In Chapter 4, we explored online sociability patterns, inquiring into the motivation for online friendship formation through exploration of relational patterns, such as homophily and proximity. We also saw in Chapter 4 that adolescents tend to create relationships not only in traditional settings such as school and neighborhood, but also online. In this chapter, we take a closer look at the use of online communication to maintain existing relationships.

In doing so, we ask how characteristics of social ties affect the likelihood of using online communication to sustain friendship networks, and the ways relational patterns of social networks affect the use of online communication with friends.

Friendship is a special type of relationship, characterized by closeness and intimacy, trust, and commitment, which are reflected in the communication channels used. Close friends are individuals with whom we share personal information, concerns, and grievances, and often get social support. True, we also discuss with our friends our everyday experiences, such as: the movies we have seen, our views on political issues, our feelings about music clips, and different experiences at school. But none of these topics requires real closeness, and all can be discussed equally with other schoolmates or neighbors. Sharing intimate information, such as our romantic feelings and our problems and misunderstandings with parents, requires a higher level of closeness that admits intimacy and trust without fear that this information will be disclosed in public and embarrass us. Attraction to friendship, its formation, and its quality in adolescence are topics that have received much sociological attention (Kandel, 1978; Crosnoe, 2000; Moody, 2001). This period in life is characterized by rapid developmental changes, and as children enter their teenage years, they interact less with their parents. Instead, peer relationships expand and

90 *ICT and existing social ties*

assume greater importance (Youniss and Smollar, 1996; Giordano, 2003). Peers act as emotional confidants, providing each other with advice and guidance, often serving as role models of behavior and attitudes (Berndt, Miller, and Park, 1989; Hartup 1997; Crosnoe, Cavanagh, and Elder, 2003). Studies found a significant relationship between the quality of an individual's friends and well-being (Hartup, 1997; Collins et al., 1999). By contrast, adolescents who lack attachment to peers are more likely to report psychological distress and low psychological well-being (Beraman and Moody, 2004), and as a result are particularly exposed to stronger effect of social influence, particularly online (Pearson and Mitchell 2009). Although parents continue to influence behaviors and decisions, the time that adolescents spend with their peers expands, and they become their most important reference group and source of social influence (Hartup, 1996; Steglich et al., 2010, 2012; Lewis, Gonzalez and Kaufman, 2012; Preciado et al., 2012; Holliday et al., 2016; Kim and Altmann, 2017; Meghanathan, 2019). At the same time, however, existing family social ties are intensified via the social media applications. As "digital natives," who are equipped with more digital skills, adolescents often entice their parents to use ICT as a medium, therefore intensifying communication frequency and quality, especially via social apps such as WhatsApp (Van Deursen and Van Dijk, 2014; Correa, 2014, 2016; Correa et al., 2015; Van Deursen and Van Dijk, 2015; boyd, 2017; Jenkins and Sun, 2019).

Sociological studies on adolescent friendship attraction, formation, and quality have mostly relied on the proximity-similarity hypothesis (Kandel, 1978; Shrum, Cheek, and Hunter, 1988). According to this perspective, homophily in social relationships is a two-step process. It results from the combination of social, geographical, and institutional proximities, which provide joint opportunities for frequent and mutual exposure and shared social status, which in turn creates attraction among similar individuals who share the same social experience and context.

Activities in which people participate in their daily life are socially structured, creating an array of opportunities that tend to bring them into frequent contact (Suitor, Pillemer, and Keeton, 1995).

Studies of close social relationships have emphasized the importance of homophily (Hartup, 1997; McPherson, Smith-Lovin, and Cook, 2002; Knecht et al., 2010; Steglich et al., 2010, 2012; Bramoullé et al., 2012; Lewis et al., 2012; Preciado et al., 2012; Holliday et al., 2016; Kim and Altmann, 2017; Meghanathan, 2019), as we indicated in Chapter 4. Homophily is frequent, because it provides—among other things—important emotional rewards. Similar individuals are likely to participate in enjoyable joint activities with others who have similar characteristics and interests, and that way to receive validation of their own attitudes

ICT and existing social ties 91

and beliefs (Aboud and Mendelson, 1996). Joining in the same activities increases the frequency of social interaction and provides social support across a wide variety of aspects of social life. Not surprisingly, similarity has been associated with stable and strong ties (Hallinan and Kubitschek, 1988; Steglich et al., 2010, 2012). When dissimilarity exists at the beginning of relationships, or ascribed social statuses are mismatched, relationships tend to be unstable and are more likely to terminate, as individuals move on to other relationships in which there is greater similarity (Hallinan and Kubitscheck, 1988; Shutts et al., 2013; Shutts, 2015; Shaw et al., 2017).

Among adolescents, proximity is also important for friendship, as it establishes the boundaries within which the individual adolescent's choice of friendship is constrained by social or geographic location. A major location for meeting and making friends is school: adolescents spend a large part of their waking hours there. But other settings might be important as well. Adolescents spend their free time in neighborhood hangouts that they frequent after school. In shopping malls, video arcades, and movie theaters, usually located in the neighborhood or nearby, groups of adolescents spend leisure time, getting to know others who might live in the same neighborhood or locality but do not attend the same school (Cotterell, 1996). In sum, homophily in social relationships can be explained as originating from a combination of opportunity for mutual disclosure and shared life experiences. Activities in which individuals participate in their daily lives are socially structured, creating an array of opportunities that tend to bring similar people into frequent contact. School, workplace, and neighborhood haunts are places where social activities are organized (learning, work, leisure). The social structuring of these activities tends to bring similar individuals into frequent contact, encouraging the development of social relationships. These different foci of activities are the structural constraints in which individual choices are made (Feld, 1981). Foci of activity, a measure of proximity, might differ in how close they bring similar individuals. Some social contexts are more homogeneous in terms of age, gender, and place of residence, such as the school, but the assumption made by school sample studies that friendships are created only at school may be criticized. Friendships can be created in other social settings. Friends, even if attending school, meet in different social contexts and their friendships outside school have migrated there. Our knowledge of adolescents' friendships may benefit also from consideration of the context of acquaintance, and how this context is related to the quality of social relationships.

Furthermore, adolescents are a segment of the population whose ICT use has dramatically increased in recent years. Theories of

92 *ICT and existing social ties*

computer-mediated communication (CMC) are skeptical about its potential use to maintain and reinforce existing relationships.

Homophily and proximity were found to be the biggest predictors of mutual selection (tie formation) and influence of changing attitudes and behavior in existing adolescents' social ties (Knecht et al., 2010; Preciado et al., 2012; Holliday et al., 2016; Kim and Altmann, 2017; Meghanathan, 2019).

A troubling peer influence is risk-taking and health-related conduct. Accumulated evidence from longitudinal studies were able to verify that risk-taking and non-risk-taking behavior are learned predominantly in the context of peer clusters. Moreover, the influence of risk-taking is conditioned by network position. Peer influence has a greater focus of influence on the selection of adolescents among those who are located on the "periphery" side of the network, in comparison to adolescents who are more central (Pearson and Michell 2009).

Theoretical perspectives on online communication

A review of CMC theories reveals a number of perspectives (Table 5.1). The first, usually referred to as the *lack of contextual clues* approach, is based on the concept that different channels of communication transmit different amounts of information (Daft and Lengel, 1984; Sproull and Kiesler, 1991; Bargh and McKenna, 2004). Information, in communication terms, refers not only to words but also to the social context or socially implicit knowledge in that communicated bundle. From this perspective, scholars argue that CMC provides a *limited social presence* as compared to face-to-face communication, and that the lack of social and contextual cues from the communicators affects the perception of the messages, the perception of the individuals sending the messages, and, eventually, the social connections between communicators (Sproull and Kiesler, 1991; Tidwell and Walther, 2002). Several theories follow this approach. For example, the basic assumption of media richness theory (Daft and Langel, 1984) is that media differ in their ability to handle rich information, embedded with socially tacit knowledge and complex meanings. The richness of a medium refers to its capacity to transfer non-verbal and verbal cues and allow immediate feedback, to its language variety, and to its use of diverse channels. Based on the assumption that face-to-face communication is a rich medium, whereas CMC is a leaner one, the theory expects rich media to be used for complex and equivocal messages and leaner media for less equivocal exchanges. According to Kahai and Cooper (2003), media richness theory emphasizes that media differ in their ability to facilitate changes in the understanding of

ICT and existing social ties 93

Table 5.1 Theories of computer-mediated communication

Theory	Postulate	Implication
Technologically deterministic		
Lack of contextual clues, limited social presence	CMC provides a limited social presence as compared with face-to-face communication	A lack of social and contextual communicators' cues affects the perception and the quality of social connections between communicators
Media richness theory	Media differ in their capacity to convey rich information, embedded with socially tacit knowledge and complex meanings	
Cues-filtered-out theory	Impersonality reduces interpersonal impressions	Inability to create communication with real personal content, but also in negative communication, such as flaming and verbal aggression
Conditional models (indeterministic)		
Hyper-personal theory	Computer-mediated communication can support more intimate communication than face-to-face communication	Frequency, duration, and commitment create intimate relations online
Social identity and de-individuation (SIDE) model	Lack of non-verbal cues in online communication is not detrimental to personal communication	Anonymity, lack of supervisory features, and availability in cyberspace of individuals who have the same specialized and shared interests, can even stimulate personal communication

messages. Face-to-face communication is richer than written communication because it facilitates changes in the understanding of messages between communicators. To facilitate communication and task performance, rich media include multiple cues in addition to words, such as voice inflection, body gestures, non-verbal messages, immediacy of feedback, and bi-directional communication. Multiple cues allow rapid message

94 ICT and existing social ties

reinterpretation, clarification, and personalization. Personal feelings and emotions are infused, and messages are tailored to the receiver's current needs. Language variety is the range of meanings that can be conveyed by the available pool of symbols in a language. The critical elements are multiplicity of cues and immediacy of feedback, which enable communicators to clarify the message.

The *social presence theory* belongs to this family and refers to the extent to which a medium is perceived as conveying the communicators' actual physical presence. Social presence depends on the communication of words, but also on a variety of non-verbal cues, such as physical distance, postures, facial expressions, and the like. According to this theory, different types of media vary in their capacity to transmit information about facial expression, direction of looking, posture, dress, and non-verbal and vocal cues. Low social presence media are used when intimate and personal communication is minimal. From the perspective of social presence theory, computer-mediated communication is unable to convey the message of emotions. For a message to be effective, two conditions must be met: multiplicity of cues and immediacy of feedback, both of which promote the clarity of the message. This theory predicts that media facilitating multiple cues and immediacy of feedback yield more frequent socio-emotional communication, communication with a *personal content*, and the formation of *meaningful personal associations*. Media that lack social presence result in communication with low personal content.

The *cues-filtered-out theory* (Sproull and Kiesler, 1986) similarly posits that social presence declines with the move from face-to-face to computer-mediated communication; messages become more impersonal. Sproull and Kiesler (1986) state that CMC reduces social context cues, aspects of the physical environment, and non-verbal hierarchical status cues, the absence of which is said to reduce interpersonal impressions.

According to Sproull and Kiesler (1986), without non-verbal tools, a sender cannot easily alter the mood of a message; communicate a sense of individuality, or exercise dominance or charisma. Moreover, communicators feel a greater sense of anonymity and detect less individuality in others. Scholars of this outlook, which evolved from early work on CMC, argue that the bandwidth is insufficient to carry all the communication signals needed to convey social, emotional, and contextual content. In text-only systems, for example, both task information and social information are carried in the same single verbal/linguistic channel, which may be adequate for most task information but cannot transmit non-verbal information such as body motions, voice tone, and so on (Sproull and Kiesler, 1986). Filtering out social, emotional, and contextual information can obviously entail important consequences for the interaction, especially when the main focus is on the development of an interpersonal relationship.

These early theories were highly deterministic technologically, assuming that limitations inherent in the text-based communication prevent the support of strong (supportive and intimate) ties but can support weak ones (that supply information). The theories do not account for the socio-structural context of existing relationships, and the emphasis is on communication features. Furthermore, only the *lack of social clues* theory considers the social context, which they assert is not clear, so the communicators experience a lack of social control. This results in an inability to create communication with real personal content, but also in negative communication, such as flaming and verbal aggression (Sproull and Kiesler, 1986).

An alternative perspective has emerged to account for the evidence that under certain circumstances, individuals communicating online are able to maintain personal and intimate relationships just as in face-to-face settings. This perspective is increasingly becoming relevant as ICT has been integrated into many user-friendly social apps, containing voice and video messaging. This perspective is usually referred to as the "socio-emotional perspective" (Kahai and Cooper, 2003). Walther (1996) developed the hyperpersonal interaction model, arguing that, in certain cases, CMC, rather than producing impersonal communication, can lead to hyper-personal or even intimate communication. The model, based on principles of social psychology, argues that CMC can support more intimate communication than face-to-face communication. According to this approach, the absence of non-verbal cues, identity cues, and temporal characteristics may prompt online users to engage in selective self-presentation and partner idealization, enacting exchanges more intimate than those that occur in face-to-face interactions (Tidwell and Walther, 2002). The hyper-personal model acknowledges the problem that CMC lacks reliable information about the communicators, but it also implies that the development of a close and personal relationship requires primarily frequent communication and time. If individuals communicate frequently, intensely, and for a long period of time, they are highly likely to develop a shared system of symbols. Online communication can reach intimacy, be personal, and support close relationships.

Spears and Lea (1992) likewise developed the *social identity and de-individuation* (SIDE) model, arguing that the lack of non-verbal cues in online communication is not detrimental to personal communication. According to this approach, the communicators' personal goals and needs are the sole determinants of its effects, and people engage in interpersonal

96 *ICT and existing social ties*

and mediated communication for purposes that are individual in nature. Different individuals are motivated in various ways to participate in the communication process, and each has a distinctive motivation, determining the communicators' willingness (or lack thereof) to disclose their offline, real, selves. The specific individual purposes determine the communication outcome, regardless of particular features of the communication channel in which the interaction takes place.

Bargh and McKenna (2004) maintain that some of the characteristics of ICT can—under certain circumstances—be conducive to the development of personal and intimate communication. According to these scholars, several qualities of the Internet, such as anonymity, lack of gating features, and the availability in cyberspace of individuals who have the same specialized and shared interests, can paradoxically stimulate personal communication. Furthermore, these authors argue that intimate relationships require anonymity to capacitate self-disclosure, which in turns, increases the experience of intimacy in social interactions. Disclosure of intimate information occurs after trust and liking have been established between partners, and intimacy is difficult to reach when one is concerned that personal and intimate information may be embarrassing should it become known to members of one's close social circle. The relative anonymity of Internet interactions greatly reduces the risk of such disclosure, particularly of intimate aspects of oneself, because here one can share inner beliefs and emotional reactions with less fear of disapproval and sanction. Such anonymity can be relevant to all people, but especially to adolescents, who under anonymous conditions can avoid the embarrassment of exposing their feeling and ideas to others, all the more so if they are members of an "invisible minority," such as homosexuals. A second reason for greater self-disclosure online is the invisibility of the usual features that obstruct the establishment of a close relationship. Easily discernible features such as physical appearance (attractiveness), evident shyness, or social anxiety are barriers in everyday life to relationship formation. These gates often prevent people who are less attractive physically or less skilled socially from developing relationships to the point where disclosure of intimate information can begin. Such features on the Internet are not initially in evidence, hence do not stop potential relationships from getting off the ground. Finally, the unique features of the Internet enable individuals easily to find others who share their specialized interests. The implications, according to Bargh and McKenna (2004), are that online communication can support closeness and intimacy. The convergence of communication media changed, particularly the use of video conversation, modifying the effect of lack of social cues in the digital space, but did not abolish it altogether. On the contrary, presentation of the user's digital self has become more architecture-based and sophisticated, especially for digital natives (Wohn and Birnholtz, 2015; Ziegele and Reinecke, 2017).

The shift of social media to smartphones, and the integration of IM into desktop, tablets, and phones have changed texting practices. Texting has undergone a change in the past several years with the advent of smartphone-based messaging apps that have added features and changed the cost, message length, and other structures around sending short messages. An impressive rate of 91 percent of teen cell users exploit text messaging—either directly through their mobile phones or through an app or a website (Lenhart et al., 2015). Pew Research found that girls are also a bit more likely than boys to use messaging apps, with 37 percent of cell-owning girls using them compared with 29 percent of boys with cell phones (Lenhart et al., 2015).

Sharing, posting, and publishing online short "stories" in visual-dominated, telephone-centric applications, provide different gratification and sense of belonging to youth and adolescents (Hassen, 2019). Research indicates that Instagram users, for example, are demonstrating intention to produce and maintain symbolic bonds on the application. Like many other social networks applications, Instagram attracts its users to compete for "gifting" online, vying for public recognition, and social capital. Like other social networks platforms, Instagram thus serves as a built-in reward system where users celebrate abundance, echoed by the nature of the online posts and stories (Hassen, 2019).

Youth social network effects in the adoption of media

In the last ten years the communication environment of Western youth has changed as youth are increasingly using the Internet for communication and social purposes. An early study in the USA found that 89 percent have access to the Internet. Most of the use is for social purposes, as 93 percent send and receive emails, 68 percent send and receive Instant Messages, 55 percent have a profile in a social networking site, 28 percent have created or work in an online journal (blog), and 18 percent visit chat rooms (Lenhart et al., 2007). These numbers have significantly increased (Smith and Anderson, 2018). The majority of Americans use social platforms, while some platforms are more popular among young adults and teens (Smith and Anderson, 2018). Adolescents' online interactions with strangers are not as common now as during the early years of the Internet. Most online interactions are with close friends: to keep in touch after school hours, exchange gossip, share information

98   ICT and existing social ties

about homework, coordinate gatherings and activities, and ask for social support (Subrahmanyan and Greenfield, 2008; Valkenburg and Taylor Piotrowski, 2017).

Online communication has become an integral part of the youth culture; the high diffusion is associated with the "network effect," the phenomenon whereby a service becomes more valuable as more people use it, thereby encouraging ever-increasing numbers of adopters. The network effect becomes significant after the number of users has reached a certain figure, usually referred to as the critical mass. The network effect often results from dissemination by word of mouth. Later on, known others play a more significant role. So while some individuals adopt the system initially because someone has told them about it, later they may adopt a service because virtually most everyone they know uses it. Then, as the number of users increases, the system becomes even more valuable and is able to attract a wider user base.

The network effect has two kinds of value. One kind is for the user, namely, the benefit that accrues from the plain fact that he or she is using the product. The other is the value of the network itself, namely, the benefits to the user resulting from others using the same product. The network effect indicates that the extensive use of email, Instant Messaging, and social networking sites by teens is the result of its diffusion through social networks, mostly face-to-face. Consistent evidence suggests that people who socially interact eventually use concurrently multiple types of communication channels (Van Cleemput, 2010). In other words, not only is the adoption of specific applications (IM, social networking sites) social, but their use may depend on the nature of the existing social networks. Close friends have a higher likelihood of communicating through a diversity of communication channels: face-to-face meetings, phone and cell phone conversations, online communication, and more (Haythornthwaite, 2002; Baym, Zhang, and Lin, 2004; Mesch and Talmud, 2006a; Van Cleemput, 2010).

It is interesting to note that both SMS and IM are used to support an important developmental task of adolescence: the creation of a sense of autonomy and belonging. SMS messages allow teenagers to work within the constraints imposed on them, such as their not driving, hence their reliance on public or parental transport, and the need to balance school and parental requirements with their social desires. SMS allows teenagers to stay in touch and communicate when doing homework and when at extracurricular activities (Ito et al., 2009). For teenagers in traditional groups that constrain cross-sex meetings without adult control, IM serves to communicate with friends of the opposite sex without the knowledge and control of parents and siblings. In a study of Arab and Jewish Israelis,

ICT and existing social ties   99

Mesch and Talmud (2007c) found that Arab youngsters blended their IM use with other computer work. If a parent or sibling approached, IM use was rendered temporarily invisible through window management, namely, by minimizing or hiding the chat window.

Studies on adolescents' Internet use consistently present the idea that Instant Messaging is used as an additional communication tool rather than displacing the telephone (Gross, 2004; Gross et al., 2002; Lenhart et al., 2001, 2005; Lenhart, 2015). Most Instant Messaging partners are friends or best friends from school. Their online interactions occur in a private setting, with friends who are part of their daily offline lives, covering ordinary yet intimate topics. Moreover, teens' communication of intimate topics may strengthen their closeness with friends, as shown in Valkenburg and Peter's (2007b) findings that adolescents with a high frequency, intensity, and rate of chatting felt closer to their friends.

Instant Messaging and social networking sites differ from other online communication channels in a variety of characteristics. As we have already mentioned, the adoption of the technology is social, as it results from a group of friends settling on a particular IM or social networking system. Social media are a fundamental component of the communication channels used by adolescents. IM is adopted mainly because of peer pressure, which helps to create a critical mass of users in an online social group. Today, as media are more converged, being part of a peer group is an essential, required engagement in perpetual communication online after school hours especially on social media such as WhatsApp. Those who do not, cannot be integral part of the peer group. Not being online or not having an IM user name means exclusion from most of the daily social interaction. Using IM requires having an active list of buddies and being on a friends list authorized by the peers. In that sense, the use of IM with strangers is uncommon as its appeal is mainly with existing friends.

Young people's use of instant and text messaging might be motivated by the need to belong to, maintain, and develop an existing social circle. In recent years, a number of studies have confirmed this argument. In a study of late adolescents' motivations for IM use, participants named mainly four. One was social entertainment, in which the user conducted IM communication to spend spare time and to stay in touch with friends. Next was task accomplishment, namely, to learn from others how to do things, generate ideas, and make decisions. The third motivation was social attention, in particular, mitigation of loneliness and getting support and affection from peers. The least frequent motivation named by the participants was meeting new people (Flanagin, 2005).

When used to connect with members of the peer group, IM promotes rather than hinders intimacy, with frequent IM conversations encouraging

100   ICT and existing social ties

the desire to meet face-to-face with friends (Hu, Fowler-Wood, Smith, and Westbrook, 2004). The main uses of IM are for socializing, event-planning, task accomplishment, and meeting people (Grinter and Pallen, 2002; Flanagin, 2005), such that IM has a positive effect when used with known friends. Conversely, visiting chat rooms expands the size of young people's networks and provides complementary social support; but this apparently is at the expense of intimacy with known friends and results in a perception of increased alienation and conflict, and decreased intimacy and companionship with face-to-face friends. These two different activities clearly serve different functions

It had been found already more than 12 years ago that adolescents' use the Internet to commutate with friends in a complex way. An early study in the USA, conducted by the Pew and American Life Project, found already in 2007 that 91 percent of all social networking teen respondents said they used the sites to stay in touch with friends whom they saw frequently; 82 percent used them to stay in touch with friends whom they rarely saw in person; and 72 percent used the sites to make plans with their friends. Only 49 percent used them to make new friends. More specifically, about a third of the surveyed teenagers talked to their friends through mobile phone, IM, and text messaging every day. Slightly fewer youngsters used social network sites (21 percent) and email (14 percent) on a daily basis. Meanwhile, the traditional ways of communication (face-to-face and landline phone) were still the most often used means for interaction (Lenhart et al., 2007). In the UK, findings were similar, although users reported massive numbers of individuals as "friends," the actual number of close friends was approximately the same as that of face-to-face friends (Smith, 2007). The research consistently found that although the sites allowed contact with hundreds of acquaintances, people tended to have around five close friends and 90 percent of the contacts were people they had met face-to-face. Only 10 percent were contacts made with total strangers (Smith, 2007). The comparative study found that on average only 17 percent of respondents with a profile in social networking sites used the site to talk with people they did not know (Ofcom, 2008).

Another study, investigating a sample of pre-adolescents, examined whether online communication reduced or increased perceived closeness to existing friends. Online communication using IM proved to exert a positive effect on perceived closeness to friends. This effect came about mainly because IM communication is conducted with friends who are known and represent an additional channel of communication that reinforces existing ties (Valkenburg and Peter, 2007b). Yet another study of pre-adolescents (7th graders) probed the role of IM in their social life. Participants reported using the application for more frequent social

ICT and existing social ties 101

interaction with their friends, for gossip, and for romantic communication. The most frequent motive, stated by 92 percent of the respondents, was hanging out with a friend after school hours. Participants described their IM partners as long-standing friends and peers, first met at school. Our study investigated the association between IM use and psychological wellbeing. Participants who reported feeling lonely at school on a daily basis were found more likely to have online sessions with individuals they met online and did not know face-to-face. Teens who felt well connected with their school friends tended to use IM to seek out additional opportunities for social interaction with them after school hours, mostly as a continuation of conversations that had started during school hours (Gross, Juvonen, and Gable, 2002). In a longitudinal study of 812 Dutch adolescents, Valkenburg and Peter (2009) found that the positive effect of IM on relational quality was entirely attributable, or could be "explained" by, the tendency to increase intimate disclosure and personal information to close friends through this medium. Although self-disclosure could be risky, with potential for detrimental usages, such as flaming and harassment, users learn over time to develop precautionary devices in their Internet use (McCowan et al., 2001), and the differences in relational quality between online and offline channels diminish as the relationships develop (Chan and Cheng, 2004), and as social media are converging into inter-operative platforms; all embedded in user-friendly smartphones. The use of smartphones has dramatically changed ICT communication frequency and quality, The Pew Institute found that in 2018, 24 percent of American teens go online "almost constantly," facilitated by the widespread availability of smartphones (Lenhart 2015), most extensively, using social networks sites. Girls dominate visually-oriented social media platforms, while boys are more likely to play online video games. Additionally, platform choice is associated with family social status: Snapchat is used most often by wealthier teens, while Facebook is most popular among lower-income youth (Lenhart, 2015; Valkenburg and Piotrowski, 2017).

Communication channel choice

Other factors are also involved in the choice of communication channel. Communication is an integral part of social relationships and takes place in a social context that includes geographic location, origin, and intensity of the relationship, and the information that is being communicated (Sproull and Kiesler, 1986). In that sense, whether already existing characteristics of a relationship and its social context affect the choice of an online or offline channel of communication is an important question. Geographic

102 *ICT and existing social ties*

location serves as a social context that provides opportunities for channel choice. People in proximity are more likely to participate in joint activities and to be physically exposed to each other; and to communicate face-to-face, people must be in geographic proximity or have easy physical access to each other. For example, among adolescents, proximity is important for friendship formation as it establishes the boundaries within which they choose friends. A major location for meeting and making friends is school, where adolescents spend many of their waking hours. Yet other settings might be important as well. Adolescents spend their available free time in neighborhood haunts after school, such as shopping malls or video arcades usually located in the neighborhood, where groups of adolescents get to know others who might live in the same neighborhood but do not attend the same school. While geographical proximity or access is a necessary condition for face-to-face communication, it does not restrict the ability to use other channels of communication. In other words, when individuals are in physical proximity due to place of residence or activity, they are more likely to use face-to-face communication. The costs involved in such communication (traveling and available time) rise with physical distance.

Strength of tie is important as well, as face-to-face meetings to socialize and spend time together are more likely with ties one feels close to. Face-to-face meetings with distant ties are more likely to be conducted in formal settings and for formal purposes. Interestingly, although computer-mediated communication facilitates global communication, it mostly serves locally based ties (Hampton and Wellman, 2001; Livingstone, 2007).

Another factor influencing the choice of communication channel is relationship origin. The use of the Internet has diversified and expanded the sources of relationship formation to the online space. Individuals make new friends in the neighborhood, school, and workplace, but also online; and often the last-named connection moves to face-to-face meetings. Relationships created online are likely to be maintained through online communication, certainly during the first steps of relationship formation; but even after the communicators have met in person they tend to continue relying mostly on online communication for small-talk and coordination of shared activities. In addition, little overlap apparently exists between those relations created offline and friendships that are created online. Individuals are very likely to create two different sets of social networks, one with individuals they have met online and the other with people with whom the relationship began offline, without much overlap between them (Mesch, 2009; boyd, 2017). This argument implies that some relationship antecedents (such as geographical proximity and

ICT and existing social ties 103

relationship origin) are instrumental in the choice of communication channel.

An important component of communication choice is multiplexity, or multiple dimensions of relational flows. It is high when individuals are connected in multiple activities and discussions. Unlike formal relationships, in which social interaction is partial and based on social status, friendship is more holistic. A friend differs from a co-worker or a relative in not being restricted to a few topics of conversation or a few shared activities. To be friends is to be together and to talk about anything. Multiplexity exists where a tie between two or more people encompasses multiple activities or topics of conversation, rather than a single activity or a shared topic. Studies show that multiplexity increases ties' strength (Boissevain, 1974; Kadushin, 2004). Additionally, multiplexity is statistically associated with social similarity (homophily) and is reported among friends of similar social background, such as age, gender, ethnicity, school, academic performance, and social status (Stoller, Miller, and Guo, 2001). Background similarity or homophily increases the likelihood of contact multiplexity (Bush, Walker, and Perry, 2017).

Multiplexity is divided into activity multiplexity (shared social actions), and content multiplexity (the number of issues shared by a pair of friends). Multiplexity is a typical indicator of village community life, and is an important indicator of intimacy and trust (Wasserman and Faust, 1995; Kadushin, 2004).

Another important element is relationship strength. Social ties differ in terms of the intensity of the relationship. Friendship, for example, is distinct from other types of social relationships because contact with friends is more intense. It seems reasonable then that strong ties will tend to communicate by a variety of communication channels. Their social interaction is more frequent and includes intimate and non-intimate conversations, and is not restricted to specific topics or activities. This holistic characteristic implies the use of a wide variety of channels, from face-to-face, through phone and cell phone, to online communication (Haythornthwaite, 2002; Baym, Zhang, and Mei-Chen, 2004).

Van Cleemput (2010) studied 15-year-old Belgian adolescents' communication patterns. Using social network analytical tools, she inquired into relational patterns between the adolescents' communication networks. The results clearly indicated that face-to-face communication was still the most prominent way for information to flow through the adolescents' network. Interactions through communication media (email, IM, text messaging, mobile phone, and landline phone), supplemented, but did not replace, this flow of information in a substantive way. Consequently,

104 *ICT and existing social ties*

communication media use patterns were characterized by multiplexity. In a typical way, close friends (strong ties) used all available communication media to connect with one another. By comparison, adolescents who were just "friends" (weak ties) preferred either face-to-face communication or social network sites. More specifically, the study found that the studied adolescents talked, on average,

> at least a few times a week to seven other students through instant messaging and sent four other students a text message with the same frequency ... instant messaging was preferred over e-mail for non-school-related interactions, while e-mail was preferred over instant messaging for school subjects ... the communication patterns for school and non-school topics were very similar. E-mail and instant messaging were followed by text messaging, making telephone calls on a mobile phone, and making telephone calls on a landline phone.

Additionally, there was a substantive overlap between all communication relations (Van Cleemput, 2010).

In our Israeli studies of adolescents' online and offline friendship ties, we investigated the extent to which social relationships originating online and offline differ. We compared these relationships on several central dimensions, in particular, duration and communication content. Multiple communication channels are a central component of any association, because they indicate "thick communicative action", shared multiple interests, intimacy, and closeness. We also asked whether relations migrate from setting to setting, blurring the boundaries between offline and online. Finally, we showed how interpersonal trust differs according to the origin of the relationship.

We found that closeness to a friend is a function of social similarity, content and activity multiplexity, and duration of the relationships. Friendships that originated on the Internet are perceived as less close and less supportive because they are relatively new, and online friends are involved in fewer joint activities and fewer topics of discussion. Furthermore, strength of ties seems to be a developmental process, becoming firmer with age; also, it is greater for boys than for girls (Mesch and Talmud, 2006a).

Our results, based on two representative samples of the Israeli adolescent population, consistently show that the diverse social contexts in which individuals reveal themselves to each other are important. The highest degree of similarity in friends was found in schools. Apparently, age-graded segregation and the fact that schools mainly depend on local enrollment combine to create a high degree of friends' similarity in age

ICT and existing social ties 105

and place of residence. Friends met in the neighborhood were less similar to the respondents, and friends met online were the least similar to them. These results indicate that the higher levels of homophily reported in previous studies, which were based on school samples alone, might overestimate the extent of friends' homophily.

Our Israeli results also indicate that adolescents' developmental factors also affect the tendency to relational similarity. Of all three indicators of similarity (gender, age, proximity), age was found to have a negative relationship to the likelihood of similarity. In other words, over and above the effect of proximity, the older the adolescent, the less likely was friendship similarity to occur. Another indication of a developmental process was the effect of length of acquaintance. The longer the time a friend was known, the more likely was social similarity to exist. Keeping friends from the past seems to reinforce the effect of proximity in the development of social similarity in adolescence; the past has an effect on the present state of friendship (Mesch and Talmud, 2006a, 2007c).

The question of maintaining online relational quality over time is particularly relevant for close, salient, and intimate friendship ties. Valkenburg and Peter (2007a) found that adolescents who communicated more often with their friends online felt closer to their existing friends than those who communicated less often online. Similarly, Blais et al. (2008) examined to what extent using the Internet for different activities affected the quality of close adolescent relationships (i.e., best friendships and romantic relationships). In a one-year longitudinal study of 884 adolescents, they tested whether visiting chat rooms, using Instant Messaging (ICQ), using the Internet for general entertainment, or participating in online gaming predicted changes in the quality of best friendships and romantic relationships. Blais et al. (2008) found that Internet activity choice influenced later relationship quality in both kinds of relationship. More specifically, using ICQ was positively associated with most aspects of romantic relationship and best-friendship quality. In contrast, visiting chat rooms was negatively related to best-friendship quality. Using the Internet to play games and for general entertainment predicted a decrease in the quality of the relationship with best friend and with romantic partner. These findings reflect the important and complex functions of online activity and virtual socialization for the development and maintenance of relationships in adolescence in the information age. Similarly, Lee (2007) found that adolescents' overall social offline relational quality determined the likelihood of online communication, and resulted in cohesive friendship ties, which in turn even led to higher school connectedness.

106 *ICT and existing social ties*

Online and face-to-face convergence

In many contexts, information and communication technologies supplement, interweave with, or replace traditional routes of communication (Hardey, 2004; Madden, 2009; Subrahmanyan and Greenfield, 2008). Table 5.2 presents the structural processes affecting online relationship maintenance. While adults tend to judge online communication against an idealized image of face-to-face conversation, young people evaluate a wide range of options—face-to-face, email, instant messaging, chat rooms, phones, SMS—according to their communicative needs. The evidence presented in this chapter shows that adolescents may in fact improve their social relationships through online communication activities, but also by using the Internet as a source of shared activities and common culture among peer groups. Some ethnographic studies suggest that children use online games together with their friends, and information and ideas gathered online are used as common topics for

Table 5.2 Structural processes affecting online relationship maintenance

Process	Feature	Outcome
Network effects on diffusion	Transitivity and homophily drive the adoption of ICT by adolescents	Rapid adoption of ICT by adolescents via peer "word-of-mouth" influence
Media choice and content choice	Multiplexity: spillover between face-to-face interaction and ICT	Multiple channels intensify relational strength and tie maintenance
More choice between media channels (IM, chat rooms, social networking site, mobile phones)	User's versatility	More communication autonomy for the adolescent user Choice is associated with relational strength
Transitivity, homophily, and proximity govern relational patterns	Online communication is mainly for maintaining existing social ties among socially similar people	Social closure and structural diversification of online networks
Convergence of face-to-face and online worlds	The division between offline and online spaces is growing blurred and fading away	Reciprocal effects of online and offline spheres

ICT and existing social ties 107

offline interaction (Valentine and Holloway, 2002; Lee, 2007; Lenhart, 2009). The conversational content among adolescent users is often mundane; being readily in touch with their friends is what counts for them (Gross, 2004).

Online communication seems to foster offline links. Online communication is rarely an escape from offline context; rather, durable online and offline ties are mutually embedded and reinforcing. The technological affordance of online relations, as well as the fact that online relational patterns are embedded in the general social structure, impacts ICT to promote rather than undermine existing social contacts with friends from school, connecting adolescents into local, rather than global, networks (Mesch and Talmud, 2006a; Lee, 2007).

Another tension in the potential outcomes of the use of online communication that needs to be addressed is between social diversification and social bonding. Certain technologies might support expansion of social relationships, including access to information, knowledge, and skills that teens cannot access due to residential segregation. Diversification is very likely to take place together with social bonding. The use of technologies that require previous knowledge, and even membership of the same social circle, can be used to coordinate group activities, to continue conversations that started at school, to express personal and intimate concerns, and to provide social support. In that sense, these technologies can support the development of peer group cohesion and the formation of a sense of solidarity and togetherness for those who are part of the social circle. Additionally, many issues typical of the adolescent developmental stage have partially become transformed from face-to-face to online interactions, or have been affected by virtual space. Both online and offline spheres involve issues of adolescents' intimacy, identity formation, peer pressure, and individual autonomy, as well as bullying, harassment, and racism (Subrahmanyan and Greenfield, 2008).[1]

Leskovec and Horvitz (2008) found that people tend to communicate online more when they are of a similar age, sharing the same language, and same location, and that cross-gender conversations are both more frequent and longer than conversations with the same gender. Transitivity and homophily, which drive the formation of social networks, may exclude others who lack access to the technologies and those who are not accepted by the group (Kadushin, 2004; Leskovec and Horvitz, 2008). The transitivity of adolescents' social networks contains an additional benefit: it can facilitate overcoming or minimizing the possibility of deceit. Mutual contacts can vouch for the offline identities of online friends. Additionally, local social networks can provide more contacts to verify online identities (Wolak, Mitchell, and Finkelhor, 2002).

108 *ICT and existing social ties*

Still, the social affordance of ICT makes remote communication easier, and is a benefit for those who in their geographically close environment have no friends with common interests. For these, the Internet serves as a compensatory device for the lack of sufficient support in their own-group.

A marginal adolescent can construct a virtual identity, thus compensating for his or her lack of support in offline ties. Adolescents were found to experiment more than adults with their identity in the virtual environment (Šmahel and Machovcová, 2006). Moreover, the Internet can facilitate like-minded strangers becoming more supportive of one another by maintaining frequent virtual interactions. A recent study on offline strangers in tightly integrated online communities who explore their passion with like-minded people showed that the integration of offline and online life supports "passion-centric" activities, such as shared hobbies or lifestyles (Ploderer, Howard, and Thomas, 2008).

Nevertheless, for adolescents, propinquity governs their relational patterns (Kadushin, 2004). That is, most of their online ties are situated in their school, their neighborhood, and same place of residence, although this regularity is higher in face-to-face relations (Mesch and Talmud, 2006b). The intricate interaction of motivations for the use of different technologies with the particular type of social circle involved has to be made clear for an understanding of the effects of information and communication technologies on the size, composition, and nature of the social relationships which characterize adolescence in the information age.

With the passage of time, the online/offline comparison is apparently becoming a faded and even false dichotomy. Many ties operate in both cyberspace and the physical realms. They do not exist only online; instead, most adolescents' Internet practice routinely uses online communication to fill the spells between face-to-face meetings, and to coordinate joint activities and work (Van Cleemput, 2010). In other words, technological convergence—user-friendly, ubiquitous social apps—facilitates social multiplicity. Computer-mediated communication supplements, arranges, and amplifies in-person and telephone communications rather than replacing them. The Internet offers ease and flexibility regarding with whom one communicates, which medium to choose, when to communicate, and the communication duration. In reality, online relationships often replace empty spots in people's lives, a process deemed important especially where residential dispersal and dual careers reduce the availability of leisure and family times.

Adolescents learn how to manage their existing ties (boyd, 2017). The spread of social apps assists them in doing so. Anthropologist Dan Miller

ICT and existing social ties 109

classifies these apps into two key scales of a dual dimension, called "scalable sociality" (Miller 2016). The first is running from the most private to the most public. The second is the scale from the smallest group to the largest groups. At one end of both of these scales we still see private dyadic conversation and at the other end we still see fully public broadcasting.

Personal effects of existing social ties

In an early study of adolescents' online ties, researchers found that receiving positive feedback on one's online profile was associated with increased self-esteem and well-being (Valkenburg et al., 2006). Others found that mobile Internet and social media have greatly changed the way that adolescents communicate. More important, adolescents' mobile social media use was associated with a higher quality of friendship, which, in turn, contributed to their formation of self-identity. In addition, gender moderated the relation between mobile social media use and friendship quality, such that this relation was stronger for males than for female (Wang et al., 2019). there is a strong and negative relationship between online activities (chatting, emailing, participating in communities or clubs and using bulletin boards) and self-reported mental health and suicidal ideation among a nationally representative sample of Korean students (Kim, 2017).

Adolescents rely then on offline and online social connections and support—-including social apps—to develop a sense of belonging and also self-esteem, emotional well-being, self-efficacy, and self-worth (Sabik, Falat, and Magagnos, 2019). But cyberspace is an integral part of adolescents' and youth's ties, and consequently the characteristics that distinguish adolescents offline also shape their online activities (Davis, 2012),

The introduction and domestication of new technologies, however, are often accompanied by a kind of moral panic, frequently fostered by popular beliefs and journalism. These beliefs suggest that, as a result of this new technology, we have lost some essential elements of our authentic humanity or genuine nature of community (Miller, 2016; Hampton and Wellman, 2018). An example of this trend is Sherry Turkle's concern that the nature of online social interactions, in particular social media, has changed the way youth connect with one another. More specifically, Turkle argues that because people in interpersonal social situations, particularly young people, are often distracted by their phones, they will pay insufficient attention to one another, creating increasingly shallow relationships (Turkle, 2011). Her argument was supported by a few quantitative studies

110 *ICT and existing social ties*

(cf. Brook, 2015). Turkle further argues that teenagers' reliance on friends' advice prevents self-reflection and, as a result, is leading adolescents to live in a less personally autonomous life (Turkle, 2011).

Certainly, social media are a means for individuals to connect with others and to seek out social support and information. The results of this connection, however, are manifold and often even paradoxical. In the early days of the Internet, it was more common to argue that the Internet had a detrimental mental effect, though not always with sufficient evidence or appropriate methodology (cf. Kraut et al., 1998). However, other evidence suggested that online social networks use was correlated with mental illness and well-being. The main point is that these effects are neither uniform or general; rather, they are conditional. Furthermore, the extent to which this effect is beneficial or detrimental depends at least partly on the quality of social factors embedded in the social environment (Bessière et al., 2010; Seabrook et al., 2016). Specifically, the negative association found between online identity expression/exploration and self-image was mediated partially by low friendship quality effects. Put differently, communicating online with one's friends appeared to play a more positive role in adolescents' sense of identity. More to this point, online peer communication affected the crystallization of the clarity of the self-concept indirectly through its positive impact on friendship quality (Spies and Margolin, 2014).

However, not all social interactions online produce positive outcomes, as we will illustrate in Chapter 7. For example, studies have found that frequent social media use may be associated with lower subjective well-being and even increased depression (Lin et al., 2016). In a systematic review exploring the effects of online technologies on adolescent mental well-being or related concepts, results show contradictory and mixed evidence. The main benefits of using online technologies were reported as increased self-esteem, perceived social support, increased social capital, safe identity experimentation, and increased opportunity for self-disclosure. In contrast, detrimental effects were reported as increased exposure to harm, social isolation, depression, and cyberbullying. The majority of studies reported either mixed or no effect of online social technologies on adolescent well-being. It is important to see that there was still a lack of robust, longitudinal analysis (Best, Manktelow, and Taylor, 2014). Many findings on attributed effects of online social networks on the mental health and well-being of adolescents have suffered from methodological problems, mainly using cross-sectional data that cannot lead to conclusive evidence regarding causality (Keles, McCrae, and Grealish, 2019). Moreover, other empirical evidence supporting the notion of negative effects of ICT is typically based on secondary analyses of large-scale social datasets with many variables, analytical flexibility, and "too powerful" statistical tests that lead to false positives (Orben and Psybilski, 2019).

Another related issue that has received public and scholarly attention is the presumed rising level of loneliness in online social networks (Twenge, Spitzberg, and Campbell, 2019). Loneliness, however, does not occur by chance. It is a function of both individual attributes and behavior, but also of the properties of social networks in which the individual is embedded. In fact, the subjective feeling of loneliness is contagious. It can be spread like a social epidemic. The gap between an individual's loneliness and the actual number of his or her connections in a social network is well known. This disparity was investigated by Cacioppo, Fowler, and Christakis (2009), who analyzed large-scale adult social networks. They investigated the spread of loneliness throughout social networks. They found that loneliness occurs in clusters, extending up to three degrees of separation. More to the point, loneliness was disproportionately represented at the periphery of social networks, and spreads through a contagious process. More importantly, and relevant to adolescents and youth as well, they revealed that the spread of loneliness was stronger than the spread of perceived social connections, stronger for friends than family members, and stronger for women than for men (Cacioppo et al., 2009). More specifically,

> loneliness is not only a function of the individual but is also a property of groups of people. People who are lonely tend to be linked to others who are lonely, an effect that is stronger for geographically proximal than distant friends yet extends up to three degrees of separation (friends' friends' friend) within the social network. The nature of the friendship matters, as well, in that nearby mutual friends show stronger effects than nearby ordinary.
>
> (Cacioppo et al., 2009)

Orben and her associates (Orben et al., 2019) recently conducted a robust, longitudinal, and comprehensive analysis of the overall effects of social media on adolescents, across three large-scale social datasets (total $n = 355,358$). They specifically examined to what extent adolescents who are using more social media, are showing different levels of life satisfaction compared with adolescents using fewer social media. They found that across all operationalizations, the median longitudinal effects were trivial in size, especially when compared to other offline factors which affect

112 ICT and existing social ties

well-being and life satisfaction (Orben, Dienlin, and Przybylski, 2019; Orben and Przybylski, 2019). It means, among other things, that many effects which are been attributed to online social ties are either indirect, confounded, or negligible, comparing to other life effects on adolescents' and youth's social reality (see also Hampton, 2019, for the adult population). In particular, Orben and Przybylski (2019) found that the association between digital technology use and adolescent well-being was negative but utterly small, explaining at most 0.4 percent of the variation in well-being, thus they concluded that "taking the broader context of the data into account suggests that these effects are too small to warrant policy change."

Summary

In this chapter, we focused on the link between ICT and existing social ties. More specifically, we explored youth social network effects in the adoption of media, by examining how social patterns affect the maintenance and endurance of adolescents' online social ties. Moreover, we illuminated three main principles governing the quantity and quality of online communication: proximity, homophily, and transitivity. In the remaining chapters, we compare a few theoretical perspectives on online communication. On the one hand, media differ in their capacity to convey rich information, embedded with socially tacit knowledge and complex meaning, while net impersonality reduces interpersonal impressions. On the other hand, it seems that computer-mediated communication can support more intimate communication than even face-to-face communication. Frequency, duration, and commitment create intimate relations online. Lack of non-verbal cues in online communication is not detrimental to personal communication. On the contrary, anonymity, lack of supervisory features, and availability in cyberspace of individuals who have the same specialized and shared interests, can even stimulate personal communication. There is spillover between face-to-face interaction and ICT communication. The existence of multiple channels tends to intensify relational strength and tie maintenance.

Adolescents' online communication is mainly used for maintaining existing social ties among socially similar people. The unexpected fundamental outcome is the emergence of social closure and structural diversification of online networks. Another key result is the convergence of face-to-face and online worlds, where the imagined divide between offline and online spaces is growing blurred and fading away. Finally, recent authoritative research suggests that while online adolescents' engagement is increasing, its net effects on adolescents' life is negligible, compared to other life events.

In Chapter 6, we address directly the implications of the integration and blurring of face-to-face and online social ties for the creation, maintenance, and modification of social capital.

Note

1 On negative social ties, see Chapter 7.

6 The impact of ICT on social network structure

Introduction

Every social network is affected by relational patterns and social regularities. In this chapter, we examine three central questions regarding the structural configuration of adolescents' online social networks. The first is how heterogeneous the composition of adolescents' social ties is becoming, and to what extent this change is linked to social and technological factors. The second is whether this change affects the strength of adolescents' social ties. The third is the effect of ICT on social capital, specifically whether ICT supports bonding or bridging social capital.

We also examine the impact of network density and Internet use on the quality of social relations among adolescents, and the impact of ICT on their ability to reconfigure their social networks and relational pattern. To put these important questions in analytic context, we start with a discussion of the digital divide and its implications.

The digital divide: from stratification to normalization and from access to skills and usage

The "digital divide" means the uneven distribution of access to, and the asymmetric utilization of, the Internet (Anderson et al., 1995; Fong, Wellman, Kew, and Wilkes, 2001). It is important analytically to differentiate ICT access from ICT use. Access is the right to use a computer that is connected to the Internet in a private space, such as the home, or at a public point of access, such as a library. Use can be of different types. In an information society, using the Internet for computer games has different implications and outcomes from using it to gather information relevant for schoolwork. The former use is expected to help the development of motor skills, the latter school-related skills.

Many conceive the Internet as an agent of change in society because it allows rapid diffusion of information, the creation of social networks,

Impact of ICT on social network structure 115

and the accumulation of social capital (Lin, 2001; DiMaggio et al., 2001; Van Dijk, 2005; Mesch and Talmud, 2007b, 2007c:). The Internet can also reduce social inequalities by lowering the cost of information and enhancing the ability of socially marginal groups to gain human capital, compete for good jobs, and otherwise improve their life chances (Anderson et al., 1995). At the same time, many scholars are concerned that the Internet is creating a post-industrial society of information haves and have-nots that increases rather than reduces existing inequalities (DiMaggio et al., 2001). Narrowing the digital divide has become a concern for social activists, non-profit organizations, political activists, and governments.

Exploring the digital divide, we must distinguish aspects of access (owning a computer, having access to the Internet and a broadband connection) from dimensions of use (general cultural literacy, degree of computer literacy, and differences in type of use (Van Dijk, 2006)). More studies have suggested that the definition of the digital divide should cover, in addition to gaps in access, inequalities in the extent of use, types of Internet use, quality of digital literacy, and the critical ability to evaluate the quality of information (DiMaggio et al., 2001; Van Dijk, 2006). These difference in views manifest by disciplinary lens: while geographers and economists tend to emphasize uneven access to the Internet; sociologists and psychologists underscore the size of gaps in Internet use.

The categories of Internet access and use may be collapsed into a multidimensional concept of Internet connectedness (Jung, Qiu, and Kim, 2001; Loges and Jung, 2001). But the utility of this multidimensional approach is doubtful, as it may hide the sources of inequality. For example, lack of any kind of access to the Internet is not the same as lack of significant usage opportunities (Van Dijk and Hacker, 2003). For the adult population, access may be defined as a continuum (Loges and Jung, 2001), but this definition seems unsuitable for the adolescent population. Most adolescents who have Internet access in the developed world have already acquired some basic computer and Internet skills and literacy. As digital access and opportunity to use the Web involve the realization of social, economic, and cognitive resources, there is a strong association between Internet access and social inequality (Van Djik, 2005, 2006).

Studies have exposed several disparities between those who do and do not use the Internet (Katz, Rice, and Aspden, 2001), structured primarily along ethnic, gender, socio-economic, age, and urban-rural lines (DiMaggio et al., 2001; Livingston, 2003; Chen and Wellman, 2004; Van Dijk, 2005; Drori, 2006). Usually, the ethnic majority reports greater access to the Internet than minorities (Hoffman and Novak, 1998; Fong et al., 2001; Chen and Wellman, 2004). It is possible that a combination of various forms of disadvantage can multiply the likelihood of sustaining or

116 *Impact of ICT on social network structure*

increasing the inequality in certain populations, because they are excluded from the computer revolution that is shaping our society (DiMaggio et al., 2001; Attewell et al., 2003). The results of the Pew Internet and American Life Project indicated that "having a college degree, being a student, being white, being employed, and having a comfortable income each independently predicts Internet use" (Lenhart et al., 2003: 41; see also OECD 2018; Pew Research Center, 2019a, 2019b).

Despite evidence that the globalization process is dominated by the values, culture, and power of the dominant Western countries in the developed world, the emergence of expansive cyber-networks using relatively low-cost computer devices suggests the possibility of a bottom-up globalization process as well (Lin, 2001; Chen and Wellman, 2004). Moreover, the rise of ICT implies a "new era of democratic and entrepreneur networks and relations where resources flow and are shared by a large number of participants with new rules and practices" (Lin, 2001: 28–29). Lin argues further, "with the increasing availability of inexpensive computers and ever-increasing web capabilities which transcend space and time, we are facing a new era of social networks in the form of global villages" (Lin, 2001: 50).

Access and use: amplification or normalization?

The ability to maintain digital exchange with close friends and to form new virtual relations with new contacts is closely connected to ICT access and literacy. It can be argued that while physical access to computers and to the Internet and mobile phones is becoming increasingly universal, at least in Western countries, the types of use differ along social stratification lines, creating a new type of digital divide with profound consequences for the future (Table 6.1). Use diversity is the most important one, because

Table 6.1 Types of digital divide

Type of digital divide	Description
Access	The degree to which a person has access to ICT at home, at work, on smartphone, or in a public place (dissipating)
Use	Kinds of use, frequency and duration of usage
Digital literacy	The degree to which a person is competent in using ICT, computers, social media, and hyper-textuality
Multi-dimensional	A combination of all three; usually applies to the adult population

digital skills and literacy are acquired mainly through informal training (Van Dijk, 2006), affecting also the ability to accrue resources, education, and skills, deemed pertinent for the future labor market and social world (Van Dijk, 2006; Van Deursen and Van Dijk, 2010, 2014; OECD, 2018; Abrahim et al., 2019). The complex relation of sociological categories of stratification to informal training in Internet skills led Van Dijk to predict that over time the Internet access and use divide would grow wider (Van Dijk, 2005; Drori, 2006). Because Internet skills and kinds of use are "soft," being structurally associated mainly with material wealth, income disparity, and the household's cultural capital, Van Dijk foresees that the rate of information and online literacy skills will continue to accelerate differentially for those who have skills and those who do not. By contrast, the diffusion, contagion, and adoption perspectives argue that over time the gaps between social categories will shrink relatively, and the digital divide in access and in use will become greatly normalized (Van Dijk, 2005). For this reason, the study of ICT (especially the Internet) needs to scrutinize skill disparities and use diversification, which are now more important than the primary divide in access. Furthermore, the knowledge-acquisition process, especially by means of digital information, is a self-reinforcing cycle (Parayil, 2005). Therefore, the effect of differential acquisition of computer skills, online use, and Internet experience will produce an over-arching digital divide in the future, expressed as differential possession of digital skills which are increasingly relevant to future labor markets. as well as to technologically embedded social lives (Van Dijk, 2006). At the same time, extensive adoption of the Internet narrows digital gaps, especially in access to ICT, to a minimum, as has been the case with smartphone use and social apps (Hampton, 2011).

We follow Van Dijk (2006) to further clarify the distinction between factors associated with various types of digital divide (Table 6.2). The

Table 6.2 Reasons for the social divide

Reasons for and obstacles to the digital divide	*Deprived category*
Gender	Girls (dissipating)
Education, ethnicity, class, socio-economic background	Low educated, lower socio-economic households, minorities
Technological infrastructure	Low-income countries, regime preventive regulations
Language barriers	Non-English speakers (dissipating)
Regional differences in development	Peripheral regions

118   *Impact of ICT on social network structure*

categorical divide is a digital divide in access or use predicted by sociological categories associated with a general social inequality in the distribution of resources, such as age, gender, ethnicity, class, race, and education. *Material access* refers to the actual physical or economic ability to be connected to the Internet, either at home or at school. *Skills access* refers to the possession of digital skills, including information retrieval and processing (Hargittai, 2010). *Usage access* refers to the dissimilar division of use and usage time. *Motivational access* refers to avid motivation to use the Internet, which in turn may influence categorical inequality, the networks to which individuals belong, or their characteristic manner of conversing via computer-mediated communication.

If the digital divide persists or deepens, it may also affect other social aspects, as computer-mediated communication is associated with the configuration of online and offline friendships and with individuals' self-image (DiGennaro and Dutton, 2006). Enlarging the digital divide may amplify the class division in individuals' self-image and diversification into distinct social networks.

Factors associated with inequalities in access

Research has identified several factors associated with gaps in Internet access and use. In general, the higher one's socio-economic status and education level, the higher one's rate of access to the Internet (Leigh and Atkinson, 2001). Income is related to Internet access, as middle-class and upper-class households are more likely to be able to afford computer ownership and Internet connection. But despite the focus of early reports on income differences, the effect of educational attainment on Internet use is twice that of income, even after the introduction of controls in multivariate analysis (Robinson et al., 2000). One possible reason for this educational effect is the positive relation of number of years of schooling to holding service-industry jobs, where the use of computers is more common; examples are finance, banking, marketing, mass communication, legal services, and the civil service. Employment in this industry increases exposure to computers, and people who are exposed develop both the positive attitude and the skills that facilitate Internet use at home as well. Family background is an important determinant of adolescents' ICT literacy and usage. An American study with young students found that those with access to a computer at home when they were younger than 10 years old showed significantly higher levels of full-spectrum ICT technology use than other demographic groups. Students' age on first encounter with computers at school had no significant impact on their full-spectrum technology use (Ching, Basham, and Jang, 2005).

Impact of ICT on social network structure 119

Disparities in Internet use may also have to do with the language of the Internet. This is predominantly English, which may be a barrier to access by groups who are not fluent in that language. In most Western societies these are usually the minorities. Although fewer than one in ten people in the world speaks English, over 80 percent of websites are in that language, which Lavoie and O'Neill (2003) see as a form of cultural imperialism. Even in the United States, English is not the dominant language in ethnic minorities. Greenspan (2002) shows that Hispanic-American Internet users tend to spend their online time using more Spanish than English. Furthermore, the dominant position of languages such as English, French, and German does not help small countries. The infiltration of the Internet into Greek society remains lower than in other European countries (Vryzas and Tsitouridou, 2002). Although slightly decreased, the Internet is still dominated by English language content. Ongoing monitoring, conducted by W3Techs, revealed that in 2015, just over 55 percent of the most visited websites had English-language homepages. Other top languages that are used at least in 2 percent of the one million most visited websites, according to W3Techs, are: Russian, German, Japanese, Spanish, French, Chinese, and Portuguese (W3Techs, 2015).

According to various reports (e.g., Spooner and Rainie, 2001), Internet use is lowest among minorities. In the USA, for example, Hispanic and African Americans are less likely to go online than whites. A Metamorphosis Project conducted in seven areas across Los Angeles (Jung et al., 2001) found that more than 70 percent of the Chinese American and Caucasian respondents had computers at home, as against 52 percent of African Americans, 50 percent of respondents of Korean origin, 23 percent of Mexican origin, and 16 percent of Central American origin.[1] An early examination of Internet access yielded a similar pattern: Internet connection varies across ethnic lines. It was reported by 63 percent of Caucasian respondents, as against 52 percent of Chinese origin, 44 percent of African Americans, 38 percent of Korean origin, and less than 20 percent of Latino origin. Ethnic minorities are more likely to belong to economically disadvantaged social groups that cannot afford a computer or the necessary Internet connection hardware. Evidence also suggests that in some cases, less affluent individuals who are users are more likely to become non-users later on (Katz and Rice, 2002a).

New information technologies can improve educational achievements. ICT may encourage learning through direct information searching and gathering. Social apps also foster education via online networks (cf. Mazer, Murphy, and Simonds, 2007; Mazman and Usluel, 2010; Meishar-Tal, Kurtz, and Pieterse, 2012; Abrahim, Mir, and Suhara, 2019). More to

120 *Impact of ICT on social network structure*

the point, for the minority of disabled people who do have access to the Internet, however, its use can lead to significantly improved frequency and quality of social interaction. A study on disabled Chinese people found that the Internet significantly reduced existing social barriers in their physical and social environment (Guo, Bricout, and Huang, 2005). The introduction of learning software in schools is deemed an important pedagogical development because it facilitates individualized learning; a step-by-step approach is taken in exposing students to school material, completing exercises, and receiving online, interactive feedback. This type of learning is conceived as superior because it involves a personalized approach to student needs. Structured socialization to ICT, as at school, where individuals have assured access, seems to offset many of the traditional ways in which the digital divide is thought of. Clearly, aspects of the digital divide are minimized in this environment (Cotten and Jelenewicz, 2006). ICT socialization can improve other kinds of literacy (Van Dijk, 2006; OECD 2018). Writing a term paper using word processing software, which includes automatic spell checking, thesaurus, and a dictionary, may improve students' writing skills as misspellings are corrected automatically and students assimilate the rules of writing word by word. The Internet can be used to search for information, encouraging students to explore and integrate numerous, diverse, and global sources of information. Schools utilize adolescents' rapid learning of computer skills and their multimedia capabilities to encourage their creativity as they work collectively on projects that combine text, color, music, pictures.

> In a digitally saturated society, media literacy is only the first step. Technical skills are increasingly important. Few teens have a basic understanding of how the computer systems they use every day work. Some are curious enough to develop this knowledge, but it takes time and effort as well as opportunities, networks, and training to become active participants and contributors.
>
> (boyd, 2017: 182)

The Internet exposes adolescents early to ideas and attitudes that create in them greater emotional and intellectual openness. Through this medium, they can observe the world in a global context and enter a space where even those from disadvantaged groups in society feel included. With knowledge resources at their fingertips, children and adolescents of the net generation consider access to, and active search for information and the expression of opinion, a fundamental right. Innovation follows, as more and more children and adolescents use the ICT to create their own worlds. The pace of the Internet makes adolescents aware of a virtual

Impact of ICT on social network structure 121

world as an extension of their own face-to-face cosmos, so that they internalize demands for fast processing and communication in real time.

In fact, there is public concern that young people who lack access to home computing may become disadvantaged because they cannot acquire the skills needed for the adult job market. Apparently, even if low-income children do gain access to ICT at home via a smartphone, children from poorer homes may not benefit as much from it as affluent children do (Attewell and Battle, 1999). In a study in the USA, an important finding is that minority adolescents tend to use the computer for games rather than developing cognitive skills relevant to school performance (Attewell et al., 2003; Van Dijk, 2005), thereby widening the existing gap in ethnic stratification. According to Attewell's early study, home computing, which held out great promise that poorer children could catch up educationally with their more affluent peers, in fact, widens the educational gap between them. One important reason for this educational gap may be the differential use of the Internet by different groups of adolescents. Some adapt ICT to their needs and may use it for purposes unrelated to school, such as games, music, and videos.

Many studies inquire into gender inequalities in frequency usage of the Internet (e.g. Ling et al., 2003). Like the adoption of many new technologies, at the early days of the Internet domestication, men appeared more likely than women to use it (Rogers, 1995; Chen and Wellman, 2004; OECD 2018; Pew Research Center, 2019a). Gender inequality starts early in life: boys are connected to the Internet more often than girls (Bimber, 2000; Terlecki and Newcombe, 2005). But multivariate analyses have shown that the gap in access to the Internet reflects male/ female differences in income and other resources (Bimber, 2000). Still, this access gap is becoming significantly narrower. In the USA, moreover, the gender gap in access to the Internet has practically closed (OECD, 2001, 2018; Pew Research Center, 2019a.) For some, it seems that that gender and income differences in aggregate Internet use (hours spent using ICT) reflect the social composition of the population rather than a true digital divide (Van Dijk and Hacker, 2003). Yet, the gender gap in Internet use clearly remains, but only in users' type of activity, but not in use duration (Van Dijk, 2005, Cotten and Jelenewicz, 2006: Van Deursen and Van Dijk, 2010, 2014; OECD 2018, Abrahim et al., 2019).

In the early days of the Internet, several studies found gaps between men and women in Internet access and in ICT use (e.g. Soukup, 1999; DiMaggio et al., 2001; Chen and Wellman, 2004; OECD, 2018; Pew Research Center, 2019a). This line of research suggests that that type of ICT use reflects gendered cultural stereotypes in Western society,

122 *Impact of ICT on social network structure*

Nonetheless, in the Western would, the gap has been dissipating (Pew Research Center, 2019a).

The digital divide is often investigated as an aspect of the "diffusion of innovation" (Rogers, 1995). As a fairly recent innovation, PC penetration and Internet access are generally lower for older than for younger people (Rogers, 1995). The pace of adoption is also faster in younger age groups across OECD countries (OECD, 2001, 2018). Scholars have found that use declines with age, but they have failed to distinguish age effects from cohort effects of the digital divide (Pew Research Center, 2019b). By contrast, gender differences in the use of new technologies appear quite small, and tend to disappear (Pew Research Center, 2019a).

The notion of digital divide is also applicable to children and adolescents. Using the National Educational Longitudinal Survey (NELS88), Attewell and Battle (1999) found that computer ownership did not predict closure of the digital gap. More specifically, eighth-grade teenagers from more affluent and educated families scored higher on math and reading tests than their poorer and less educated peers who had computers at home (Attewell et al., 2003).

We found in our early Israeli studies that in 2001 the digital divide in Israel was a function of the level of parental education, nationality, gender, and age. By contrast, by 2004, the observed differences were only partially related to socio-economic standing; apparently, cultural factors, a propensity for social networks, and gender expectations explain the digital gap in the types and magnitude of use. Analysts of social stratification and cultural capital predict that the digital gap will grow wider over time (Van Dijk, 2006), but we do not find evidence of a widening digital divide. Instead, we find a subtler diversification of Internet use according to the adolescent user's type of interest and social location. Internet gaps in access and especially in use, we conclude, are embedded in the social structure.

Age differences are clearly evident as well. As with other technologies, younger individuals are more likely to adopt it (Rogers, 1995). Computer literacy, degree of software competence, and ability to use the Web are clearly conversely related to age. This finding is consistent across all age groups (Kraut et al., 1998; Hargittai, 2001). As ICT has consistently become more domesticated, embedded in and converged with many user-friendly smartphone apps, the age gap has been significantly declining, but it is still persisting (Pew Research Center, 2019b).

It is important to note that macro variables affect the permeability of the digital divide. OECD statistics consistently show how firm characteristics, especially firm size, rate of ICT penetration into the country, and the urban-rural divide, affect access to the Internet and frequency of Internet use (OECD, 2001). The aggregate statistics of access and use are affected by macro-level variations, but also by individual-level variations. Wilson et al. (2003) have shown that community resources and infrastructure interact with personal resources, skills, and attitudes to facilitate or delay the adoption of new technologies.

Aspects of a digital divide also exist in terms of whether one uses the Internet for specific purposes; however, once individuals begin using the Internet, few racial differences exist. Internet experience and gender affect particular types of Internet usage, suggesting that the digital divide is a complex, multilayered phenomenon (Barzilai-Nahon, 2006; Cotten and Jelenewicz, 2006; Vehovar et al., 2006; Van Dijk, 2006; Van Deursen and Van Dijk, 2010, 2014). Social location in the stratification system is closely associated with Internet skills and computer literacy. Competent Internet users can employ the new media strategically as an alternative to existing communication channels, and to expand or maintain their social networks. Thus, ICT users may choose to replace or complement the communication channels they use to connect with close friends (Cho, de Zuniga, and Shah, 2003).[2] We have reported elsewhere (Mesch, 2001; Mesch and Talmud, 2006a) that online friendships are formed to expand existing social networks or to compensate for their deficiencies. The motivation to use the Internet varies according to the type of social activity one is engaged in or the type of social network to which one belongs (Steinfield, Ellison, and Lampe, 2008). Adolescents have the time, flexibility, and know-how to cope with new media (Katz and Rice, 2002a). But their patterns of Internet access and use may also have to do with their family socio-economic status, ethnic background, cultural frameworks, their communicative styles, their peer group's norms, and particularly their socio-psychological needs. Like any other social activity, the Internet can be classified into distinct network clusters, as we will show later. Online social engagement and peer-group climate affect their Internet use over and above the cultural and social dimensions of stratification.

The various theoretical positions, discussing the social impact of the Internet, are derived from arguments about social affordability, which are dominated by two contrasting views: technological determinism and social constructivism. In the Introduction we showed that these two perspectives are at two polar extremes regarding the relative impact of technological vs. social factors in the use of ICT for the formation and maintenance of online social ties. Assuming the technological determinism of ICT, early conceptualizations described the weakness of electronic media in supporting social ties. This early perspective was skeptical of the ability of CMC to support strong ties. Because CMC provides

124 *Impact of ICT on social network structure*

access to a wider audience of individuals who may share interests and hobbies, it has been suggested that the environment of reduced social cues on which CMC is based is better suited to supporting weak ties by reducing the risks associated with contacting unknown individuals (Sproull and Kiesler, 1986; Rice and Love, 1987).

Social constructivists, by contrast, argue that aspects of online communication, such as anonymity, isolation, and the absence of "gating features," facilitate finding others with the same interests, making it easier for individuals to form strong ties (McKenna et al., 2002; Joinson, 2008). The relative anonymity of the Internet reduces the risks of such disclosure, especially of intimate information (McKenna et al., 2002). Hampton and Wellman (2018) succinctly summarize that "With the withering of traditional community, networks of supportive relations have undergone two major changes. The first change [is] to the 'networked individualism.'" Hampton continues: "The second, more recent change, which is only now being recognized, is a result of 'relational persistence' and 'pervasive awareness'" (Hampton 2016).

The network affordances of persistence and awareness are increasingly possible because of the permanence of email addresses and mobile phone numbers, social media that allow for the articulation of social ties, and continued awareness—online and off—of the opinions and daily activities of community members. The result of these shifts is that people continue to be embedded in communities that provide informal watchfulness and awareness of an enduring set of relations" (Hampton and Wellman (2018)

From divide to diversification: differential use of social capital

The rapid diffusion of ICT, especially in the form of Internet technology of Web 2.0 applications and cellular phones, makes the convergence between ICT media more possible and more comprehensive. Content originating from one medium can be directly linked to other digital media (Katz and Rice, 2002a). As digital information becomes more available, inequalities in access appear to narrow down (Van Dijk, 2005).

A great deal of scholarly attention has recently been devoted to the impact of the Internet on quality of life. There are two contradictory outlooks: a *dystopian school*, which regards individualization, urbanization, and globalization, combined with the rapid incorporation of ICT in households, as destructive of the social fabric, and a *utopian perspective*, depicting the ICT as significantly contributing to the emancipation of individuals and of identity groups from constraints of time and space, and even from critical elements of the social structure such as gender, race, geographic boundaries, and

Impact of ICT on social network structure 125

class background (Wellman et al., 2003; Boase and Wellman, 2006). Yet even proponents of the dystopian view, such as Cummings, Butler, and Kraut (2002), admit that [though] "online relationships are less valuable than off-line ones, indeed, their net benefit depends on whether they supplement or substitute for offline social relationships."

An effective way to examine these schools is to scrutinize how ICT in general, and the digital divide in particular, are linked to adolescents' social capital. An important element in assessing the quality of life in modern society is the nature of social relations. This has been a central tradition in sociology and related disciplines. Since the seminal work of Emile Durkheim, all theories of social relations, but most specifically network models of social structure, have been concerned with structural measures of relational quality and the effects of relational quality on significant outcomes. In his classic study, Durkheim (1952) shows that social cohesion has a curvilinear association with social pathologies. Too dense social ties or too sparse a social system result in elevated societal rates of suicide. By contrast, moderate social cohesion is a necessary condition for a healthy social fabric.

Social scientists have been intrigued by the possible effect of dense networks on social processes (Monge and Contractor, 2003). But social network and community theorists differ over the presumed effect of social ties on relational quality. The theory of structural holes, derived from Georg Simmel's image of the modern city (Simmel, 1990), posits that individuals' degrees of freedom intensify insofar as they have many "non-redundant" ties (Burt, 1992). In other words, to the extent that individuals are connected to others, who in turn are not connected to one another, they enjoy "structural autonomy." In this sense, the very disconnection from one's peers is one's social capital. To the extent that individuals have many unconnected others they can manipulate contacts, information flow, gossip, timing, control and social differentiation, and gain rewards from social interactions. According to this view, being positioned among "structural holes" provides leverage power.

The structural holes perspective claims that sparse networks can be social capital; individuals can accumulate it and profit from it. Studies have found that even individual's psychological wellbeing is associated with the number of strangers in one's networks (Burt, 1992). At the community level, Granovetter (1973) claimed that societal integration was possible precisely because of the existence of weak ties. Tocqueville's notion of the "art of association" as a condition for individual freedom is also relevant here. In this view, a "healthy individual" is engaged in a social group, which saves one from selfishness. At the same time, the plurality of social groups ensures that no strict control is exercised over the individual (Tocqueville, [1835] 1954; Hampton and Wellman, 2018).

126 *Impact of ICT on social network structure*

The "art of association," learned by adolescents of the net generation and enacted through their social relations, is a basic element in promoting an adult life of civic engagement (Putnam, 2000). At the psychological level, scholars celebrate the emancipation of the individual, particularly members of minority groups, by means of Internet access. These scholars echo the idea that low density, that is, the segmentation of social ties, is a necessary condition for individual autonomy and freedom from social constraints, which is particularly relevant for hidden or invisible minorities (McKenna et al., 2002). Individuals who have many non-overlapping social ties occupy a position that enables them to experience relative autonomy in their actions (Burt, 1992). Density is considered a conventional measure of group cohesion, but many scholars have used density as an oversimplified measure of the degree centrality index (Wasserman and Faust, 1995: 181–182).

At the other theoretical pole, students of social and community integration emphasize the effect of dense social networks on the viability of individuals' moral, occupational, and political behavior. An individual who is locked into a cohesive group and possesses many dense, transitive ties experiences a high level of confidence, coherence, and social control. Coleman (1988) underscores the contribution of "social closure" to children's educational attainments. Robert Putnam (1995) emphasizes the importance of dense social networks for public morality and civic engagement. Rafaeli and colleagues demonstrate how social density benefits the community of Internet users (Rafaeli et al., 2003), and Woolcock (1998), among many others, shows the value of *bonding social capital* on the collective production of national wealth. This perspective also echoes the "community lost" notion, which holds that the introduction of ICT accelerates the segmentation of social ties (White and Guest, 2003; Hampton and Wellman, 2018). Table 6.3 presents the social consequences of the digital divide.

These two perspectives could not be more diametrically opposed. The theory of "structural holes" asserts that the individual profits from *bridging social capital* across social disconnection in sparse networks. By contrast, the perspective of "network integration" maintains that individuals,

Table 6.3 Social consequences of the digital divide

Theory	Prediction
Amplification	The rich get richer; digital divide augments other forms of social inequality, especially education and skills.
Normalization	Low-cost ICT can reduce other kinds of social inequality

Impact of ICT on social network structure   127

groups, and communities gain collective and individual rewards from their *bonding social capital*, typically through their social interconnection throughout dense networks.

Bonding social capital and relational strength are associated (Ellison, Steinfield, and Lampe, 2007). Granovetter (1973) argued that most bridging ties are weak (although most weak ties are not necessarily bridges). Bridging social capital consists mainly of weak ties because these are not transitive, hence they go beyond the individual's immediate network clusters. By contrast, strong ties tend to be more cohesive and closely knit. They tend to be more prevalent in close-knit clusters of cohesive peer groups. Still, there is little doubt that global, virtual, social connections, transcending the confines of time and space, contribute to the emergence of a "networked individual," who has a much greater capacity to increase his or her bridging social capital (Wellman et al., 2003; Kennedy and Wellman, 2007). As Nan Lin (2001) claims:

> There is little doubt that the hypothesis that social capital is declining can be refuted if one goes beyond the traditional interpersonal networks and analyzes the cyber-networks ... We need to compile basic data and information on the extent to which individuals are spending time and effort engaging others over cyber-networks, as compared to the use of time and effort for interpersonal communications, other leisure activities (TV watching, travel, eating out, movie- and theater-going) ... We need to estimate the amount of useful information gathered through cyber-networks as compared to traditional media.
>
> (Lin, 2001)

We have already shown in previous chapters that peers act as emotional confidants, providing each other with advice and guidance, and serving as models of behavior and attitudes. In adolescence, individuals are inclined to spend more time with their peers, treating one another as their most important reference group (Hartup, 1997).

There is evidence, especially in health matters, that online communication promotes social support and expansive social interactions (Kavanaugh et al., 2002) rather than isolation and depression, as previously had been argued (e.g., Kraut et al., 1998; Nie, Hillygus, and Erbring, 2002). Additionally, Ito (2005) argues that adolescents are substituting poorer quality social relationships (i.e., weak ties) for strong ties that provide better relational quality.

Chan and Cheng (2004) found significant differences between relationships formed through CMC and offline. Online relationships

128 *Impact of ICT on social network structure*

proved shallower than offline relationships, although the difference diminished as the relationships continued to develop (Chan and Cheng, 2004). We have also shown in previous chapters that social similarity and residential proximity serve as important factors in the formation and maintenance of social ties among adolescents. These structural conditions—conformity, homophily, proximity—foster the emergence of social cliques among adolescents' networks.

Adolescents' online social networks slightly increase social heterogeneity, and enlarge relations across geographic location (Mesch and Talmud, 2007b). Social networks websites are used predominantly to enlarge bridging social capital. Ellison and colleagues (2007) found that young adults used social networking sites (such as Facebook) to maintain large and heterogeneous networks of friends. Similarly, Steinfield, Ellison, and Lampe (2008) found a relatively high number of contacts for Facebook users (mean of 223 in 2006 and 339 in 2007). They concluded, "emerging adults are using Facebook to maintain large, diffuse networks of friends, with a positive impact on their accumulation of bridging social capital" (Steinfield, Ellison, and Lampe, 2008: 444). Because they performed a longitudinal study, they could assert that the technology facilitates the expansion of bridging social capital. Moreover, they found that online social networking sites provide the technological affordances to expand network size, deemed especially beneficial for those with lower self-esteem who otherwise are hard-pressed to form and maintain large and heterogeneous social networks. In other words, social networks sites provide an avenue for enlarging bridging social capital, serving also as a compensatory device for youngsters who lack offline social networks. Accordingly, digital differentiation can be observed in the virtual world, contrary to offline ties. Online social networks are more permeable, diversified, fragmented, and fluid (Hampton et al., 2011).

ICT is used also to maintain existing relations with closed ties. Adolescents' closed friendships are more prevalent in cohesive social circles. To what extent do social cohesion and transitive ties affect adolescents' relational quality? What are the effects of dense networks around individual adolescents on their social capital?

Social network density

As described in the Preface, density is a key structural dimension of social networks, measuring the extent to which members of social networks know one another. More specifically, it measures the proportion of actual ties to all possible ties. Network density increases with transitivity in social relations. Given that member A knows member B and member B knows member C, if the conditional probability of member A also knowing member C (or vice versa, assuming network symmetry) is high, then transitivity is prevalent (Wasserman and Faust, 1995). High density typically occurs in cohesive groups, and it is more likely to be pronounced in small communities. Figure 6.1 shows that the number of links (lines) between actors (points) is higher in Network A, which is consequently denser than Network B.

In terms of social capital, the white node (actor) in Network B enjoys actual or potential benefits, accruing to her through her position in structural holes (Burt, 1992). These benefits include access to non-redundant information (Burt, 1992), control over information flows, quicker

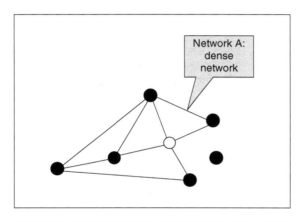

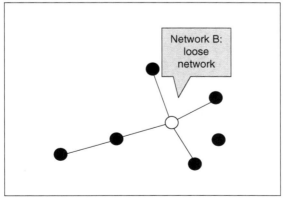

Figure 6.1 Bonding and bridging social capital

130   Impact of ICT on social network structure

communication timing, and the ability to manipulate information flows (Burt, 2005).

By contrast, actors in Network A are situated in a dense social network, hence are deemed to enjoy actual or potential "profits" typical of bonding social capital: interpersonal trust, shared norms, and a tendency to closeness, tie stability, reciprocity, and a joint capacity to seek help from one another (Lin, 2001; Kadushin, 2004).

The relational quality of adolescents in the information age

We propose that there has been a gradual shift from the digital divide to a more complex phenomenon of digital social network diversification, amplified by both technological applications of ICT and by adolescents' tendency to create ties—even among strangers—with similar others, due either to social similarity or to shared interest in a topic.

Narrowing the physical digital divide in accessing ICT technology leads to widening heterogeneity in adolescents' digital social networks. As inequalities in access to CMC fade, and ICT becomes more widespread, more individual adolescents bear fewer social constraints and fewer costs in forming new social relations via ICT. As the basic social propensity is to form contacts with similar others, the structural end result is more heterogeneous social networks, or diversification of online space.

Bridging social capital and *bonding social capital* are both nested in the human propensity for homophily (Table 6.4). But there are significant differences. Certainly, network ties, consisting of bridging social capital, have less relational strength, social homophily, and geographic proximity than ties consisting of bonding social capital. Yet even bridging social capital is more likely to occur among adolescents with the same kind of interests and tastes. Another important feature of ICT is the complementary use of online social networks to extend offline social networks; through ICT even isolated individuals can compensate for a dearth of offline ties, while central individuals can deepen their everyday contacts with their close peers and expand their communicative devices by means of multiple communication media (face-to-face, Internet, mobile phone) (Cohen, Lamish and Schejter, 2008), while at the same time expanding their social ties, mainly through their Internet access. Put differently, the use of social capital depends on the individual's position in her networks. ICT has a great potential for recombining adolescents' online and offline social networks, where they operate according to net-generational "networked individualism" (Wellman et al., 2003).

Impact of ICT on social network structure 131

Table 6.4 Two theories of social capital

Theory	Bridging social capital	Bonding social capital
Social morphology	Broad range, a variety of kinds of friends, many weak ties, connecting network clusters	Homogeneous networks, closely knit, dense social ties; stable, durable, transitive social ties
Presumed benefits	Information broker, cognitive flexibility, broad reach of tastes, fashion, and innovation, weak ties, individual autonomy	Trustful strong relations, mutually committed, social and emotional support
Presumed costs	Shallow relations, lack of emotional support	Social control, peer pressure

Online and offline social networks tend to expand as the young people grow older (Mesch and Talmud, 2007a; Davis, 2012). Their groups seem more cohesive than those of typical modal adults. More important, online exchanges appear also to widen adolescents' circles and diversity of friendships (Davis, 2012).

Social media users have more social capital, including more acquaintances and interactions, as compared to individuals who do not use social media (Steinfield et al., 2008), and it is generally accepted that greater interpersonal activity may account for an increase in well-being (Pittman and Reich, 2016). This may contribute to many positive outcomes. Kim (2017) found a strong and negative relationship between online activities (chatting, emailing, participating in communities or clubs and using bulletin boards) and self-reported mental health and suicidal ideation among a nationally representative sample of Korean students. This finding supports the theoretical notion that health outcomes are partly shaped by social or network variables, as predicated by social capital and public health scholars (Kim, 2017).

Like many other social phenomenon, online networks are unevenly distributed and used. Additionally, the growth of social ties reflects inequality in the previously held amount of social capital. In other words, the advantage of social ties rises with direct relations with the existing stock of social capital. Abbas and Mesch (2018) revealed that the laws of preferential attachment are valid also to adolescents' ties in Facebook. According to this perspective, the rate of accumulation of social capital is a function of the social resources that adolescent users had already accrue. Analyzing a representative sample of Palestinian teenagers

132 *Impact of ICT on social network structure*

(n = 567), they found positive correlation between the use of active and passive communication features and perceived online social capital. Accordingly, their results support the rich-get-richer model. Even among socially disadvantaged group, the teenagers who already had a stock of social capital offline benefitted more from using Facebook (Abbas and Mesch, 2018).

Being located in a relatively cohesive group, especially in offline relation, while being able to expand relational circles via the Internet leads to an important question: to what extent can they trust and share secrets with one another in a cohesive group, where peers' social control over the individual is tighter?

In our study of Israeli adolescents, we found that adolescents' relational strength was inversely associated with network density. In other words, social closure diminishes adolescents' relational quality. Paradoxically, even among adolescents, membership of too dense a social cluster apparently reduces their emotional affiliation and attachment to their peer group; conversely, individuals situated in a sparse social network have more intense ties with the group. This evidence corroborates the predictions of the structural holes perspective, that individuals' autonomy will be directly connected to their wellbeing (Burt, 1992). We found Internet use inversely related to relational strength and social capital, a result consistent with our previous findings showing that Internet use increased the heterogeneity of ties and proximity among peers. It furnishes moderate and partial support for the dystopian perspective of the effects of ICT on relational quality.

The effect of the Internet on social capital is conditioned by social structural variables as well as personal attributes. Youths' structural position determines the resources they exchange over the Internet as well as in face-to-face relations, creating through joint social activity shared sentiments and a sense of mutual support. Transitive ties are a robust indication of both social support and social control. In the adolescents' society, their relational quality is therefore associated with the structural condition of personal autonomy.

Being connected to different network clusters elevates adolescents' relational quality. This finding also corroborates Burt's argument that structural autonomy is positively associated with wellbeing and personal welfare (Burt, 1992). It could also be connected to the arguments raised by prominent psychologists that sometimes online relations with strangers contribute to adolescents' development (Subrahmanyam and Greenfield, 2008). Future studies should also inquire into the associations of network density, social support, popularity, and rejection. These relations may be

Impact of ICT on social network structure 133

contingent on larger social contexts, and should therefore be examined in different cultures.

ICT is often used by adolescents as a compensatory device. Social ties which solely exist through the Internet probably have less relational strength and communicative depth. Ties accessible only on the Internet are perceived as "external" to the participants' already existing social networks. Adolescents who use the Internet to create bigger networks do so at the cost of weaker relationships. Although strong ties are a common source of emotional support and intimacy, they also are a mechanism of social control, making the individual subject to the pressures exerted by her peer group. This is especially true of transitive ties, which are the foundation of adolescents' social networks. Transitive social ties amplify imitation, social influence, and social selection (Pearson, Steglich, and Snijders, 2006). So to safeguard their wellbeing, many adolescents choose non-redundant ties, where their online and offline friends are not attached. In network analytic terms, having non-redundant ties enhances the individual's "structural autonomy" (Simmel, 1990; Burt, 1992), and minimizes the social constraints and social control of their conduct exercised by their peers.

There is some evidence that those who occupy positions containing bridging social capital tend to have certain personality traits, especially higher degrees of extroversion and a capacity for self-monitoring (Burt, Jannotta, and Mahoney, 1998; Kalish and Robins, 2006). More research is needed to examine the relations of personality traits, network position, and social resources' acquisition and exchange.

In this chapter, we have shown the shift from a binary digital divide in access to social network diversification through ICT. As the latter is both a technological and a social device (Katz and Rice, 2002b), using CMC assists adolescents to reshape their relationship configuration across ICT platforms and face-to-face interactions.

We also raised a key outcome of ICT, considered highly pertinent to adolescents' new capacity for relational configuration: the adolescent's ability to mold his or her network is less costly and more flexible. This novel ability has positive outcomes: Valkenburg and colleagues (2006) found that the more people used social network sites, the greater the frequency of interaction with friends, to the benefit of users' self-esteem and life satisfaction. Often, using ICT increases social support and self-esteem. Valkenburg and Peter (2007a) found that unlike non-socially anxious adolescent respondents, socially anxious respondents perceived the Internet as more valuable for intimate self-disclosure, which led to more online communication. Using ICT technology, a teenager can nowadays

134 *Impact of ICT on social network structure*

expand his or her network size by forming contacts with strangers. This ability is not restricted to bridging social capital. Adolescents can compartmentalize their communication with close peers with very little difficulty, under the aegis of computer-mediated communication.

Moreover, the diversification of social networks through expansion of online weak ties is accompanied by deepening stronger ties via multiple communication channels (Hampton et al. 2011). Social media is promoting "networked, supportive, persistent, and pervasive community relationships" (Hampton and Wellman, 2018). The end structural result is the upsurge of many "islands" composed of closely knit social clusters, which are bridged by weak ties.

An increasing number of people have become users of social media, mostly looking for social contacts, and networking in social networks sites can increase students' social capital in many ways, such as in the form of peer support groups and learning environments, and enhance bonding and communality in them (Uusiautti and Maatta, 2014).

Williams (2019) conducted a systematic review of the peer-reviewed literature and conference material published between January 1, 1997 and March 31, 2018, regarding the extent to which the use of online social networking sites cultivates and nurtures an individual's bonding social capital. He found out that 85 empirical studies (out of the total 116 studies examined) had confirmed that individual bonding social capital had been cultivated and nurtured via use of online social networking sites (Williams, 2019).

Though the bonding social capital is related to ICT usage, there are still open research puzzles. As the network size of Internet users grows larger, future studies should investigate how the social bridging and bonding kinds of social capital are associated with relational quality in other settings, using comprehensive research instruments, dedicated to registering ICT users' behavior in real time (Cohen, Lamish, and Schejter, 2008). More specifically, such studies should examine how the co-evolution of online and offline network construction, selection, mixing, and peer influence affects adolescents' network reconfiguration, and how existing attitudes to technology and the net generation's rising digital literacy affect the relational quality of contemporary youth.

Summary

In this chapter, we explored how social regularities affect the configuration and composition of adolescents' online networks. We linked various dimensions of digital divide to online sociability, and discussed the possible social consequences of the digital divide. Finally, we contrasted two

Impact of ICT on social network structure 135

perspectives on social capital, bridging and bonding, to examine the relational quality of the structure of adolescents' ties. In Chapter 7, we will describe the negative consequences of adolescents' online usage.

Notes

1 The study inferred ethnicity based on neighborhood, and therefore overestimated its effect on Internet access by the ecological fallacy.
2 In addition to connection and interaction, people may use the Internet for learning, acquisition, and consumption, but it is beyond the scope of this study to discuss these patterns of use and needs.

7 Online communication and negative social ties

Introduction

In this book we have taken a social network perspective for the understanding of adolescents' social world. Nowadays, this social environment is comprised of the social groups to which youth belong: parents, peers, classmates, and friends in the neighborhood. All are linked by online and face-to-face social networks. In general, youth's social networks are positive outcomes that are almost always emphasized and linked to the development of a positive social bond to social institutions, developing social skills, as through social interaction we internalize social norms, expectations, and social values.

At the same time, we should recognize that social ties can carry negative outcomes, commonly thought to be the result of lack of social ties alone. Not belonging to a large network, not experiencing closeness to existing ties, or belonging to a low density network are all assumed to be conducive to deterioration in mental health. Negative outcomes may result from being involved in negative social ties—negative in the sense of hostile, aggressive, and humiliating interactions. In this chapter we focus on negative social network sources: cyberbullying, online harassment, the specific impact of online cyberbullying on adolescents' well-being, and the role of parents and peers in the prevention—and increase—of cyberbullying and harassment.

The social network perspective focuses on exchanges (or the lack of) between pairs of actors. A social network relation denotes the type of exchange or interaction between any pair of actors in a system of actors. The network approach differs from other approaches mainly in its focus on exchanges and interactions between actors, not on the individual characteristics of the actors engaged in the exchange of resources. Social network analysis is used to describe the network and to explain how involvement in a particular network helps to explain its members' attitudes and behavior. As most social networks reflect exchanges that

Online communication: negative social ties   137

provide companionship, social support, information, and social identity, most analysis has naturally centered on the positive or socially accepted resources that are available through them (Wei and Jonson-Reid, 2011).

However, social network analysis has also been used to study networks of deviant behavior, such as drug use, criminal involvement, and bullying (Wei and Jonson-Reid, 2011). Most of this book has taken a social network perspective to understand the changes in social structure of young adolescents' social networks. From the perspective of social diversification, we have discussed how online networks affect the size, composition, social similarity, and range of contact of young adolescents. At the same time, we should note that since the use of information and communication technologies began to expand, there has been social concern with the potential negative effects of these networks, particularly regarding youth. In one famous case in the USA, the use of identity deception to harass a young female through a social networking site resulted in the tragedy of suicide. Meigan Meier had been instant messaging with a "cute" boy she had met over the social networking site MySpace. She struck up a friendship with "Josh" and the pair exchanged dozens of messages. Josh was the fake name used by an adult female neighbor who lived in the same street. When "Josh" told her "he" didn't want to be her friend and called her a "liar and slut," she became depressed. She committed suicide a few days later after her online friendship ended. In another case, Ryan Patrick Halligan was bullied for months online. Classmates sent the 13-year-old boy instant messages calling him gay. He was threatened, taunted, and insulted incessantly online. Eventually, in 2003, Ryan killed himself. These, of course, are extreme cases; online harassment for the most part has consequences, but not so radical (Kowalski, Giumetti, Schroeder and Lattanner, 2014). In this chapter we address this issue, the main task being to sort out what is new about cyberbullying from what is not and belongs to more traditional forms of peer harassment known before the advent of information society. The aims are to identify incidents of cyberbullying and harassment, to categorize the personal and family characteristics of youth who are the victims of such experiences, and to describe some consequences of such victimization.

Cyberbullying from a social network perspective

In our understanding of the role of youth social networks, it is positive outcomes that are almost always emphasized. From a normative social perspective, social networks have an important role at the individual and social levels. At the individual level, the existence of social ties is linked to the development of a positive social bond to social institutions. Having

138   *Online communication: negative social ties*

friends means developing social skills, as through social interaction we internalize social norms, expectations, and social values (Sasson and Mesch, 2014). At the aggregate level, social ties link individuals to society and support the development of a common identity and social solidarity. Through social interaction, namely, exposure to other people, individuals develop mutual obligations, trust, and commitment.

Social norms theory suggest that peers have an influence on adolescents' involvement in cyberbullying. This influence is rooted in the adolescents' belief about norms that are prevalent among peers. Such norms dictate how to dress and behave, as well as expectations about the types of media to use and on how these media influence their friends' attitudes and behavior. The social norms approach distinguishes between descriptive norms and injunctive norms. Descriptive norms are beliefs about what is actually done by most people in one's social group. These norms imply that if one believes that everybody is engaging in a certain behavior, one is prompted to engage in the same behavior. Injunctive norms can be defined as beliefs about the approval of a certain behavior by one's peers, namely, whether one's friends approve or disapprove of this behavior. In a study that collected data from students in the sixth to eleventh grades, respondents were asked to indicate if they had ever sent an insulting message online. It was found that the perceptions of one's peers approve the behavior, thus supportive norms in the peer group increase the likelihood of sending insulting messages online. The results indicate that youth who engage in bullying behavior online believe that their friends approve of such behavior (Sasson and Mesch, 2014).

The existence of social ties affords the individual access to companionship, information, and romantic involvement. In the literature on youth, social bonds with other peers have indeed been associated with compliance with social values and social norms, but with the avoidance of deviant behavior as well.

Supportive and mutual ties have been linked to keeping clear of engagement in deviant and non-normative behavior both offline and online, to avoid the negative consequences of suffering social sanctions at the hands of significant others. On the role of strength of ties in the formation of positive online ties, in a study based on youth in the USA, a positive relationship was found between the number of weak ties and describing a positive experience in meeting a contact online. The number of strong ties did not have a statistical relationship to describing positive experiences meeting strangers online. Interestingly enough, in the same study, the strength of ties differed for ethnic groups. African American youth reported weaker ties than White youth (Mesch, 2018b).

Online communication: negative social ties 139

At the same time, we should recognize that social ties can carry negative outcomes, commonly thought to be the result of lack of social ties alone. Not belonging to a large network, not experiencing closeness to existing ties, or belonging to a low density network are all assumed to be conducive to deterioration in mental health (Beraman and Moody, 2004). Note, however, that negative outcomes may result from being involved in negative social ties—negative in the sense of hostile, aggressive, and humiliating interactions (Beran and Li, 1995; Berson, Berson, and Ferron, 2002). A study that investigated dyadic relationships among youth found that a significant proportion (25–30 percent) of bullying events occurs in the context of perceived friendship. Most of the relationships involving friendship and bullying were categorized as unilateral nominations of aggressors as friends by victims. These findings have consequences for how and when friends can be regarded as a protective resource and reject the idea of bullying occurring outside of friendships. In fact, having a friend does not necessarily guarantee protection and support, and some friends are actually aggressive and abusive (Wei and Jonson-Reid, 2011).

In this chapter we address these adverse aspects, and focus on their prevalence, sources, and consequences.

From bullying to cyberbullying

Bullying is a serious social issue as it is a vicious threat to a welcoming and supportive educational environment. Grave consequences have been identified for victimized people, including suicide attempts, eating disorders, running away from home, depression, dropping out of school, and aggressive behavior in adulthood (Borg, 1998; Kaltiala-Heino et al., 1999; Hawker and Boulton, 2000; Olweus, 1994).

Historically, bullying is a common form of youth violence that affects children and teenagers, mostly when engaged in age-related activities, such as going to school and traveling to or from school or when in public places such as hangouts (Patchin and Hinduja, 2006). Accordingly, in the past, bullying has been extensively studied as a behavior enacted in children's and adolescents' natural habitats such as the neighborhood and school, and in social gathering places. As to the prevalence of bullying, the data show that 10–15 percent of students aged 12–18 years had been bullied in the previous 30 days (Devoe et al., 2002; Galinsky and Salmond, 2002). Prevalence rates of bullying and cyberbullying are highly variable because of how it is defined and the time parameter used to determine if the behavior has occurred (Brochado, Soares, and Fraga, 2016).

Bullying is conceived of as an act of aggression with the attempt to exert domination through inducing fear. According to dominance theory

140 *Online communication: negative social ties*

(Hawley, 1999), students use aggression against weaker fellows to gain access to resources, including high sociometric status among peers. Bullies therefore will occupy more central network positions and hold more physical and social power, while victims will probably not be at the center but will be more peripheral in the network than their classmates. Mouttapa et al. (2004) found that victims received fewer friendship nominations and occupied less central positions in the friendship network than other members. Socially, for different reasons, they were less integrated into the school groups and of an inferior social status in the school network.

An issue more relevant to our argument is the major importance of the youth network as a protective factor. During adolescence, an attempt is made to attain social status in the peer network. Achieving good grades, participating in extracurricular activities, socializing, and displaying cultural symbols are in part tools for adolescents striving to achieve social status. Targets of bullying at school tend to be children who are not well integrated into their social networks and are known to be lonely or isolated. Well-integrated children are not targeted, as they are more likely to be in their friends' company and the friends can intervene in threatening situations (Mesch, Fishman, and Eisikovits, 2003). Network analysis has been used to investigate whether school sociometric status is associated with bullying victimization. Centrality, an index of popularity, is linked to both pro-social and anti-social behaviors. In their study of fourth- and sixth-grade males, Rodkin, Farmer, Peral and Van Acker (2000) found that boys perceived as nonaggressive, cooperative, and leaders, and boys perceived as aggressive, equally occupied a central position in their classmates' social network. Some studies have specifically examined bullies' and victims' sociometric characteristics. Victims were often found to be rejected by their peers and more eccentric than other student. There is evidence that a display of reciprocal friendships (e.g., students nominate a friend, and receive a friendship nomination from that friend) protects students against victimization (Boulton, Trueman, Chau, Whiteland, and Amatya, 1999).

Many young people are able to avoid the experience of bullying at school mainly due to parental support (Nansel et al., 2001; Mesch, Fishman, and Eisikovits, 2003; Fanti, Demetriou, and Hawa, 2012). Peers represent a support system, and studies on social networks and bullying have shown that victims are more likely to have friends who are nonaggressive, and offenders have ties to others who are aggressors (Mouttapa et al., 2004). Another notable result of these studies is the importance of the closeness of children to parents: when children inform their parents of bullying experiences, the parents are able to intervene and inform the

Online communication: negative social ties 141

school authorities (Farrington, 1993; Mesch et al., 2003). These findings indicate the relevance of studying social networks for the understanding of bullying.

Concomitant with increased use of the Internet has been increased reporting of cyber-harassment, sexual solicitation, and cyberbullying (Berson, Berson, and Ferron, 2002; Li, 2006; Patchin and Hinduja. 2006). Cyberbullying involves the use of information and communication technologies such as email, cell phone, social networking sites to support deliberate, repeated, and hostile behavior by an individual or group—all intended to harm others (Rosen, 2007).

By using information and communication technologies, bullying enjoys the advantage of several characteristics of the medium that transform the essence of the phenomenon as we know it. First, online communication in its very nature might induce bullying behavior (Giuseppe and Galimberti, 2001). Communication that lacks non-verbal cues, status symbols, and proximity to the victim may produce a behavior that is self-oriented and not concerned with the feelings and opinions of others. Self-orientation may lead to a lack of inhibition and negative perceptions of others, resulting in an increase in online bullying. Second, offenders exploit the Internet's relative anonymity, through the use of screens or nicknames, to hide their true identity. An overall feeling of fear is generated in the victim, not knowing the perpetrator's identity; he or she does not know whether the perpetrator is or is not a classmate or a person met online (Li, 2007). Fear of unknown cyberbullies harms the educational and accepting environment essential to the classroom. The school is perceived as a hostile environment where victims feel unsafe, and such a child might avoid this by not attending classes. Third, the online environment provides a potentially large audience for the aggressive actions. This might appeal to perpetrators, and furnish them with positive feedback for their actions. Fourth, the large audience may amplify the negative effects of online bullying on the victim, as the harassment is being watched by all known acquaintances even beyond the school and neighborhood. In sum, we may conclude that a salient difference between school and cyberspace is that, in the latter, a large number of perpetrators can be involved in the abuse, and classmates who eschew bullying at school will engage in it in cyberspace, hiding behind anonymity.

Past studies on real-life bullying have shown the importance of the audience, as 30 percent of bystanders were found to express attitudes supporting the aggressors rather than the victims. The longer the bullying persists, the more bystanders join, and the more the bystanders join, the worse are the consequences (Boulton et al., 1993; Saarento and Salmivalli, 2015).

Prevalence and consequences of cyberbullying

An early survey in Canada showed one quarter of young Internet users reported they had experienced receiving messages containing hateful things about others (MNET, 2001). Ybarra and Mitchell (2004) conducted a large study of young Internet users in the USA and found that 19 percent of the adolescents reported being bullied online. More recent studies show a similar level of prevalence. A study of US high school students found that 16 percent reported being victims of cyberbullying in the past 12 months (Kessel-Schneider, O'Donnell, Stueve, and Coulder, 2012).

Victims of online bullying were more likely than non-victims to be the target of offline bullying as well, but the correlation was far from perfect. Individuals involved in cyberbullying are also involved in traditional bullying (Smith, 2015). Researchers have questioned the extent that cyberbullying contributes a unique variance to negative outcomes, even after controlling for traditional bullying victimization (Olweus and Limber, 2018). Online bullying seems to be increasing over the years. A study by the Crimes Against Children research center that compared the results from two US national youth Internet surveys in 2000 and 2005 found that self-reported online victimization of bullying increased from 6 to 9 percent of those surveyed. Also, the percentage of children reporting cyberbullying others online increased from 14 to 28 percent. In that study, being cyberbullied was defined as receiving mean, nasty messages, being threatened with bodily harm, being called names, and having others tell lies about the victim on the Internet. Inspecting in more detail the types of online bullying to which youth are exposed online, a study in the USA found that 13 percent had experienced a situation of others spreading a rumor online about them, 6 percent a situation in which someone posted an embarrassing picture of them online without their permission, and 13 percent had received a threatening or aggressive email or text message.

As to risk factors, studies have indicated that the higher the frequency of Internet use, the higher the risk of cyberbullying (Patchin and Hinduja, 2006; Mitchell, Ybarra, and Finkelhor, 2007; Rosen, 2007). Risk factors appear to differ according to age. Among elementary school children, online gaming is a high risk factor. Among adolescents, social networking sites are increasingly common venues of cyberbullying (Kowalski, Limber, and McCord, 2019). These findings are consistent with earlier studies as well. Victimization occurs more often in Internet spaces used for communication with unknown individuals such as chat rooms, online gaming and social networking sites than through email (Hinduja and Patchin, 2008). A secondary analysis was conducted by the 2006 Pew American Life and Study of Parents and Teens on the link between teenagers' Internet

Online communication: negative social ties 143

activities and victimization. When types of Internet activities were divided into searching for information, entertainment (playing games online), and communication, it was found that only using the Internet for communication was associated with the likelihood of cyberbullying. In particular, youth who had a profile on a social networking site or a clip-sharing site (such as YouTube) and participated in non-moderated chat rooms were at higher risk than youth who did not participate in these activities. An online profile on social networking and clip-sharing sites provides personal characteristics, disseminates contact information, and exposes the adolescent to potential contact with motivated offenders, probably unknown to them. This private information is the raw material that might be used by potential offenders to call youngsters names, threaten them, and ridicule them. Consistent with this approach, the same study showed that attitudes supporting disclosure of personal information predicted the likelihood of cyberbullying victimization. Youths who reported greater willingness to disclose personal information to other individuals when meeting for the first time were more likely to report being victims of cyberbullying (Mesch, 2009).

On entering online space some adolescents are more willing than others to disclose personal information without being asked. A study of young people's public profiles in social networking sites showed that these contained personal information, such as pictures of themselves, with friends or family. A number of youth inserted pictures of themselves posing in swimsuits and underwear. Information on habits such as smoking and alcohol use could be found. Some even included their contact information such as the school they attended and phone numbers. Public disclosure of such information increases the risk of cyberbullying (Hinduja and Patchin, 2008). Not surprisingly, participation in chat rooms heightens the risk of cyberbullying still more, as participants are likely to engage in conversations with strangers, some of whom may be offenders. Studies have already found that online conversations tend to develop intimacy, and individuals are more likely to share private and personal information online because of the relative anonymity of the medium. Interestingly, playing online games was not found to be associated with risk of cyberbullying. Individuals engaged in this activity are most probably oriented to a less expressive and more instrumental form of communication, focused not on personal characteristics but on characteristics of the game (Mesch, 2009). Table 7.1 lists the risk factors associated with online victimization.

The findings direct our attention to the role of online social networks, as online victimization is associated with the use of social media. This means mobile applications that are used for communication, in particular,

144 *Online communication: negative social ties*

Table 7.1 Summary of risk factors of online victimization

Risk factor	Definition
Online bullying	An act of aggression, willful and repeated harm, including making nasty comments, spreading rumors, sending offensive text messages and posting embarrassing clips or photographs
Individual risk factor	Victim of bullying at school Lack of supportive social ties
Exposure factors	High frequency of Internet use Willingness to share personal and intimate information online
Online activities	Participation in chat rooms Participation on forums Having a profile on a social networking site
Technology-induced	Internet anonymity Reduced inhibition in making aggressive comments Large Internet audience

those that expose youth to networks of individuals who are unknown, or who are known but may use a false identity that facilitates their aggression.

Results of cyberbullying

For several reasons the effects of cyberbullying might be more pronounced than those of traditional bullying. An important characteristic of bullying is that when moving from physical to virtual space, its intensity increases. In traditional bullying the possibility exists of physical separation between the aggressor and the victim, but in cyberbullying, physical separation does not guarantee cessation of acts such as sending text messages and emails to the victim. Second, with the Internet the abuser has a sense of anonymity and often believes that there is only a slim chance of detection of the misconduct. Third, when bullying is technologically supported, the aggressor is not aware of the consequences of the aggression. The screen does not allow a view of the victim's emotional expression. Anonymity and absence of interaction may make the aggressor still less inhibited and increase the frequency and power of cyberbullying (Heirman and Walrave, 2008). Cyberbullying is associated with a variety of negative consequences for both victims and perpetrators. Among the negative consequences are higher levels of anxiety, depression, loneliness, greater suicidal ideation, and poor academic performance (Kowalski et al., 2019).

Online communication: negative social ties 145

Victims are also more likely to engage in high risk behaviors such as low school commitment, neglect of grades, and alcohol and cigarette consumption (Finkelhor, Mitchell, and Wolak, 2000). An emotional aspect also exists, and after a bullying event the victim reports feeling angry and upset, and has difficulty concentrating on schoolwork. Online bullying has proven to have a negative effect on parent–child relationships and on relations with friends (Patchin and Hinduja, 2006). Regarding actions taken by victims, most respondents said they took none, 20 percent decided to stay offline, and only 19 percent went to their parents and told them about the incident (Patchin and Hinduja, 2006). As these data show, the aggressors' perception that their acts incur no consequences seems to reflect the low likelihood that victims will take any action and report such incidents to teachers and parents. Thus, aggressors continue with their misdeeds because they do not face any negative social reaction.

From time to time, the danger has increased with the establishment of social network sites that provide platforms for publishing hate and cyberbullying. Examples are Enemybook, Snubster, and Hatebook. These utilities describe themselves as anti-social; subscribers may add to the Friend feature, adopted from the basic idea of Facebook, an additional feature of enemies, the reasons for choosing them as enemies and spreading their secrets, and can invite others to join them in their bullying (Hammond, 2007).

Explaining cyberbullying

The explanation of online victimization requires a socio-technical framework incorporating patterns of Internet use, the nature of computer-mediated communication, and individual characteristics that affect the quality of ties. The pivotal element is the existence of opportunities for an aggressor; these are likely to arise as young people conduct their regular activities online: cyberbullying is possible only for adolescents who have access to the Internet. That said, even for Internet users, the likelihood of being victims of cyberbullying varies according to the amount of daily time use, types of Internet use, and extent of disclosure of information. The concept of diversification is useful; we have shown in previous chapters that Internet use for communication purposes is an important element in youngsters' social life. Participation in online communication is an important component in the explanation of cyberbullying. Consistent with our argument, frequent Internet use and high level of Internet skills increase the risk of being bullied online (Kowalski et al., 2019).

Participation through social media has an effect on the size, composition, and quality of social ties, increasing exposure of youth to them. The

146 *Online communication: negative social ties*

effect varies according to each application, and the risk of exposure to victimization varies accordingly. Participation in chat rooms and forums and exchange of emails exposes youth to new ties with unknown others. With some of them the exposure can have positive consequences as youth are able to meet others who share their interests and concerns and are able to exchange resources that are not located in the existing network. At the same time, Internet activity enlarges the youth network; hence the risk of exposure to others with whom negative relationships may develop.

Here it is important to note the role that friending with parents on social network sites may have. A study examined the role of a parent–child connection on social networking sites on negative online experiences of young adolescents. Using data from a secondary analysis of teenagers (aged 12–17 years old) who participated in the 2011 Teens and Digital Citizenship Survey, and controlling for their participation in risky online activities and socio-demographic factors, the study establishes that children who reported having a parent as a social networking friend are less likely to be victims of cyberbullying. Furthermore, the parent–child connection on social networking sites apparently has a specific protective effect that might result from the children's disclosure of information to their parents through the mechanism of friending (Mesch, 2018b).

The more unknown individuals become part of the social network, the greater the likelihood of meeting some who might become aggressors. The risk may also intensify due to the heterogeneity of the expanding network's composition; this raises the likelihood of the adolescent meeting others who are socially different (in age, race, ethnicity) from him or her, and social heterogeneity might be a further source of aggression. Some older individuals might express interest in associating with teens to harass them or solicit them sexually. Also, the addition of online ties to the youth network might temporarily decrease the strength of existing ties, reducing the sources of social support available to the individual. The extent that cyberbullying is carried out by strangers remains to be assessed as existing evidence is more anecdotal than based on large-scale studies. Due to the anonymity of the medium, it is difficult to establish perpetrators' identities or if they belong to the victims' social network or not. As most of the adolescents use the Internet to connect with schoolmates and members of their peer group, it is plausible that the offenders are more likely to belong to the immediate social circle and less to be unknown strangers.

The use of social media to maintain existing ties, and keeping a profile and communicating with friends through social networking sites expose youth to the risk of online victimization, but by a different mechanism. The incorporation of social networking sites into adolescents' lives

Online communication: negative social ties 147

transforms their relationship with peers. When teens arrive home every day, rather than disconnecting from their friends, they enter a state of perpetual connection as smartphones are on all the time, text messages arrive, and conversations continue. In this case online bullying becomes an extension of school bullying, conducted after school hours through electronic communication. Now the possibility of after-school disconnection from or avoidance of contact with aggressors decreases. Cyberbullying often starts at the school or in the neighborhood and it continues online, as affirmed by adolescents themselves. In one study, US teens were asked where they thought someone of their age was more likely to be bullied or harassed. It is interesting that while 29 percent replied that it was more likely to happen online, the vast majority of these young Internet users, 67 percent, thought that it happened more often offline. Only 3 percent thought that it happened equally online and offline. For teenagers, online bullying can be emotionally debilitating, particularly because it is mainly a continuation at home of the aggression in the playground by known others from their social network. With traditional bullying, on arriving home the youngster felt safe and there was a respite from the aggression; now the aggression follows the adolescent home and can go on 24 hours a day. There is no place for the youngster to hide, even at home, from the persistent aggression (Rosen, 2007).

Important too is that online bullying requires some knowledge of the victim. When conducting online activities, individuals differ in their readiness to share personal information. Some are less willing to provide contact and personal information than others. Providing personal information can be considered a risk factor for victimization, particularly when it is given to strangers.

Another significant element is the way the Internet is perceived; this affects the user's behavior. In many ways the effect of the added value of communication technologies to face-to-face bullying is the well-known disinhibition effect, often associated with the use of these technologies. Suler (2004) noted that cyberspace can be conducive to behaviors that may not be revealed in the offline world. Various factors contribute to creating a subjective perception that fosters the disinhibition effect. Among the most salient characteristics are anonymity, asynchronicity, and dissociative imagination. Anonymity means the individual's subjective perception that the use of a nickname online separates him or her from the real world and his or her real identity is not known to others. This sense of anonymity might give rise to actions for which the actor does not feel responsible, at least not in the way he or she feels responsible for actions performed in a social circle in which his or her identity is known to friends, teachers, and parents. Asynchronicity means that often individuals interact online

148 *Online communication: negative social ties*

not at the same time, especially when communicating through email, forums, and social networking sites. Not interacting in real time means that individuals do not experience in real time the reactions of others, or get immediate negative feedback for their actions. This lack of interactivity might multiply aggressive acts against others as their reactions and feelings are not revealed immediately or as part of the social interaction between the teens.

Dissociative imagination means a situation in which some individuals evaluate online events differently and separately from face-to-face events. Certainly anonymity may reinforce this feeling that online norms of behavior unacceptable in a face-to-face situation are acceptable online; this is sensed as a different sphere, less real, or with fewer real consequences, for the victims. Disinhibition can be linked to the "lack of social cues" perspective, which holds that the deficit of online communication lies in the lack of social cues, of non-verbal signals that denote social status, and of the emotions of the participants in interpersonal communication. Accordingly, in the case of cyberbullying, the victim's emotional reactions are not present. The aggressor is unaware of the victim's distress, fear, tears, and other emotional reactions; he or she is thus likely to increase the aggression attempts without setting limits on it that would otherwise derive from interpersonal contact and interactivity. These perceived characteristics cannot be taken as the sole factors responsible for all online bullying activity. They work in combination with the aggressor's personality and family characteristics, which they interact with to amplify their effect.

Linking traditional bullying and cyberbullying

Is cyberbullying independent of bullying at school and the neighborhood? Some observers have advanced the idea that cyberbullying is a new phenomenon, largely the result of children and adolescents coming into contact with strangers and unknown individuals in open chat rooms online. In these spaces of conversation and social interaction strangers hold conversations with young people, making derogatory ethnic and sexual comments, or deriding their contributions. However, recent studies point more and more to a link between school bullying and cyberbullying. A study in Canada found that the most important predictor of cyberbullying victimization was victims being bullied at school (Li, 2007).

Bullying and cyberbullying are closely related, and in many cases the bullying possibly started at school and/or in the neighborhood and then spread to cyberspace. In fact, cyberspace serves bullies as yet another venue in which to harass others, as they take advantage of the high rate

Online communication: negative social ties 149

of Internet use among youth. Another possibility is that bullying starts online, and later the perpetrators take it into the real world, converting it into face-to-face bullying.

In trying to resolve this issue we face the problem of identifying the aggressor. As the Internet often provides anonymity, victims do not always know who the perpetrator of the aggressive behavior is. A study reported that 25.6 percent of the respondents said that they were cyberbullied by schoolmates, 12.8 percent by people outside school. The most surprising finding was that 46.6 percent did not know who cyberbullied them (Li, 2006).

Over time, online bullying seems to be on the rise. The percentage of victims of cyberbullying has increased despite the decrease in participation in open chat rooms and forums and an increase in the participation in IM and social networking sites. These results provide an additional indication that cyberbullying is aggression by known others, such as schoolmates, taking advantage of social networking media (e.g., Instant Messaging, social network sites, SMS). As noted earlier, a study by the Crimes against Children research center compared the results of two national Youth Internet safety surveys in 2000 and 2005 and found that the amount of cyberbullying had increased. In Rosen et al.'s study (2008), although only 11 percent of the teens reported being harassed, 57 percent of parents and 34 percent of teens reported that they were concerned about harassment on MySpace. Clearly, the use of communication channels that link youth with friends and friends of friends is associated with an increase in cyberbullying; this supports the argument of a link between this and offline bullying. Rather than being new, cyberbullying seems to be a supplement to school aggression.

Online harassment

We have already argued that the Internet is a space of social activity; youth activities include participating in online games, online discussions, online social support, and social networks. Participation in this social space might expose youth to the risk of online harassment. This notion refers to unwelcome and uninvited comments or attention. The comments provoke negative emotions, and are insulting because of their gender or ethnic content. This can take the form of offensive sexual or racist messages, jokes, and remarks purposely initiated by the harasser to humiliate the victim. Youth are victims of this type of online harassment. A study in the USA reported that 62 percent of youth participating in a representative national survey reported receiving unwanted sex-related emails (Mitchell, Wolak, and Finkelhor, 2007).

150   *Online communication: negative social ties*

A form of harassment that creates public concern is online sexual solicitation. Several large-scale studies have been conducted to assess the prevalence of online sexual solicitation. Regarding the frequency of harassment, a US study found that 13 percent of youths aged 10–17 years reported experiencing an unwanted sexual solicitation on the Internet in the previous year (Wolak, Mitchell, and Finkelhor, 2003). In the UK, 9 percent of children and youth aged 9–17 reported having received unsolicited sexual material online, and 7 percent reported receiving sexual comments online (Livingstone and Bober, 2004). In Canada, a study asked about the frequency and place of sexual harassment in the previous year, providing us with a rare opportunity to compare the frequency of sexual harassment in different social contexts. According to the data, overall 12 percent of adolescents in grades 7–11 reported having experienced sexual harassment in the previous year. There was a significant gender difference. Nine percent of the boys and 14 percent of the girls report sexual harassment. When asked about the space in which the harassment occurred, 8 percent said on the Internet, 6 percent at school, 2 percent on the phone, and 2 percent on the cell phone. The study also asked about the relationship with the offender, and found that 52 percent reported that the harasser was known from the real world while 48 percent did not know who the harasser was (Wing, 2005). The results are consistent in other countries as well. A study conducted in Australia asked 502 young children aged 8–13 years about the extent they were exposed to different experiences; it found that 5 percent were exposed to obscene language (Kidsonline@home, 2005).

The studies that investigated online sexual solicitation indicate that the likelihood of being a victim of this aggression depends on the application that teenagers use. One study found that the locations where youth most frequently reported online sexual solicitation were social networking sites and chat rooms (Ybarra and Mitchell, 2008). But blogging in general was not related to sexual solicitation. Bloggers who customarily interacted with unknown others were the only ones found to be at risk of sexual solicitation (Ybarra and Mitchell, 2008). Adolescents who blogged proved more likely than youth who did not blog to post personal information online, including their real names, age, and pictures of themselves, as well as disclosing personal experiences. Yet as the study shows, blogging in itself is not related to increased risk of online sexual solicitation. The risk of sexual solicitation becomes high only when the teen interacts with people met online. Furthermore, most of the youths who write a blog do not interact with people they meet online and do not respond to their messages (Ybarra and Mitchell, 2008).

Adolescents' choice of Internet applications probably reflects a selectivity effect. Youngsters who have unsatisfactory ties with parents and friends choose to use chat rooms to compensate for this by engaging in communication with unknown others. Such activity is a risk factor for online sexual solicitation. For example, a study that compared adolescents who used chat rooms with those who did not found that chat room users were more likely to have low self-esteem, not to feel safe at school, and to have been physically abused in the past. Thus, the study reported that for boys and girls alike, chat room use was significantly associated with adverse psychological characteristics. In contrast, other Internet activities did not show a consistent pattern of positive associations with these factors (Beebe, Asche, Harrison and Quinlan, 2004).

Racial and ethnic online harassment has been reported in studies conducted in chat rooms in which adolescents participate. The anonymity of online interactions may lower control of racist remarks. A study that compared moderated and non-moderated adolescents' chat rooms reported that in the latter an individual had a 59 percent chance of being exposed to racial and ethnic harassment remarks, and in the former a 19 percent chance (Subrahmanyam and Greenfield, 2008).

The aggressor in this type of online harassment is usually an unknown, other online user who was met briefly in a forum or chat room; he or she identified his or her intended victim's social status characteristics, and set about harassing him or her. A follow-up study that investigated risk factors of online harassment found that the likelihood of exposure to sexual solicitation and sexual harassment was associated with exposure variables: high frequency of Internet use and high frequency of participation in risky sites. Age was also related, as young adolescents were more likely than older ones to undergo this experience (Fleming, Greentree, Cocotti-Muller, Elias, and Morrison, 2006).

Summary

Cyberbullying and harassment have not just moved from physical to virtual space, their intensity has magnified as well. Physical separation of aggressor and victim does not guarantee disengagement and cessation of acts of bullying—not in terms of frequency, scope, or severity of the inflicted harm. With the advent of Web 2.0, cyberbullying includes the use of email, chat, Instant Messaging, clips, and blogs, which serve to embarrass and threaten, to make rude or vicious comments, and to spread rumors or clips and photographs of the victim in embarrassing situations. Cyberbullying, a serious form of cyber-harassment, has a number of important components: (1) cyber-bullies are aggressors who seek implicit

152   Online communication: negative social ties

or explicit pleasure through the mistreatment of other individuals; (2) cyberbullying (like bullying) involves repetitious harmful behavior; (3) a power differential between bullies and victims should be expected, and in the case of the electronic environment this differential might also be observed in computer literacy. Internet users often believe that there is only a slim chance of misconduct being detected online, so threats and harassment have become prevalent among young users.

Inquiry into young people's social networks today requires study of the patterns of Internet adoption and of online and face-to-face networks. Adolescents' adoption and use of the Internet are related to the social network to which each of them belongs. The choice of Internet social applications such as forums, chat rooms, email, Instant Messaging, and social networking sites depends on which online activities are carried out by others who belong to the peer group. A member's engaging in online communication requires that the other members have adopted the Internet for communication purposes.

Internet adoption and integration into routine communication with others have an effect on a youth's access to positive and supportive ties, but also on the extent of his or her exposure to negative encounters and persistent harassment, with all its negative consequences for his or her well-being. From the studies reviewed, it is clear that some adolescents become exposed to repetitive aggression and harassment. Such exposure depends on the online activities being conducted. The motivation to use forums and chat rooms is undoubtedly different from the motivation to use Instant Messaging and social networking sites. From the psychology literature we learn that shy individuals with higher levels of social anxiety are more likely to use forums and chat rooms. From the sociological literature we learn that individuals wishing to expand their networks and access to others who share their interests and concerns are more likely to do use them. Through these applications youth are better able to establish social ties with others who share their interests and hobbies, but at the same time they become exposed to strangers who may belong to a socially different group, hence to some risk of harassment by strangers.

The motivations to use social networking sites are apparently different, having more to do with an attempt to maintain and reinforce existing social ties with present friends met at school and in the neighborhood. The greatest danger of cyberbullying thus seems to be less from strangers than from known others; and as noted, cyberbullying is less likely to be a new behavior than aggression that has acquired an additional medium: cyberspace. The use of the Internet accordingly amplifies negative behavior, allowing it to be conducted at school and after school hours as well.

Online communication: negative social ties 153

These conclusions should be qualified, as online bullying is a relatively new and developing behavior that has to be monitored over time. As new applications are being developed, including social networking sites that openly instigate calling friends names and identifying them as enemies, we must follow the progress of cyberbullying and its connection with face-to-face and online behaviors. What is new about cyberbullying seems to be the diversification of sources of risk (online activities) and the diversification of kinds of bullying (using a new medium to bully).

8 Conclusion

Introduction

In this final chapter, we summarize the book's main arguments and findings, discuss their implications, and draw a few conclusions on the following points:

- the social effects of online adolescents' usage and sociability and the emergence of new kind of literacy;
- the relations between online network size and relational depth;
- the consequences of social diversification and network closure;
- the possible outcomes of the digital divide;
- the feasible negative and positive effects of adolescents' online use over time;
- technological convergence and social incorporation of ICT in everyday life.

Since the expansion of ICT use, and especially following the increasing integration of the Internet and mobile phones, academic discourse on the implications of CMC for social interaction has risen dramatically. A large group of scholars, mainly studying the Internet as a novel cultural artefact, suggested that ICT represents a social sphere in itself, a space for dwelling, capable of generating and sustaining new and complex forms of social interaction and activity. Youth have been given various appellations, from the "net-generation" through the "millennium generation" to "digital natives" (Tapscott, 1998; Prensky, 2001). These labels attempt to identify young adolescents as a unique cohort who have grown up during the expansion of the Internet and have been exposed since early childhood to a media-rich environment. They use computers, play online games, and constantly communicate with and are connected to their friends by electronic devices. They are immersed in these technologies, using digital spaces for social interaction, identity expression, and media production and

Conclusion   155

consumption. Simply put, the argument is that the Internet has created a new generation of young people who possess sophisticated knowledge and skills in information technologies which express values that support learning by experience and the creation of a culture in a digital space, and they have particular learning and social preferences.

Another stream of scholars argued that ICT has not affected any basic social patterns and has not created a new youth culture (Herring, 2007). Proponents of this view see ICT as a cultural artefact, an object immersed in a social context; they consider how the technology is incorporated into people's everyday lives, and how it is used as a means of communication within an offline social world (Howard, Rainie and Jones, 2002; Katz and Rice, 2002a). According to this approach, the information and communication technologies have not generated novel and different experiences, but are principally a new venue to conduct old things. For these researchers, the social uses of ICT are mostly restricted and similar to the use of other communication technologies, such as landlines and cell phones. Their purpose is merely to connect individuals already known to one another. Youth who use the Internet are not a unique generation; the fundamental developmental issues they have to cope with, such as identity formation, autonomy, social participation, and socialization, are the same as those of all young people in previous eras before the arrival of the Internet. They are handled in the same traditional ways, and technology supports the accomplishment of these developmental tasks (Herring, 2007).

So, while the transformative view focuses on online ties only, the "no change" view focuses on how people who have face-to-face contact use ICT to sustain these relationships over time and space.

We expanded and modified both the above views of ICT, using the concept of social diversification, that is, maintenance but more especially expansion of the size and composition of the social network, beyond the structural factors that limit adolescents' associations. At the center of the diversification approach is a conceptualization of ICT as a space for activity and social interaction

We presented ICT as an object around which joint activities are organized, no different from the neighborhood or the school. Our approach sees ICT as an arena that reflects existing social ties, but that can also modify individuals' social involvement in personal relationships. More specifically, the objective of this book was to explore how the use of ICT and how online relationships both affect the structure, content, and closure of adolescents' social circles. We asked what the social motivations to form online social relationships are, and whether online ties diversify youth's social circles, providing access to additional resources and

156 *Conclusion*

social capital. The concept of diversification implies that the innovative aspect of the Internet is to provide additional opportunities for activities that induce social interaction, resulting in a space for meeting new individuals and deepening communication channels with friends.

Societies are characterized by varying levels of social segregation. Social stratification processes and social norms segregate youth from other age groups and from youth of a different ethnic and social class group. As a result, adolescents tend to socially associate with individuals of similar social characteristics such as age, gender, marital status, ethnicity, religion, residential proximity, and nationality. This similarity may replicate existing social inequalities and block access to information and skills not available in the restricted social circle. Among adolescents, proximity is important for friendship formation because it establishes the boundaries within which they choose friends. Every individual occupies several separate but overlapping social worlds, each a potential sphere for association. A key location for meeting and making friends is school, where adolescents spend a large part of their waking hours. But other settings may be important as well. Adolescents spend their free time in neighborhood hangouts that they frequent after school. In shopping malls, video arcades, and movie theaters, usually in the neighborhood or nearby, groups of adolescents get to know others who live in the same neighborhood but do not attend the same school (Cotterell, 1996; Miller, 2016; boyd 2017; Hampton and Wellman, 2018). Unlike groups who are geographically more mobile and exposed to more diverse foci of activity, adolescents lack geographic mobility and are trapped in social relationships that involve individuals similar to themselves.

Diversification is a concept that can be linked to social capital. Although there are several accepted definitions and operationalizations of this concept, it is agreed that social capital refers to network ties that provide mutual support, shared language, shared norms, social trust, and a sense of mutual obligation from which people can derive value (Nahapiet and Ghoshal, 1998; Lin, 2001; Huysman and Wulf, 2004). The definition emphasizes the central role of the size, structure, composition, and trust in social networks. Based on these qualities, networks provide differential access to resources that include opportunities, skills, information, social support, and sociability. In the diversification perspective, the Internet is conceived as a social arena of shared activities that provides an opportunity for maintenance of bonds in existing friendships, but also for the expansion of the social circle to others who provide linkage to resources not available in the socially segregated and similar peer group. Unlike earlier researchers, who sought a general effect of ICT use on people's social involvement, we focused on a comparative analysis of adolescents' associations based in the origin of their settings: online or face-to-face.

Conclusion 157

ICT reflects social structure and at the same time exerts significant transformative effects on relational patterns. Conceptualizing ICT as foci of activity, we were able to produce a review illustrating that ICT is embedded in social structure. It is yet another sphere of social interaction and action, where adolescents play games, exchange information, offer social support, and share other instrumental and expressive resources. Like the more realistic synopian perspective put forward by Katz and Rice (2002a), we argued that online activities are therefore closely associated with offline social behavior, where the driving forces of social interaction are shared interests and adolescents' need of diversification of their social circle. Online friendship formation is associated with the social similarity of existing ties, indicating that the motivation to expand an adolescent's network is to diversify her or his social circle. This trend carries important implications for the changing nature of adolescence in the information society. First, using information and communication technologies, adolescents incorporate into their social circles friends who are more likely to be socially different from themselves, in contrast to their more homogeneous offline relations. A speculative question is how different from current patterns future social mechanisms of friendship formation and sociability via ICT will be. Second, contemporary online friendship formation is not a deviant case but is becoming increasingly common. It potentially exposes young individuals to new sources of information, social support, acquaintance and friendship ties, expanding their social capital. Third, study of the organization of adolescent peer groups requires a novel approach, one that should integrate social networks ties made at school, in the neighborhood, and through ICT. Such integration might produce research results different from those that have mounted up over the years in respect of societies in which young people's friendships were geographically bounded (Hampton and Wellman, 2018). Fourth, the Internet is a challenge to parent–adolescent relationships. The search for autonomy, as a developmental task, continues to be salient, but the Internet changes parents' ability to control the adolescent's exposure to values, activities, and social connections. In low-income households, adolescents become technology experts and parents must rely on their skills. The sources of teens' information become diversified and might challenge parental values. Online activities are difficult to control and monitor and access to individuals belonging to a different social circle exposes youth to alternative viewpoints and experiences.

The use of different social media to stay perpetually in contact with peers raises the question of how youth accommodate online participation in their full schedules. With the abundance of social media and

158   *Conclusion*

the extensive use of computers and smartphones, multitasking has become part of the way teens manage a busy life. Media multitasking can be defined as engaging in more than one media activity at a time, switching constantly between such activities as email, IM, web search, and sending text messages to friends (Foehr, 2006; Miller, 2016; boyd, 2017). Certainly, some multitasking existed in the past, with adolescents doing homework and listening to music at the same time. But now it has been expanded from media to social multitasking, namely, conducting various conversations simultaneously with different members of the peer group and using different channels: doing homework while participating in online chats and contacting friends by SMS. In that sense, the involvement of youth in peer groups and social networks has become more intensive and intermittent, most likely strengthening the bond of young people to their social networks and intensifying their mutual expectations. One question that will need to be addressed in the near future is how media multitasking and perpetual contact with peers affect family time and family communication, which are the building blocks of the family socialization process (Turkle, 2011, 2015b).

Certainly, online social engagement is still associated with general traditional sociological variables such as ethnicity, gender, age, family background, and residential location. That is, diversification is limited by existing material conditions and in that sense it raises important questions of social marginality. In earlier chapters we indicated that access to, and use of information and communication technologies are a source of youth empowerment. Social media are adopted through networks, as peers make a decision to adopt a specific IM provider, a specific game site, or a specific social networking site. In that way a central component of peers' interaction moves online and escapes parental and school control. Youth thereby obtain spaces of interaction that support the development of existing ties, the making of new ties, and access to diverse and novel source of information. Furthermore, youth have the opportunity to go from passive consumption of media to active engagement in the co-production of information in the information society. One important development in the Internet culture is a change in the connection of youth and media. Today youth are active participants in the creation of media content. The advent of Web 2.0 has increased youngsters' ability to become active creators of and contributors to information and content online, as well as passive consumers. The lower costs of coordinating creative efforts and distributing materials allow individuals to generate their own content and to collaborate with others in social, economic, and political activities. Social media platforms facilitate various ad hoc and formal online communities, small as well as large-scale. There user-generated-content (UGC)

Conclusion 159

flourishes: bloggers post news and analysis, independent musicians distribute their music (MySpace, SoundCloud), and amateur photographers post their photos (Flickr, Snapshot, Instagram), or distribute their videos (YouTube, Instagram). Youth today are actively involved in web production and tend to appropriate portions of it and to convert them into youth zones (Miller, 2016). Additionally, teens produce unique, stand-alone content for the web, like blogs, which allow a more interactive dialog. Weblogs are a kind of diary shared with a larger audience; they present details of people's everyday lives, daily concerns, thoughts and emotions, consumer talk and television and movie critiques. As such, weblogs are a popular way of building identity, socialization in the information-based society, and social interaction. All these considerations produce the need to develop an understanding of some youths' marginalization in the information society. Access and use are not universal; by cultural choice or due to socio-economic circumstances a section of adolescents is disadvantaged. Their lack of access to communication and information technologies might result in disconnection from mainstream society. While the consequences of access and use have been studied extensively, the social and developmental consequences of "disconnection" require the development of research programs (Katz and Rice, 2002a; Van Dijk, 2005). In particular, there is a need to address the psychological and sociological consequence that not having access, or not having fast access to the Internet might result in social isolation from peer-group members who coordinate their activities through Internet social applications.

Lack of access or restricted access to the Internet also has implications for the acquisition of skills in the information society. The use of social media is becoming a regular requirement for new employees. Social networking sites are more and more instrumental in the job-hunting process and applicants are more and more recruited through social networking sites. Employers no longer rely completely on word of mouth or print ads to display the jobs they post. Information on job openings is becoming more and more available through social networking sites and micro-blogging. Social networking skills were always important in finding a job; the significant change is that social networking is now conducted online, diversifying the number and type of employees and employers who can be approached. As stated, social media skills are becoming required in many jobs. Firms are realizing that customers are expressing their views on products online and need to have a picture of customers' view of their products and for marketing their products. Social media skills can in the near future become an additional literacy required of employees. Lack of access or restricted access to the Internet might be a limitation in an applicant's skills and reduce the chances of being offered a job.

160 *Conclusion*

Cyberspace is a distinct focus of activity, where specific rules and norms of behavior are applied and where different kinds of communication occur. Although ICT is a distinct sphere of action, it cannot be wholly reduced to communication. And although ICT is socially embedded, it cannot be wholly reduced to components of social structure. At the same time, we have specified the transformative role that ICT plays in social interaction. The supporters of the "no change" perspective have attempted to evaluate how online and offline relationships affect one another. Informed by earlier research on media effects such as television, their studies focused on how ICT affected the size of social circles, the extent of involvement in social, family, and community activities, and the use of other communication devices. That research was guided by the assumption of displacement, meaning that time invested in media was at the expense of time devoted to social activities such as school learning, extracurricular activities, and family time (Nie et al., 2002). But that approach fails when one considers that the central use of ICT is interpersonal communication, linking individuals who are already in the same social circle, supporting previous friendships, creating new acquaintances, and moving from online to multi-channel communication. Accordingly, we searched for transformative effects, namely, how ICT use and online friendship formation affect the social composition and structure of adolescent friendships, finding evidence for diversification in the network structure of adolescent social ties. Furthermore, scholars have assumed—without empirical evidence—that online ties are inevitably weak. But we reviewed studies showing that online ties over time often become face-to-face ties, and therefore bear a remarkable resemblance in terms of the trust and social support they proffer.

At the current stage of ICT diffusion, online relationships are weaker because they lack certain characteristics. First, they are recently created social ties, and they need time to build up a joint history, common identity, and collective memory; previous studies have found these to be associated with the strength of ties. Second, they are created around specific and shared interests, and in some cases start slowly, moving to more generalized topics of discussion and joint activities. Thus, online ties are temporarily weaker, representing an early historical period of development; but as time goes by they provide more generalized activities and topics of interest (Mesch and Talmud, 2006a, 2006b). Our argument and findings imply that online social ties are incorporated into an individual's life, but not at the expense of close and intimate relationships. Thus, online relationships expand the size of the social networks, supporting the diversification approach.

Early approaches to computer-mediated communication were technological determinism and social constructivism. The former assumes that

Conclusion 161

CMC has an intrinsic effect of its own, reshaping social relations inside and outside cyberspace; the latter ignores the unique nature of media, depicting offline relations as primarily more relevant. Similarly, technological determinism attributes either dystopian or utopian content, either liberating or alienating characteristics, to ICT, while social constructivism overlooks ICT's technological ingredient entirely, assigning it unlimited interpretative flexibility, which can be infinitely be molded by social forces (Katz and Rice, 2002a).

In contrast to these two perspectives, we have presented a sociological approach to digital social ties, asserting that online social interaction is embedded in the larger social structure, and that individual social resources are associated with offline and online relations. More specifically, we cited some research inquiring into the social etiology of ICT activity and virtual relations, as well as the implications of virtual social capital for individual social resources and for relational quality.

As "new adopters," adolescents have dramatically increased their ICT use. Furthermore, adolescents have a fresh outlook or novel "cohort effect" in that their digital skills and cultural surroundings take for granted the very existence of digital means and a multi-media environment, and they use these media mainly for social purposes (Lenhart, Rainie, and Oliver, 2001; Gross et al., 2002). ICT is highly important also for accessing and transferring information and knowledge. Theories of the digital divide distinguish inequality in access, mainly attributed to inequality in material and physical well-being, from inequality in use, mainly ascribed to the cultural, motivational, and skill gaps in the ability to appropriate ICTs. Over time, the existence of the digital divide has become associated not only with differential access by social groups to technology but also with greater general social inequality. ICT use is regarded as connected to the accumulation of cultural capital, knowledge resources, and social capital (Van Dijk, 2005). The social stratification or amplification perspective argues that unequal distribution of social and economic resources is associated with uneven access to ICT, and in turn may in the future amplify disparity in skills, education, social literacy, and civic participation between those who have and who do not have access (Van Dijk, 2005). In contrast, the normalization hypothesis argues that the rapid diffusion of ICT may in time narrow the digital divide as more and more population segments and social categories possess and have access to it, as has been observed in other media such as television and phones (including mobile phones) (Katz and Rice, 2002a). Yet ICT use is also socially embedded: the intrinsic technological and dynamic characteristics of ICT may be used differently by various social categories. The erosion of the digital divide among youth is good news, as it may minimize prospective gaps

162 *Conclusion*

in important processes such as status attainment and civic participation in the future mature population, but the unrelenting diversification in ICT use also raises questions regarding prospective significant personal differences in social capital and social standing of the current adolescent generation. A literature review suggests the conversion of the traditional digital divide into a subtler diversification of ICT use and online sociability according to kind of interest and friendship similarity of adolescent users. In other words, users are adopting ICT in different spheres and ways according to their cultural predispositions. Future research should focus on the extent to which diversification in ICT adoption and use will affect life chances.

Adolescents use ICT mainly for social purposes. Undergoing a critical and troublesome developmental stage, adolescents need support outside of their family households. As their relations with other family members change, as they seek separation and individuation, family authority and rules are repeatedly challenged and reconfigured, and social support and social interaction with peers are vital for the adolescent's adjustment and well-being. Significant numbers of parents regard ICT as a potential risk, exposing their children to hazards involved in contact with unknown individuals (Cohen, Lamish, and Schejter, 2008 Valkenburg and Taylor Piotrowski, 2017). Beyond these legitimate concerns, ICT is not just another arena of family conflict over entertainment resources, time allocation, and wherewithal, but also a space of social interaction where adolescents can increase their social capital through access to knowledge and the construction of new social ties. Ongoing negotiation within families over ICT use is closely linked to existing family boundaries and family conflicts in other spheres of life, affecting, in turn, adolescents' online network conduct and structure. In other words, family mediation of ICT use is relevant to the differences in the extent that ICT supports adolescents' diversification of social networks (Valkenburg and Taylor Piotrowski, 2017).

Young people nowadays use multiple channels of communication for social relations, from face-to-face meetings, SMS and IM to social networking sites, to maintain and create new social ties. Adolescents' trust in online friends is still less than in to face-to-face relations, but it seems to be increasing. Adolescent Internet users' ability to reconfigure the personal network is less costly, more flexible, and much more feasible than is non-Internet users'. This novel capacity has mostly positive outcomes. Some adolescents extend their range of contacts, expanding their bridging social capital by forming new ties in ICT platforms, while others use ICT to compensate for a fragile social position. Additionally, ICT is primarily used to solidify close friends' ties by multiplex communication, and to

Conclusion 163

extend bonding social capital among adolescents. Especially during adolescence, network closure and cohesive social ties are necessary "building blocks" for the construction of "bonding social capital," enjoying the benefits of trust, social support, mutual commitment, identity maintenance and fortification, and reciprocal resource exchange.

ICT is a sphere of social activity but with specific autonomous technological features. ICT ties tend to be age-homogeneous, but a significant portion of them are quite heterogeneous in terms of residence location and gender. Adolescents' social networks can be predictive of deviant behavior, school dropping-out, and academic performance (Cairns, Cairns, Neckerman, and Gariepy, 1989). The relatively influential contagion effect and imitation conduct by an ego's alters could be constitutive. During adolescence a stable network of social support and peer influence is functionally necessary (Valkenburg and Taylor Piotrowski, 2017).

Still, the ICT may add new acquaintances to an ego's network, but this is correlated with lower network density. More importantly, ICT use reduces relational quality, but it gains in expanding social ties. Social resources are positively associated with adolescents' network heterogeneity (see Lin, 2001: 207). The steady application of the principle of social similarity shows that network expansion does not occur at random: adolescents are more likely to form social ties with others who share their interests, but at the same time they are exposed to strangers who may belong to a socially different group; they are thus be exposed to some risk of bullying (even from schoolmates), stranger harassment, and verbal violence. As ICT's technological features lower costs, some adolescents become exposed to recurrent aggression and harassment. The likelihood of being exposed to negative online conduct depends on the kinds of online activity pursued and the ICT channel chosen. The risk of a negative tie depends on motivation, personality, and kind of use. Isolated and timid individuals who mainly aim at compensating their lower stock of offline social capital by expanding their networks are more likely to do be exposed to negative ties.

Katz and Rice claim that ICT use in itself is an indication of social capital, as it enables networked individuals to activate social relations by using digital technology and linking various spheres of life (Katz and Rice, 2002a: 337–339). ICT compensates for sparse social capital, and increases sociability, because its network is less costly, more elastic and fluid, and can be a kind of peer-to-peer or group-based formations (Monge and Contractor, 2003: 318–321).

ICT ties and telephone ties may be conceived as similar, but they are quite different in some important respects (Cohen, Lamish and Schejter,

164   *Conclusion*

2008). ICT operation is affected by social categories, the unique nature of information technology, and the individual's social networks (Katz and Rice, 2002a: 345–346). People make different use of it according to their various social locations and according to nationality, gender, and religion. Moreover, though virtual relations are cost-free, and can be formed in principle almost at random, they are not like offline social ties. In both media—Internet and telephone—social structure governs the formation and reconfiguration of relational patterns. Moreover, technology adoption itself is socially embedded. Over and above cost and barriers to physical access, digital complexity is a continuing source of digital divide and network diversification (Katz and Rice, 2002a). The blending of technological complexity and network diversification intensifies the variety and richness of adolescents' online social networks. The integration of information technology with everyday social life has created a complex phenomenon, where social contexts, information channels, and network properties interact (Katz and Rice, 2002a). The virtual arena is at the same time socially embedded, but operates under autonomous technical rules. The hyper-textual nature of this medium, the modularity of its components, its tendency to reduce hidden social cues, and the unique literacy of its users are bound to raise important questions about the scope of the ICT use in future generations. It cannot therefore be understood without close attention to the processes of social affordance.

Conclusion

The emergence of a new kind of literacy

The spread of ICT in the household, school, and inter-personal relations, as well as the partial integration of the Internet with mobile phones, have led to a dramatic rise in adolescents' computer literacy. The integration of the Internet and mobile phones has yielded an extraordinary increase in adolescents' personal autonomy in choice of media channel as well as choice of online friends.

As the net generation, adolescents' digital and mobile orientation is more "embodied" in their taken-for-granted reality. ICT technological features *per se* cannot effect communication patterns; instead, people's perception of the technology creates their tendency to indeed activate these technical characteristics (Valkenburg and Peter, 2009). For contemporary adolescents of the "information age," their positive ICT orientation enables them to maneuver their relational management in "real" and virtual space, and to develop their social skills online and offline. In fact,

Conclusion 165

the net generation's conduct seems to epitomize the modal "networked individual" (Wellman et al., 2003).

Network size and relational depth

Adolescents who participate in online networks increase their overall network size. Though the ability to reach a physically remote person online is virtually technologically boundless, the ability to make new online acquaintances is hampered by social constraints: physical proximity, social similarity, and transitivity are still the over-arching principles of adolescents' online social networks. Consequently, most adolescents' frequent communication links are with their peers, close friends, of the same age, same gender, and same residential area.

Although most online ties are shallower than close and meaningful offline relationships, ICT amplifies relational quality with close friends, and to a lesser extent with remote ties with shared interests. For some adolescents, online relations serve as a compensatory outlet for their relative lack of face-to-face emotional support from their peer group—support deemed essential for their vulnerable and confusing developmental stage.

Diversification vs. closure

The combination of social and technological attributes of ICT—highlighted by the theory of social affordance—enables similar friends (demographically or sharing similar interest) to be connected in homogeneous networks. The facilitation of expanding ties to similar others is augmented by the social networking sites, where a friend of one's friend tends to become one's friend as well. The combination of homophily and transitivity dramatically diversifies ICT networks into homogeneous clusters. In fact, face-to-face networks tend to be less homogeneous than social networking sites.

The digital divide

We denoted two possible outlooks on the digital divide. The first states that the diffusion of the ICT is far from evenly distributed or uniform. Moreover, gaps in ICT access, use, and literacy are parallel to many other sources of social and economic inequalities. As a result, digital divides lead to the amplification of other inequalities, as social and academic skills will depend closely on digital access, use, and literacy (Van Dijk, 2005; Correa, 2014, 2016; Van Deursen, and Van Dijk, 2014, 2015; Correa et al., 2015; boyd, 2017; Jenkins and Sun, 2019). By contrast, the normalization

166   *Conclusion*

scenario puts forward the view that in the foreseeable future, inexpensive diffusion of the ICT will make it available for all social strata and places, albeit not in the same proportion. As a result, many digital divides will decrease in scope, intensity, and quality (Katz and Rice, 2002a).

Negative and positive effects over time

Like dark streets at night, virtual dark alleys can be full of detrimental effects and potential hazards for the adolescent users. Still, over time ICT users learn to develop precautionary devices, especially regarding disclosure of intimate and personal information and conduct with strangers. As most new contacts are made according to principles of transitivity, mutual friends can vouch for a contact's trustworthiness or attest to her or his abusive behavior. Additionally, many websites develop the institution of new users' social norms and technological devices for misconduct (reporting abuse, users' blocking, etc.), which minimize the detrimental effects of online networks. It seems to us that future generations will learn safe surfing, as in their other walks of life. Prospective digital literacy and higher awareness of ICT uses and misuses will go hand in hand in the future.

Technological convergence and social integration of ICT into everyday life

Though ICT has unique communicative characteristics, many of its key features cannot totally abolish the effect of social structure on adolescents' relational capacity. Though ICT ties are generally weaker, sparse, and shallower, to the extent that a medium is richer, relational quality is more similar to face-to-face interaction. Additionally, to the extent that an online relation is frequent and durable, its pattern is more akin to a face-to-face relationship.

ICT is mostly positive for sociability, for resources exchange, for acquiring heterogeneous contacts, and for social support. ICT use is both social and technological. It contains both a positive potential and a negative threat to the quality of adolescents' social lives. Online spaces are used as a continuation of everyday communication, to reflect on events at school and to plan joint activities. At the same time, online experience of conducting multiple activities and conversations with others is incorporated into youngsters' approach to daily life. As a result, the binary depiction of the boundaries between offline and online is deemed less relevant and meaningful. Demarcating the boundaries of virtuality and reality has become ever more difficult and vague, as ICT and social

Conclusion 167

structure mutually affect each other in various ways. These reciprocal effects will continue to be at the center of social and technological policies, public discourse, and scientific investigation.

The impact of algorithmic regulation on adolescents online

Like adults, adolescents are directed online with computer interface and by algorithms. A growing concern has been already risen regarding the implications of adolescent interaction not only through ICT by also with computer, bits, and algorithms (Turkle, 2011, 2015). Algorithmic filtering refers to how developers prioritize the selection, sequence, and visibility of posts (Bucher, 2012). It is well documented in communication research that the communicative algorithms, embedded in online social platforms, are consistently narrowing the users' attention focus and span to their already present worldview (Bucher, 2012; Loader, Vromen, and Xenos 2016; Gillespie, 2018). A platform's functionality can "dispose networked publics toward particular behaviors" (Papacharissi and Easton, 2013: 176). More important, Vaterlaus, Barnett, Roche, and Young (2016) have found that contravening the "unwritten rules" of Snapchat can adversely impact interpersonal relationships among youths. In other words, algorithmic mediation may exacerbate the already selective biases inherent in social ties of homophily, proximity, and assortativity. Moreover, it seems that this effect is deemed especially detrimental for adolescents who are in a critical stage of development and socialization, wherein their cyberspace is an integral part of their entire sociality. The precise effects of algorithmic mediation on the selection, formation, maintenance, and mixing of youth and adolescents' social ties should be further explored by future research.

Bibliography

Aarsand, P.A. (2007) Computer and video games in family life: the digital divide as a resource in intergenerational interactions, *Childhood*, 14(2), 235–256.

Abbas, R. and Mesch, G. (2018) Do rich teens get richer? Facebook use and the link between offline and online social capital among Palestinian youth in Israel, *Information, Communication and Society*, 21(1), 63–79.

Aboud, F.E. and Mendelson, M.J. (1996) Determinants of friendship selection and quality: developmental perspectives, in W.M. Bukowski, A. Newcomb, and W.W. Hartup (Eds.), *The Company They Keep: Friendship in Childhood and Adolescence*, New York: Cambridge University Press, pp. 87–112.

Abrahim, S., Mir, B.A., Suhara, H., Mohamed, F.A., and Sato, M. (2019) Structural equation modeling and confirmatory factor analysis of social media use and education, *International Journal of Educational Technology in Higher Education*, 16, 32. https://doi.org/10.1186/s41239-019-0157-y.

Achenbach, T.M. (1991) *Manual for the Child Behavior Check List 14–18 and 1991 Profile*, Burlington, VT: University of Vermont Press.

Adedokun, O.A. and Balschweid, M.A. (2008) Community social interactive processes and rural adolescents' educational outcomes: what we know and what we need to know, *The Online Journal of Rural Research and Policy*, 2, 1–19.

Agnew, R. (1993) Why do they do it? An examination of the intervening mechanisms between social control variables and delinquency, *Journal of Research in Crime and Delinquency*, 30, 245–266.

Ahn, J. (2012) Teenagers' experiences with social network sites: relationships to bridging and bonding social capital. *The Information Society*, 28(2), 99–109.

Amato, P.R. and Rivera, F. (1999) Paternal involvement and children's behavior, *Journal of Marriage and Family*, 61(2), 375–384.

Anderson A.L. (2013) Adolescent time use, companionship, and the relationship with development, in C. Gibson and M. Krohn (Eds,), *Handbook of Life-Course Criminology*, New York: Springer.

Anderson, R.H., Kedzie, C., Bikson, T.K., Keltner, B.R., Law, S.A., Panis, C. Mitchell, B.M., Pliskin, J., and Srinagesh, P. (1995) *Universal Access to E-Mail: Feasibility and Societal Implications*, Santa Monica, CA: RAND Corporation.

Bibliography 169

Antheunis, M.L., Schouten, A.P., and Krahmer, E. (2016) The role of social networking sites in early adolescents' social lives, *The Journal of Early Adolescence*, 36(3), 348–371.

Antheunis, M.L., Valkenburg, P.M., and Peter, J. (2012) The quality of online, offline, and mixed-mode friendships among users of a social networking site, *Cyberpsychology: Journal of Psychosocial Research on Cyberspace*, 6(3), Article 6. https://doi.org/10.5817/CP2012-3-6.

Attewell, P. and Battle, J. (1999) Home computers and school performance, *The Information Society*, 15, 1–10.

Attewell, P., Suazo-Garcia, B., and Battle, J. (2003) Computers and young children: social benefit or social problem? *Social Forces*, 82, 277–296.

Baorong, G., Bricout, J.C., and Huang, J. (2005) A common open space or a digital divide? A social model perspective on the online disability community in China, *Disability and Society*, 20(1), 49–66.

Bargh, J.A. and McKenna, K.Y.A. (2004) The internet and social life. *Annual Review of Psychology*, 55, 573–590.

Bargh, J.A., McKenna, K.Y.A., and Fitzsimons, G.M. (2002) Can you see the real me? Activation and expression of the "true self" on the internet, *Journal of Social Issues*, 58, 33–48.

Barzilai-Nahon, K. (2006) Gaps and bits: conceptualizing measurements for digital divide, *The Information Society*, 22(5), 269–278.

Bassani, C. (2007) Five dimensions of social capital theory as they pertain to youth studies, *Journal of Youth Studies*, 10(1), 17–34.

Baumeister, R.F., and Leary, M.R. (1995) The need to belong: desire for interpersonal attachments as a fundamental human motivation, *Psychological Bulletin*, 117(3), 497–529. https://doi.org/10.1037//0033-2909.117.3.497.

Baym, N.K., Zhang, Y.B., and Lin, M.C. (2004) Social interactions across media: interpersonal communication on the internet, telephone and face-to-face, *New Media and Society*, 6, 299–318.

Beebe, T.J., Asche, S.E., Harrison, P.A., and Quinlan, K.B. (2004) Heightened vulnerability and increased risk-taking among adolescent chat room users: results from a statewide school survey, *Journal of Adolescent Health*, 35(2), 116–123.

Beraman, P.S. and Moody, J. (2004) Adolescents' suicidability, *American Journal of Public Health*, 94, 89–95.

Beran, K.M. and Li, A. (1995) Bully and victim problems in elementary schools and students beliefs about aggression, *Canadian Journal of School Psychology*, 11, 153–65.

Berardo, F. (1998) Family privacy: issues and concepts, *Journal of Family Issues*, 118(19), 4–1.

Berndt, T.J. and Ladd, G.W. (1989) *Peer Relationships in Child Development*, New York: John Wiley & Sons.

Berndt, T.J., Miller, K., and Park, K. (1989) Adolescents' perceptions of friends' and parents' influence in other aspects of their school adjustment, *Journal of Early Adolescence*, 9, 419–435.

170 *Bibliography*

Berson, I.R., Berson, M.J., and Ferron, J.M. (2002) Emerging risks of violence in the digital age, *Journal of School Violence*, 2, 51–71.

Bessière, K., Pressman, S., Kiesler, S., and Kraut, R. (2010) Effects of internet use on health and depression: a longitudinal study, *Journal of Medical Internet Research*, 12(1), e6. https://doi.org/10.2196/jmir.1149.

Best, P., Gil-Rodriguez, E., Manktelow, R., and Taylor, B.J. (2016) Seeking help from everyone and no-one: conceptualizing the online help-seeking process among adolescent males, *Qualitative Health Research*, 26(8), 1067–1077.

Bimber, B. (2000) Measuring the gender gap in the internet, *Social Science Quarterly*, 81, 868–876.

Blais, J.J., Craig, W.M., Pepler, D., and Connolly, J. (2008) Adolescents online: the importance of internet activity choices to salient relationships, *Journal of Youth Adolescence*, 37, 522–536.

Bliemel, M.J., McCarthy, I.P., and Maine, E. (2014) An integrated approach to studying multiplexity in entrepreneurial networks, *Entrepreneurship Research Journal*, 4(4), 367–402.

Boase, J., Horrigan, J.B., Wellman, B., and Rainie, L. (2006) *The Strength of Internet Ties*, Washington, DC: Pew and American Life Project.

Boase, J. and Wellman, B. (2006) Personal relationships: on and off the internet, in D. Perlman and A.L. Vangelistihe (Eds.), *Handbook of Personal Relations*, Cambridge: Cambridge University Press.

Boissevain, J. (1974) *Friends of Friends: Networks, Manipulators and Coalitions*, New York: St. Martin's Press.

Bolton, R.N., Parasuraman, A., Hoefnagels, A., Michels, N., Kabadayi, S., Gruber, T., and Solnet, D. (2013) Understanding generation Y and their use of social media: a review and research agenda, *Journal of Service Management*, 24, 245–267.

Boneva, B., Kraut, R. and Frohlich, D. (2001) Using e-mail for personal relationships: the difference gender makes, *American Behavioral Scientist*, 45(3), 530–549.

Borg, M.G. (1998) The emotional reaction of school bullies and their victims, *Educational Psychology*, 18, 433–444.

Borzekowski, D.L.G., Fobil, J.N. and Asante, K.O. (2006) Online access by adolescents in Accra: Ghanaian teens' use of the internet for health information, *Developmental Psychology*, 42(3), 450–458.

Boulton, M., Trueman, M., Chau, C., Whiteland, C., and Amatya, K. (1999) Concurrent and longitudinal links between friendship and peer victimization: implications for befriending interventions, *Journal of Adolescence*, 22, 461–466.

Boulton, M.J., and Underwood, K. (1992) Bully/victim problems among middle school children, *British Journal of Educational Psychology*, 62(1), 73–87.

boyd, d. (2008) Friends, in I. Mizuko et al. (Eds.), *Hanging Out, Messing Around, Geeking Out: Living and Learning with New Media*, Boston: MIT Press.

boyd, d. (2017) *It's Complicated: The Social Lives of Networked Teens*, New Haven, CT: Yale University Press.

Bibliography 171

boyd, d., Hargittai, E., Schultz, J., and Palfrey. J. (2011) Why parents help their children lie to Facebook: unintended consequences of the 'Children's Online Privacy Protection Act,' *First Monday*, 16(11), November.

Bradley, K. (2005) Internet lives: social context and moral domain in adolescent development, *New Directions for Youth Development*, 108, 57–76.

Bramoullé, Y., Currarini, S., Jackson, M.O., Pin, P., and Rogers, B.W. (2012) Homophily and long-run integration in social networks, *Journal of Economic Theory*, 147(5), 1754–1786. https://doi.org/10.1016/j.jet.2012.05.007.

Brochado, S., Soares, S., and Fraga, S. (2016) A scoping review on studies on cyberbullying prevalence among adolescents, *Trauma, Violence and Abuse*, 18, 523–531.

Brooks, B., Hogan, B., Ellison, N., Lampe, C., and Vitak, J. (2014) Assessing structural correlates to social capital in Facebook ego networks, *Social Networks*, 38, 1–15.

Brooks, S. (2015) Does personal social media usage affect efficiency and well-being? *Computers in Human Behavior*, 46, 26–37. https://doi.org/10.1016/j.chb.2014.12.053.

Brown, G. and Michinov, N. (2017) Cultural differences in garnering social capital on Facebook: French people prefer close ties and Americans prefer distant ties, *Journal of Intercultural Communication Research*, 46, 579–593.

Brown, P.J. and Peterson, G.L. *Benefits of Leisure*, State College, PA: Vantage, pp. 215–301.

Bucher, T. (2012) Want to be on the top? Algorithmic power and the threat of invisibility on Facebook, *New Media and Society*, 14(7), 1164–1180.

Bundon, A. and Hurd Clarke, L. (2014) Unless you go online, you are on your own: blogging as a bridge in para-sport, *Disability and Society*, 30, 185–198.

Buote, V.M., Wood, E. and Pratt, M. (2009) Exploring similarities and differences between online and offline friendships: the role of attachment style, *Computers in Human Behavior*, 25, 560–567.

Burt, R.S. (1992) *Structural Holes: The Social Structure of Competition*, Cambridge, MA: Harvard University Press.

Burt, R.S. (2005) *Brokerage and Closure: An Introduction to Social Capital*, New York: Oxford University Press.

Burt, R.S., Jannotta, E.J., and Mahoney, T.J. (1998) Personality correlates of structural holes, *Social Networks*, 20(1), 63–87.

Bush, A., Walker, A., and Perry, B. (2017) "The framily plan": Characteristics of ties described as both "friend" and "family" in personal networks, *Network Science*, 5(1), 92–107. https://doi.org/10.1017/nws.2017.2.

Bybee, C., Robinson, D. and Turow, J. (1982) Determinants of parental guidance of children's television viewing for a special subgroup: mass media scholars, *Journal of Broadcasting*, 26, 697–710.

Byrne, D. and Osland, J.A. (2000) Sexual fantasy and erotica/pornography: internal and external imagery, in L.T. Szuchman and F. Muscarela (Eds.), *Psychological Perspectives on Human Sexuality*, New York: Wiley, pp. 283–305.

172 Bibliography

Cacioppo, J.T., Fowler, J.H., and Christakis, N.A. (2009) Alone in the crowd: the structure and spread of loneliness in a large social network, *Journal of Personality and Social Psychology*, 97(6), 977–991. https://doi.org/10.1037/a0016076.

Cairns, R.B., Cairns, B.D., Neckerman, H.J., and Gariepy, J.-L. (1989) Growth and aggression, *Developmental Psychology*, 25 (March).

Carter, R. and Pogarsky, G. (2011) One bad apple may not spoil the whole bunch: best friends and adolescent delinquency, *Journal of Quantitative Criminology*, 27(2), 197–223.

Carvalho, J., Fonseca, G., Francisco, R., Bacigalupe, G., and Relvas, A. (2016) Information and communication technologies and family: patterns of use, life cycle and family dynamics, *Journal of Psychology and Psychotherapy*, 6(1), 240. https://doi.org/10.4172/2161-0487.1000240.

Carvalho, J., Francisco, R., and Relvas, A.P. (2015) Family functioning and information communication technologies: How do they relate? A literature review, *Computers in Human Behavior*, 45, 99–108.

Castells, M. (1996) *The Rise of the Network Society*, Oxford: Blackwell Publishers.

Castells, M. (2000) Materials for an exploratory theory of network society, *British Journal of Sociology*, 51, 5–24.

Centola, D (2015) The social origins of networks and diffusion, *American Journal of Sociology*, 120(5), 1295–1338.

Chan, D.K.S. and Cheng, G.H.L. (2004) A comparison of offline and online friendship qualities at different stages of relationship development. *Journal of Social and Personal Relationships*, 21(3), 305–320.

Chen, W., Boase, J., and Wellman, B. (2002) The global villagers, in B. Wellman and C. Haythornthwaite (Eds.), *The Internet in Everyday Life*, Oxford: Blackwell, pp. 74–113.

Chen, W. and Wellman, B. (2004) The global digital divide-within and between countries, *IT and Society*, 1(7), 39–45.

Chesley, N. (2005) Blurring boundaries? Linking technology use, spillover, individual distress, and family satisfaction, *Journal of Marriage and Family*, 67(5), 1237–1248.

Ching, C.C., Basham, J.D., and Jang, E. (2005) The legacy of the digital divide: gender, socioeconomic status, and early exposure as predictors of full-spectrum technology use among young adults, *Urban Education*, 40(4), 394–411.

Cho, J. (2015) Roles of smartphone app use in improving social capital and reducing social isolation, *Cyberpsychology, Behavior, and Social Networking*, 18(6), 350–355.

Cho, J., De Zuniga, H.G., Rojas, H., and Shah, D. (2003) Beyond access: the digital divide and internet uses and gratifications, *IT and Society*, 1(4), 46–72.

Christakis, D.A. (2014) Infants and interactive media use—reply, *JAMA Pediatrics*, 168(10).

Clark, L.S. (2013) *The Parent App: Understanding Families in the Digital Age*, New York: Oxford University Press.

Bibliography 173

Cochran, M., Larner, M., Riley, D., Gunnarsson, L., and Henderson, C.R., Jr. (1993) *Extending Families: The Social Networks of Parents and their Children*, Cambridge: Cambridge University Press.

Cohen, A.A., Lamish, D., and Schejter, A.M. (2008) The wonder phone in the land of miracles: mobile telephony in Israel, *New Media: Policy and Social Research Issues*, Cresskill, NJ: Hampton Press.

Cohen, L.E. and Felson, M. (1979) Social change and crime rate trends: a routine activity approach, *American Sociological Review*, 44, 588–608.

Coleman, J. (1988) Social capital and the creation of human capital, *American Journal of Sociology*, 94, 95–120.

Collins, W.A., Maccoby, E.E., Steinberg, L., Hetherington E.M., and Bornstein, M.H. (2000) Contemporary research on parenting: the case for nature and nurture annual progress in child psychiatry and child development, *American Psychologist*, 55, 125–154.

Collins, W.A. and Russel, G.J. (1991) Mother-child and father-child relationships in middle-childhood and adolescence: a developmental analysis, *Developmental Review*, 11, 99–136.

Corrales, J. and Westhoff, F. (2006) Information technology adoption and political regimes, *International Studies Quarterly*, 50, 911–933.

Correa, T. (2014) Bottom-up technology transmission within families: Exploring how youths influence their parents in the usage of digital media with dyadic data, *Journal of Communication*, 64, 103–124.

Correa T. (2016) Digital skills and social media use: how Internet skills are related to different types of Facebook use among 'digital natives', *Information, Communication and Society*, 19(8), 1095–1107. https://doi.org/10.1080/1369118X.2015.1084023.

Correa, T. and Jeong, S.H. (2011) Race and online content creation: why minorities are actively participating in the Web, *Information, Communication and Society*, 14(5), 638–659.

Correa, T., Straubhaar, J.D., Chen, W., and Spence, J. (2015) Brokering new technologies: the role of children in their parents' usage of the Internet, *New Media and Society*, 17(4), 483–500,

Cotten, S.R. and Jelenewicz, J.M. (2006) A disappearing digital divide among college students? Peeling away the layers of the digital divide, *Social Science Computer Review*, 24(4), 497–506.

Cotterell, J. (1996) *Social Networks and Social Influences in Adolescence*, London: Routledge.

Cottrell, L., Branstetter, S., Cottrell, S., Rishel, C., and Stanton, B.F. (2007) Comparing adolescent and parent perceptions of current and future disapproved internet use, *Journal of Children and New Media*, 1, 210–226.

Coyne, S., Padilla-Walker, L.M., Day, R.D., Harper, J., and Stockdale, L. (2014) *Cyberpsychology, Behavior, and Social Networking*, 17, 8–13. http://doi.org/10.1089/cyber.2012.0623.

174 *Bibliography*

Crosnoe, R. (2000) Friendships in childhood and adolescence: the life course and new directions, *Social Psychology Quarterly*, 63(4), 377–391.

Crosnoe, R., Cavanagh, S., and Elder, G.H. (2003) Adolescent friendships as academic resources: the intersection of friendship, race, and school disadvantage, *Sociological Perspectives*, 46(3), 331–352.

Cummings, J.N., Butler, B., and Kraut, R. (2002) The quality of online social relationships, *Communications of the ACM*, 45(7), 103–108.

Cummings, J.N., Lee, J.B., and Kraut, R. (2006) Communication technology and friendship during the transition from high school to college, in R. Kraut, M. Brynin, and S. Kiesler (Eds.), *Computers, Phones, and the Internet: Domesticating Information Technology*, New York: Oxford University Press, pp. 809–851.

Daft, R.L. and Lengel, R.H. (1984) Information richness: a new approach to managerial behaviour and organizational design, in L.L. Cummings and B.M. Staw (Eds.), *Research in Organizational Behavior*, Greenwich, CT: JAI, pp. 191–233.

Daly, K.J. (1996) *Families and Time: Keeping Pace in a Hurried Culture*, Thousand Oaks, CA: Sage.

Davis, K. (2012) Friendship 2.0: adolescents' experiences of belonging and self-disclosure online, *Journal of Adolescence*, 35(6), 1527–1536.

DeAndrea, D.C., Ellison, N.B., LaRose, R., Steinfield, C., and Fiore, A. (2012) Serious social media: on the use of social media for improving students' adjustment to college, *The Internet and Higher Education*, 15, 15–23.

Derks, D., Bakker, A.B., Peters, P., and Van Wingerden, P. (2016) Work-related smartphone use, work–family conflict and family role performance: the role of segmentation preference, *Human Relations*, 69(5), 1045–1068.

Devoe, J.F., Peter, K., Kaufman, P., Ruddy, S.A., Miller, A.K., Planty, M., Snyder, T.D., and Rand, M.R. (2002) *Indicators of School Crime and Safety*, NCES 2004-004/NCJ 201257, Washington, DC: U.S. Departments of Education and Justice.

DiGennaro, C. and Dutton, W.H. (2006) The internet and the public: online and offline political participation in the United Kingdom, *Parliamentary Affairs*, 59, 299–313.

DiMaggio, P. and Hargittai, E. (2001) From the digital divide to the digital inequality, Working Paper, Princeton University.

DiMaggio, P., Hargitai, H., Neuman, W.R., and Robinson, J.P. (2001) Social implication of the internet, *Annual Review of Sociology*, 27, 307–336.

DiPrete, T.A., Gelman, A., McCormick, T., Teitler, J., and Zheng, T. (2011) Segregation in social networks based on acquaintanceship and trust, *American Journal of Sociology*, 116(4), 1234–1283.

Dooris, J., Sotireli, T., and Van Hoof, S. (2008) Distant friends online? Rural and urban adolescents' communication on the internet, *Tijdschrift voor Economische en Sociale Geografie*, 99(3), 293–302.

Drori, G. (2006) *Global E-Litism: Digital Technology, Social Inequality, and Transnationality*, New York: Worth Publishers.

Bibliography 175

Dubas, J.S., and Gerris, J.R.M. (2002) Longitudinal changes in the time parents spend in activities with their adolescent children as a function of child age, pubertal status, and gender. *Journal of Family Psychology*, 16(4), 415–427.

Duggan, M. and Brenner, J. (2013) *The Demographics of Social Media Users, 2012*. Washington, DC: Pew Research Center.

Dunbar, R.I.M. (1993) Coevolution of neocortical size, group size and language in humans, *Behavioral and Brain Sciences*, 16(4), 681–735.

Durkheim, E. (1952) *Suicide: A Study in Sociology*, Edited with an Introduction by G. Simpson, London: Routledge and Kegan Paul.

Dutton, W.H., Blumler, J.G., and Kraemer, K.L. (1987) *Wired Cities: Shaping the Future of Communications*, Boston, MA: G.K. Hall and Co.

Dutton, W.H. and Shepherd, A. (2003) Trust in the Internet: the social dynamics of an experience technology. Research Report No. 3, Oxford: Oxford Internet Institute.

Eastin, M., Greenbers, B.S., and Hofschire, L. (2006) Parenting the internet, *Journal of Communication*, 56, 486–504.

Elkind, D. (1994) *Ties that Stress: The New Family Imbalance*, Cambridge, MA: Harvard University Press.

Ellison, N.B., Steinfeld, C., and Lampe, C. (2007) The benefits of Facebook "friends:" social capital and college students' use of online social network sites, *Journal of Computer Mediated Communication*, 12, 1143–1168.

Eshet-Alkalai, Y. (2004) Digital literacy: a conceptual framework for survival skills in the digital era, *Journal of Educational Multimedia and Hypermedia*, 13(1), 93.

Fallon, B.J. and Bowles, T.V. (1997) The effect of family structure and family functioning on adolescents' perceptions of intimate time spent with parents, siblings and peers, *Journal of Youth and Adolescence*, 26, 25–43.

Fanti, K.A., Demetriou, A.G., and Hawa, V.V. (2012) A longitudinal study of cyberbullying, *The European Journal of Developmental Psychology*, 9, 168–181.

Farrington, D. (1993) Understanding and preventing bullying, in M. Tony (Ed.), *Crime and Justice: A Review of Research*, Chicago: University of Chicago Press, pp. 381–458.

Fehr, B.A. (1996) *Friendship Processes*, Thousand Oaks, CA: Sage Publications.

Feld, S.L. (1981) The focused organization of social ties, *American Journal of Sociology*, 86(5), 1015–1035.

Feld, S.L. (1982) Social structural determinants of similarity among associates, *American Sociological Review*, 47(6), 797–801.

Ferlander, S. and Duncan, T. (2006) Bridging the dual digital divide: a local net and an IT-café in Sweden, *Information, Communication and Society*, 9(2), 137–159.

Finkelhor, D., Mitchell, K., and Wolak, J. (2000) *Online Victimization: A Report of the Nation Youth*, Center for Missing and Exploited Children. Available at: www.unh.edu/ccre/youth_internet_info_page.html.

Fischer, C.S. (1977) Perspectives on community and personal relations, In C.S. Fischer, S. Jackson, A. Stueve, G.L.J. McCallister, and M. Baldassare (Eds.), *Networks and Places: Social Relations in Urban Setting*, New York: Free Press.

176 *Bibliography*

Fischer, C.S. (1982) *To Dwell among Friends: Personal Networks in Town and City*, Chicago: University of Chicago Press.

Fischer, C.S. and Shavit, Y. (1995) National differences in network density: Israel and the United States, *Social Networks*, 17, 129–145.

Flanagin, A.J. (2005) IM Online: Instant Messaging use among college students, *Communication Research Reports*, 22(3), 175–187.

Fleming, M.J., Greentree, S., Cocotti-Muller, D., Elias, K.A., and Morrison, S. (2006) Safety in cyberspace: adolescents' safety and exposure online, *Youth and Society*, 38(2), 135–154.

Flood, M. (2007) Exposure to pornography among youth in Australia, *Journal of Sociology*, 43, 45–60.

Foehr, U. (2006) *Media Multitasking among American Youth: Prevalence, Predictors and Pairings*, Washington, DC: Henry J. Kaiser Family Foundation.

Fong, E., Wellman, B., Kew, M., and Wilkes, R. (2001) *Correlates of the Digital Divide: Individual, Household and Spatial Variation*, Report to Office of Learning Technologies, Human Resources Development, Canada.

Fuligni, A.J. (1998) Authority, autonomy, parent–adolescent conflict and cohesion, *Developmental Psychology*, 4, 782–792.

Galinsky, E. and Salmond, K. (2002) *Youth and Violence: Students Speak out for a More Civil Society*, New York: Families and Work Institute.

Garton, L., Haythornthwaite, C., and Wellman, B. (1997) Studying online social networks, *Journal of Computer-Mediated Communication*, 3(1), 1–27. Available at: www.usc.edu/dept/annenberg/vol3/issue1/garton.html

Garton, L., Haythornwaite, C., and Wellman, B. (1999) Studying online social networks, in S. Jones (Ed,), *Doing Internet Research*, Thousand Oaks, CA: Sage, pp. 75–105.

Gershuny, J. (2003) Web use and net nerds: a neo-functionalist analysis of the impact of information technology in the home, *Social Forces*, 82, 141–168.

Gillespie, T. (2018) *Custodians of the Internet: Platforms, Content Moderation, and the Hidden Decisions that Shape Social Media*, New Haven, CT: Yale University Press.

Giordano, P.C. (2003) Relationships in adolescence, *Annual Review of Sociology*, 29, 257–281.

Giuseppe, R. and Galimberti, C. (2001) *Towards Cyber-Psychology: Mind, Cognitions and Society in the Internet Age*, New York: IOS Press.

Gladstone, B., Thompson C., and Zuckerman, E (2009) On the media. Available at: www.onthemedia.org/transcripts/2009/09/04/06.

Gonzales, A., McCrory Calarco, J., and Lynch, T. (2018) Technology problems and student achievement gaps: a validation and extension of the technology maintenance construct, *Communication Research*. https://doi.org/10.1177/0093650218796366.

Granovetter, M. (1973) The strength of weak ties, *American Journal of Sociology*, 78, 1360–1380.

Bibliography   177

Greenfield, P.M. (2004) Inadvertent exposure to pornography in the Internet: implications for peer to peer file sharing networks for child development and families, *Applied Developmental Psychology*, 25, 741–750.

Greenspan, R. (2002) American surfers keep it simple. Available at: http://cyberatlas.Internet.com/big_picture/geographics/article/0_5911_1466661_00.Html.

Griffiths, M. and Wood, R.T.A. (2000) Risk factors in adolescence: the case of gambling, videogame playing and the internet, *Journal of Gambling Studies*, 16(2–3), 199–225.

Grinter, R.E. and Palen, L. (2002) Instant messaging in teen life. Paper presented at the CSCW '02, New Orleans, Louisiana.

Gross, E.F. (2004) Adolescent Internet use: what we expect, what teens report. *Journal of Applied Developmental Psychology*, 25(6), 633–649.

Gross, E.F., Juvonen, J., and Gable, S.L. (2002) Internet use and well-being in adolescence, *Journal of Social Issues*, 58(1), 75–90.

Guerrero, L. and Afifi, W. (2013) What parents don't know: topic avoidance in parent-child relationships, *Parents, Children, and Communication*, 175, 233–260.

Guillén, M.F. and Suárez, S.L. (2005) Explaining the global digital divide: economic, political and sociological drivers of cross-national internet use, *Social Forces*, 84(2), 681–708.

Gunasekaran, V. and Harmantzis, F.C. (2007) Emerging wireless technologies for developing countries, *Technology in Society*, 29(1), 23–42.

Guo, B., Bricout, J.C., and Huang. J. (2005) A common open space or a digital divide? A social model perspective on the online disability community in China, *Disability and Society*, 20(1), 49–66.

Hallinan, M. and Kubitschek, W.K. (1988) The effects of individual and structural characteristics on intransitivity in social networks, *Social Psychology Quarterly*, 51, 81–92.

Hamburger, Y.A. and Ben-Artzi, E. (2000) The relationship between extraversion and neuroticism and the different uses of the Internet, *Computers in Human Behavior*, 16, 441–449.

Hammond, E. (2007) No place to hide, *Financial Times*, November 5. Available at: www.ft.com/content/f6182bc8-85e4-11dc-b00e-0000779fd2ac.

Hampton, K N. (2011) Internet as a leveler between advantaged and disadvantaged communities, in P. Nyden, L. Hossfeld, and G. Nyden (Eds.), *Public Sociology: Research, Action, and Change*, Thousand Oaks, CA: SAGE Publications, pp. 205–210.

Hampton, K.N. (2016) Persistent and pervasive community: new communication technologies and the future of community, *American Behavioral Scientist*, 60(1), 101–124.

Hampton, K N. (2018) Social media or social inequality: Trump's 'unexpected' election, in P.J. Boczkowski and Z. Papacharissi (Eds.), *Trump and the Media*, Cambridge, MA: MIT Press, p. 159–166.

178 Bibliography

Hampton, K.N. (2019) Social media and change in psychological distress over time: the role of social causation, *Journal of Computer-Mediated Communications*, 24, 205–222.

Hampton, K.N., Lee, C.J., and Ja Her, E. (2011) How new media afford network diversity: direct and mediated access to social capital through participation in local social settings, *New Media and Society*, 13, 1031–1049.

Hampton, K.N. and Ling, R. 2013. Explaining communication displacement and large scale social change in core networks: a cross-national comparison of why bigger is not better and less can mean more, *Information, Communication and Society*, 16, 561–589.

Hampton, K.N., Lu, W., and Shin, I. (2016) Digital media and stress: cost of caring 2.0, *Information, Communication and Society*, 19, 1267–1286.

Hampton, K.N., Sessions, L.F., Her, E.J., and Rainie, L. 2009. *Social Isolation and New Technology*, Washington, DC: Pew Internet and American Life Project.

Hampton, K. and Wellman, B. (2001) Long distance community in the network society: contact and support beyond Netville, *American Behavioral Scientist*, 3, 476–495.

Hampton, K.N. and Wellman, B. (2002) The not so global village of Netville, in B. Wellman and C. Haythornthwaite (Eds.), *The Internet in Everyday Life*, Oxford: Blackwell, pp. 345–372.

Hampton, K.N. and Wellman, B. (2018) Lost and saved … again: the moral panic about the loss of community takes hold of social media, *Contemporary Sociology*, 47(6), 643–651. https://doi.org/10.1177/0094306118805415.

Hansen, D.M., Larson, R.W., and Dworkin, J.B. (2003) What adolescents learn in organized youth activities: a survey of self-reported developmental experiences, *Journal of Research on Adolescence*, 13(1), 25–55.

Hardey, M.L. (2004) Mediated relationships: authenticity and the possibility of romance information, *Communication and Society*, 7(2), 207–222.

Hargittai, E. (2001) Second-level digital divide: mapping differences in people's online skills, *arXiv preprint cs/0109068*.

Hargittai, E. (2010) Digital na(t)ives? Variation in internet skills and uses among members of the 'net generation'. *Sociological Inquiry*, 80(1), 92–113.

Hargittai, E. and Hsieh Y.P. (2010) Predictors and consequences of differentiated practices on social network sites, *Information, Communication and Society*, 13, 515–536. https://doi.org/10.1080/13691181003639866.

Hartup, W.W. (1997) The company they keep: friendships and their developmental significance, *Annual Progress in Child Psychiatry and Child Development*, 63–78.

Hassen, H. (2019) Social exchanges in the digital media, thesis submitted for the degree of Doctor of Philosophy at the University of Leicester.

Hawker, D.S.J. and Boulton, M.J. (2000) Twenty years' of research on peer victimization and psychological maladjustment, a meta analysis, *Journal of Child Psychology and Psychiatry*, 41, 441–445.

Hawley, P.H. (1999) The ontogenesis of social dominance: a strategy-based evolutionary perspective, *Developmental Review*, 19(1), 97–132.

Bibliography 179

Haythornthwaite, C. (2002) Strong, weak, and latent ties and the impact of new media, *Information Society*, 18, 385–402.

Haythornthwaite, C. (2005) Social networks and internet connectivity effects, *Information, Communication and Society*, 8, 125–147.

Haythornthwaite, C. and Kazmer, M. (2002) Bringing the internet home: adult distance learners and their internet, home and work worlds, in B. Wellman, and C. Haythornthwaite (Eds.), *The Internet in Everyday Life*, Oxford: Blackwell, pp. 461–463.

Haythornthwaite C. and Wellman, B. (1998) Work, friendship and media use for information exchange in a networked organization, *Journal of the American Society for Information Science*, 49, 1101–1114.

Heirman, W. and Walrave, M. (2008) Assessing concerns and issues about the mediation of technology in cyberbullying, *Cyberpsychology: Journal of Psychosocial Research on Cyberspace*, 2(2), 1.

Helsen, M., Vollebergh, W., and Meeus, W. (2000) Social support from parents and friends and emotional problems in adolescence, *Journal of Youth and Adolescence*, 29, 319–335.

Helsper, E.J. (2008a) Gendered internet use across generations and life stages in the UK. Paper presented at AOIR Conference, Copenhagen, October.

Helsper, E.J. (2008b) Perceptions of security and risks on the internet: experience and learned levels of trust. Presentation slides from IT Security in Practice Conference, Aarhus University, January 24.

Herring, S.C. (2007) Questioning the generational divide: technological exoticism and adult constructions of online youth identity, in D. Buckingham (Ed.), *Youth, Identity, and Digital Media*, Cambridge, MA: The MIT Press, pp. 71–92.

Hertlein, K.M. (2012) Digital dwelling: technology in couple and family relationships, *Family Relations*, 61, 374–387.

Hill, R.A. and Dunbar, R.I.M. (2003) Social network size in humans, *Human Nature*, 4, 53. https://doi.org/10.1007/s12110-003-1016-y.

Hinduja, S. and Patchin, J.W. (2008) Personal information of adolescents on the internet: a quantitative content analysis of MySpace, *Journal of Adolescence*, 31, 125–146.

Hine, C. (2005) Internet research and the sociology of cyber social scientific knowledge, *The Information Society*, 21, 239–248.

Hiniker, A., Schoenebeck, S., and Kientz, J.A. (2016) Not a dinner table: parents' and children's perspectives on family technology rules. *CSCW'16*, February 2016, 1376–1388.

Hirschi, T. (1969) *Causes of Delinquency*, Berkeley, CA: University of California Press.

Hofferth, S.L. and Sandberg, J.F. (2001) How American children spend their time, *Journal of Marriage and Family*, 63, 295–308.

Hoffman, D. and Novak, T.P. (1998) Bridging the racial divide on the internet, *Science*, 280, 390–391.

180 *Bibliography*

Holliday, J., Suzanne, A., Campbell, R., and Moore, L. (2016) Identifying well-connected opinion leaders for informal health promotion: the example of the Assist Smoking Prevention Program, *Health Communication*, 31(8), 946–953.

Holloway, S. and Valentine, G. (2003) *Cyber-kids: Youth Identities and Communities in an On-Line World*, London: Routledge.

Holme, P., Edling, C.R., and Liljeros, F. (2004) Structure and time-evolution of an internet dating community, *Social Networks*, 26, 155–174.

Horst, H. (2008) Families, in M. Ito et al. (Eds.), *Hanging Out, Messing Around, Geeking Out: Living and Learning with New Media*, Boston: MIT Press, pp. 123–156.

Howard, P.E.N., Rainie, L., and Jones, S. (2002) Days and nights on the internet, in B. Wellman and C. Haythornwaite (Eds.), *The Internet in Everyday Life*, Oxford: Blackwell, pp. 45–74.

Hu, Y., Fowler-Wood, J., Smith V., and Westbrook. N. (2004) Friendship through IM: Examining the relationship between IM and intimacy, *Journal of Computer Mediated Communication*, 10(1), JCMC10111.

Huffaker, D. (2004) Spinning yarns around the digital fire: storytelling and dialogue among youth on the internet information technology, *Childhood Education Annual*, 63–75.

Hughes, T.R. and Hans, J.G. (2001) Computers, the internet and families, *Journal of Family Issues*, 22, 776–790.

Huisman, S., Edwards A., and Catapano, S. (2012) The impact of technology on families, *International Journal of Education and Psychology in the Community*, 2(1).

Huysman, M. and Wulf, W. (2004) *Social Capital and Information Technology*, Cambridge, MA: MIT Press.

Igarashi, T., Takai, J., and Yoshida, T. (2005) Gender differences in social network development via mobile phone text messages: a longitudinal study, *Journal of Social and Personal Relationships*, 22(5), 691–713.

Indeok, S., Larose, R., Eastin, M.S., and Lin, C.A. (2004) Internet gratifications and internet addiction: on the uses and abuses of new media, *Cyber Psychology and Behavior*, 7, 384–394.

Ito, M. (2005) Mobile phones, Japanese youth, and the re-placement of social contact, in *Mobile Communications*, London: Springer, pp. 131–148.

Ito, M. et al. (2009) *Hanging Out, Messing Around, Geeking Out: Living and Learning with New Media*, Cambridge, MA: MIT Press.

Jackson, L.A., Von Eye, A., Barbatsis, G., Biocca, F., Zhao, Y., and Fitzgerald, H.E. (2003) Internet attitudes and internet use: some surprising findings from the HomeNetTOO project, *International Journal of Human Computer Studies*, 59, 355–382.

Jenkins, K. and Sun, K.C.Y. (2019) Digital strategies for building spiritual intimacy: families on a "Wired" Camino. *Qualitative Sociology*. https://doi.org/10.1007/s11133-019-09432-0.

Bibliography 181

Jerusalem, M. and Schwarzer, R. (1986) Selbstwirksamkeit [Self-efficacy scale], In R. Schwarzer (Ed.), *Skalen zur Befindlichkeit und Personlichkeit*, Berlin: Freie Universitat, Institut für Psychologie, pp. 15–28.

Joinson, A.N. (2008) Knowing me, knowing you: reciprocal self-disclosure in internet-based surveys, *Cyber-Psychology and Behavior*, 4(5), 587–591.

Juhaňák, L., Zounek, J., Záleská, K., Bárta, O., and Vlčková, K. (2019) The relationship between the age at first computer use and students' perceived competence and autonomy in ICT usage: a mediation analysis, *Computers and Education*, 141(November), 103614.

Jung, J.Y., Kim, Y.C., Lin, W.Y., and Cheong, P.H. (2005) The influence of social environment on internet, connectedness of adolescents in Seoul, Singapore and Taipei, *New Media and Society*, 7(1), 64–88.

Jung, J.Y., Qiu, J.L., and Kim Y.C. (2001) Internet connectedness and inequality: beyond the divide, *Communication Research*, 28(4), 507–535.

Kadushin, C. (2004) *Understanding Social Networks: Theories, Concepts, and Findings*. Oxford: Oxford University Press.

Kahai, S.S. and Cooper, R.B. (2003) Exploring the core concepts of media richness theory: the impact of cue multiplicity and feedback immediacy on decision quality, *Journal of Management Information Systems*, 20(1), 263–299.

Kaiser Family Foundation (2003) *Growing up Wired: Survey of Youth and the Internet in the Silicon Valley*, Washington, DC: The Henry J. Kaiser Family Foundation.

Kalish, Y. and Robins, G. (2006) Psychological predispositions and network structure: the relationship between individual predisposition, structural holes and network closure, *Social Networks*, 28(1), 56–84.

Kaltiala-Heino, R., Rimpela, M., Martunen, M., Rimpela, A., and Rantanen, P. (1999) Bullying, depression, and suicidal ideation in Finnish adolescents, *British Medical Journal*, 319, 348–351.

Kandel, D.B. (1978) Homophily, selection, and socialization in adolescent friendships, *American Journal of Sociology*, 84, 427–436.

Kanter, M., Afifi, T., and Robbins S. (2012) The impact of parents "friending" their young adult child on Facebook on perceptions of parental privacy invasions and parent–child relationship quality, *Journal of Communication*, 62(5), 900–917.

Katz, J.E. and Aspden, P. (1997) A nation of strangers?, *Communications of the ACM*, 40, 81–86.

Katz, J.E. and Rice, R.E. (2002a) *Social Consequences of Internet use, Access Involvement and Interaction*. Cambridge, MA: MIT Press.

Katz, J.E. and Rice, R.E. (2002b) Syntopia: access, civic involvement, and social interaction on the Net, in B. Wellman and C. Haythornthwaite (Eds.), *The Internet in Everyday Life*, Oxford: Blackwell, pp. 114–138.

Katz, J.E., Rice, R.E., and Aspden, P. (2001) The internet 1995–2000, access civic involvement and social interaction, *American Behavioral Scientist*, 45, 405–419.

Kautiainen, S., Koivusilta, L.K., Lintonen, T., Virtanen, S.M., and Rimpela, A.H. (2005) Use of information and communication technology and the prevalence of overweight and obesity among adolescents, *International Journal of Obesity*, 29, 925–933.

182 *Bibliography*

Kavanaugh, A. and Patterson, S.J. (2002) The impact of community computer networks on social capital and community involvement in Blacksburg, in B. Wellman and C. Haythornthwaite (Eds.), *The Internet in Everyday Life*, Oxford: Blackwell, pp. 325–345.

Kayany, J.M. and Yelsma, P. (2000) Displacement effects of online media in the socio-technical contexts of households, *Journal of Broadcasting and Electronic Media*, 44(2), 215–230.

Kef, S., Hox, J.J., and Habekothe, H.T. (2000) Social networks of visually impaired and blind adolescents, structure and effect on well-being, *Social Networks*, 22(1), 73–91.

Keles, B., McCrae, N., and Grealish, A. (2020) A systematic review: the influence of social media on depression, anxiety and psychological distress in adolescents, *International Journal of Adolescence and Youth*, 25(1), 79–93.

Kennedy, T.L.M., Smith, A., Wells, A.T., and Wellman, B. (2008) *Networked Families*, Washington, DC: Pew and American Life Project.

Kennedy, T.L.M. and Wellman, B. (2007) The networked household, *Information, Communication and Society*, 10(5), 645–670.

Kerr, M., Stattin, H., and Burk, W.J. (2010) A reinterpretation of parental monitoring in longitudinal perspective, *Journal of Research on Adolescence*, 20(1), 39–64. https://doi.org/10.1111/j.1532-7795.2009.00623.x.

Kessel Schneider, S., O'Donell, L., Stueve, A., and Coulter, R.S. (2012) Cyberbullying, school bullying, and psychological distress: a regional census of high school students, *American Journal of Public Health*, 102(1), 171–177.

Khan, S., Gagné, M., Yang, L., and Shapka, J. (2016) Exploring the relationship between adolescents' self-concept and their offline and online social worlds, *Computers in Human Behavior*, 55, 940–945.

Kidsonline@home (2007) *Internet Use in the Australian Homes*, Sydney: Australian Broadcasting Authority.

Kiesler, S., Zdaniuk, B., Lundmark, V., and Kraut, R. (2000) Troubles with the internet: the dynamics of help at home, *Human-Computer Interaction*, 15, 322–351.

Kim, H.H.S. (2017) The impact of online social networking on adolescent psychological well-being (WB), a population-level analysis of Korean school aged children, *International Journal of Adolescence and Youth*, 22(3), 364–376. https://doi.org/10.1080/02673843.2016.1197135.

Kim, K. and Altmann, J. (2017) Effect of homophily on network formation, *Communications in Nonlinear Science and Numerical Simulation*, 44, 482–494.

Kim, W.Y., Baran, S.J., and Massey, K.K. (1988) Impact of the VCR on control of television viewing, *Journal of Broadcasting and Electronic Media*, 32(3), 351–359.

Knecht, A., Snijders, T.A.B., Baerveldt, C., Steglich, C.E.G., and Raub, W. (2010) Friendship and delinquency: selection and influence processes in early adolescence, *Social Development*, 19, 494–514.

Koltay, T. (2011) The media and the literacies: media literacy, information literacy, digital literacy, *Media, Culture and Society*, 33(2), 211–221.

Bibliography 183

Kowalski, R.M., Giumetti, G.W., Schroeder, A.N., and Lattanner, M.R. (2014) Bullying in the digital age: a critical review and meta-analysis of cyberbullying research among youth, *Psychological Bulletin*, 140(4), 1073.

Kowalski, R.M., Limber, S.P., and McCord, A. (2019) A developmental approach to cyberbullying: prevalence and protective factors, *Aggression and Violent Behavior*, 45, 20–32.

Kraut, R., Kiesler, S., Boneva, B., Cummings, J., Helgeson, V., and Crawford, A. (2002) Internet paradox revisited, *Journal of Social Issues*, 58, 49–74. https://doi.org/10.1111/1540-4560.00248.

Kraut, R., Patterson, M., Lundmark, V., Kiesler, S., Mukopadhyay, T., and Scherlis, W. (1998) Internet paradox: a social technology that reduces social involvement and psychological well-being?, *American Psychologist*, 53, 1011–1031.

Kvasny, L. (2006) Cultural (re)production of digital inequality in a us community technology initiative information, *Communication and Society*, 9(2), 160–181.

Kwon M.-W., D'Angelo, J., and McLeod, D.M. (2013) Facebook use and social capital, *Bulletin of Science, Technology & Society*, 33(1–2), 35–43.

La Greca, A.M. and Lopez, N. (1998) Social anxiety among adolescents: linkages with peer relations and friendships, *Journal of Abnormal Child Psychology*, 26, 83–94.

Larson, R.W. and Verma, S. (1999) How children and adolescents spend time across the world: work, play, and developmental opportunities, *Psychological Bulletin*, 125, 701–736.

Latzer, M. (2013), Media convergence, in R. Towse, and C.N. Handke (Eds.), *Handbook of the Digital Creative Economy*, Cheltenham: Edward Elgar, pp. 123–133.

LaVoie, D. and O'Neill, H. (2003) Trends in the evolution of the public Web: 1998–2002, *D-Lib Magazine*, 9(4). Available at: http://webdoc.sub.gwdg.de/edoc/aw/d-lib/dlib/april03/lavoie/04lavoie.html.

Lawson, H. and Leck, K. (2006) Dynamics of internet dating, *Social Science Computer Review*, 24(2), 189–208.

Leander, K.M. and Lovvorn, J.F. (2006) Literacy networks: following the circulation of texts, bodies, and objects in the schooling and online gaming of one youth, *Cognition and Instruction*, 24(3), 291–340.

Leander, K.M. and Mckim, K.K. (2003) Tracing the everyday 'sitings' of adolescents on the internet: a strategic adaptation of ethnography across online and offline spaces education, *Communication and Information*, 3(2), 211–238.

Lee, P.S.N. and Leng, L. (2008) Assessing displacement effects of the internet. *Telemetric and Informatics*, 25, 145–155.

Lee, S.J. (2007) The internet and adolescent social capital: who benefits more from internet use, PhD Dissertation, The University of Texas at Austin.

Lee, S.J. and Chae, Y.G. (2007) Children's' internet use in a family context: influence on family relationships and parental mediation, *Cyber Psychology and Behavior*, 10(2), 640–644.

184   *Bibliography*

Lee, W. and Kuo, E.C. (2002) Internet and displacement effect: children's media use and activities in Singapore, *Journal of Computer Mediated Communication*, 7(2).

Lee, Y. (2020) Facebooking alone? Millennials' use of social network sites and volunteering, *Nonprofit and Voluntary Sector Quarterly*, 49(1), 203–217. https://doi.org/10.1177/0899764019868844.

Leigh, A. and Atkinson, R.D. (2001) Clear thinking on the digital divide, *Policy Report*, 43, 1–20.

Lenhart, A. (2009) It's personal: similarities and differences in online social network use between teens and adults. Available at: www.pewinternet.org/Presentations/2009/19-Similarities-and-Differences-in-Online-Social-Network-Use.aspx.

Lenhart, A. (2015) *Teens, Social Media and Technology Overview 2015*, Washington, DC: Pew Research Center.

Lenhart, A., Horrigan, J., Reinie, L., Allen, K., Boyce, A., and Madden, M. (2003) *The Ever-Shifting Internet Population: A New Look at Internet Access and the Digital Divide*, Washington, DC: Pew and American Life Project.

Lenhart, A., Madden, M., and Hitlin, P. (2005) *Teens and Technology: Youth Are Leading the Transition to a Fully Wired and Mobile Nation*, Washington, DC: Pew and American Life Project.

Lenhart, A., Madden, M ., Rankin, A., and Smith, M.A (2007) *Teens and Social Media*, Washington, DC: Pew and American Life Project.

Lenhart, A., Raine, L., and Lewis, O. (2001) *Teenage Life Online: the Rise of the Instant-message Generation and The Internet's Impact on Friendships and Family Relationships*, Washington, DC: Pew and American Life Project.

Leskovec, J. and Horvitz, E. (2008) Planetary-scale views on a large instant-messaging network, in *Proceedings of the 17th International Conference on World Wide Web*, pp. 915–924.

Lewis, K., Gonzalez, M., and Kaufman, J. (2012) Social selection and peer influence in an online social network, *Proceedings of the National Academy of Sciences of the U.S.A.*, 109(1), 68–72.

Lewis, K., Kaufman, J., Gonzalez, M., Wimmer, A., and Christakis, N. (2008) Tastes, ties, and time: a new social network dataset using Facebook.com, *Social Networks*, 30, 330–342.

Li, Q. (2006) Cyber bullying in schools: a research of gender differences, *School Psychology International*, 27, 157–170.

Li, Q. (2007) Bullying in the new playground: research into cyber-bullying and cyber-victimization, *Australasian Journal of Educational Technology*, 23(3), 435–454.

Lin, L., Sidani, J.E., Shensa, A., Radovic, A., Miller, E., Colditz, J.B., Hoffman, B.L., Giles, L.M., and Primack, B.A. (2016) Association between social media use and depression among U.S. young adults, *Depression and Anxiety*, 33(4), 323–331. https://doi.org/10.1016/j.chb.2012.01.016.

Lin, N. (2001) *Social Capital: A Theory of Social Structure and Action*, New York: Cambridge University Press.

Bibliography   185

Lin, N. (2005) A network theory of social capital, in D. Castiglione, J.Van Deth, and G. Wolleb (Eds.), *Handbook on Social Capital*, Oxford: Oxford University Press.

Lin, S.S.J. and Tsai, C.C. (2002) Sensation seeking and internet dependence of Taiwanese high school adolescents, *Computers in Human Behavior*, 18(4), 411–426.

Ling, C., Gen-Cai C., Chen-Guang, C., and Chuen, C. (2003) Using collaborative knowledge base to realize adaptive message filtering in collaborative virtual environment. Paper presented at International Conference on Communication Technology Proceedings, 2003. ICCT 2003. Available at: http://ieeexplore.ieee.org/servlet/opac?punumber=8586.

Liu, H., Shi, J., Liu, Y., and Sheng, Z. (2013) The moderating role of attachment anxiety on social network site, *Psychological Reports*, 112(1), 252–265.

Livingstone, S. (2007) Strategies of parental regulation in the media-rich home, *Computers in Human Behavior*, 23, 920–941.

Livingstone, S. (2008) Taking risky opportunities in youthful content creation: teenagers' use of social networking sites for intimacy, privacy and self expression, *New Media and Society*, 10(3), 393–411.

Livingstone, S. and Bober, M. (2003) *U.K. Children Go On-line: Listening to Young People's Experiences* [Online], London: LSE Research Online. Available At: http://Eprints.Lse.Ac.Uk/Archive/0000388.

Livingstone, S. and Bober, M. (2004) *U.K. Children Go Online*, London: London School of Economics.

Livingstone, S. Bober, M., and Helsper, E. (2005) Active participation or just more information?: Young people's take up of opportunities to act and interact on the internet, *Information, Communication and Society*, 8(3), 287–314.

Livingstone, S. and Bovill, M. (2001) *Children and Their Changing Media Environment: A European Comparative Study*, London: Lawrence Erlbaum Associates Publishers.

Livingstone, S., D'Haenens, L. and Hasebrink, U. (2001) Childhood in Europe: contexts for comparison, in S. Livingstone and M. Bovill (Eds.), *Children and the Changing Media Environment: A European Comparative Study*, London: Lawrence Erlbaum Associates Publishers, pp. 3–31.

Livingstone, S. and Helsper, E. (2007) Taking risks when communicating on the internet, *Information, Communication and Society*, 5, 619–644.

Livingstone, S., and Helsper, E.J. (2008) Parental mediation of children's Internet use, *Journal of Broadcasting and Electronic Media*, 524, 581–599.

Loader, B.D., Vromen, A., and Xenos, M.A. (2014) The networked young citizen: social media, political participation and civic engagement, *Information, Communication and Society*, 17, 143–150.

Loader, B.D., Vromen, A., and Xenos, M.A. (2016) Performing for the young networked citizen? Celebrity politics, social networking and the political engagement of young people, *Media, Culture and Society*, 38(3), 400–419.

Loges, W.E. and Jung, J.Y. (2001) Exploring the digital divide: internet connectedness and age, *Communication Research*, 28, 536–562.

186 *Bibliography*

Ma, C.M.S. and Shek, D.T.L. (2013) Consumption of pornographic materials in early adolescents in Hong Kong, *Journal of Pediatric and Adolescent Gynecology*, 26(Suppl. 3), S18–25.

Maczewski, M. (2002) Exploring identities through the internet: youth experiences online, *Child and Youth Care Forum*, 31(2), 111–120.

Madden, M. (2009) *Eating, Thinking and Staying Active with New Media*, Washington, DC: Pew Research Center. Available at: www.pewresearch.org/.../06/02/eating-thinking-and-staying-active-with-new-media.

Madden, M., Lenhart, A., Cortesi, S., Gasser, U., Duggan, M., Smith A, and Beaton, M. (2013) *Teens, Social Media, and Privacy*, Pew Internet and American Life Project, Washington, DC: Pew Research Center.

Malamuth, N.M. and Impett, E.A. (2001) Research on sex and media: what do we know on the effects on children and adolescents? In D.G. Singer and J.L. Singer (Eds.), *Handbook of Children and Media*, Thousand Oaks, CA: Sage, pp. 269–287.

Marsden, P. and Campbell, K.E. (1984) Measuring tie strength, *Social Forces*, 63(2), 482–501. https://doi.org/10.1093/sf/63.2.482.

Martin, S.P., and Robinson, J.P. (2007) The income digital divide: trends and predictions for levels of internet use, *Social Problems*, 54(1), 1–22.

Matsuda, M. (2000) Wakamono no yujin kankei to keitai denwa riyou: kankei kihakuka ron kara sentakuteki kankei ron he [Interpersonal relationships among young people and mobile phone usage: from attenuate to selective relationships], *Shakai Jyouhougaku Kenkyu* [*Japanese Journal of Social Informatics*], 4, 111–122 [In Japanese, cited in *Journal of Social and Personal Relationships*, 2005, 22, 691.

Mazer, J.P., Murphy, R.E., and Simonds, C.J. (2007) I'll see you on Facebook: The effects of computer-mediated teacher self-disclosure on student motivation, affective learning, and classroom climate, *Communication Education*, 56(1), 1–17

Mazman, S.G. and Usluel, Y.K. (2010) Modeling educational use of Facebook, *Computers and Education*, 55(2), 444–453.

Mazur, E. and Kozarian, L. (2010) Self-presentation and interaction in blogs of adolescents and young emerging adults, *Journal of Adolescent Research*, 25(1), 124–144. https://doi.org/10.1177/0743558409350498.

McCowan, J.A., Fischer, D., Page, R., and Homant, M. (2001) Internet relationships: people who meet people, *Cyber-Psychology and Behavior*, 4(5), 593–596.

McKenna, K.Y., Green, A.S., and Gleason, M.E. (2002) Relationship formation on the Internet: what's the big attraction? *Journal of Social Issues*, 58, 9–31.

McLauglin, M., Osborne, K.K., and Smith, C.M. (1995) Standards of conduction usenet, in S.G. Jones (Ed.), *Cyber-society*, Thousand Oaks, CA: Sage, pp. 57–72.

McMillan, S.J. and Morrison, M. (2006) Coming of age with the internet: a qualitative exploration of how the internet has become an integral part of young people's lives, *New Media and Society*, 8(1), 73–95.

Bibliography 187

McPherson, M., Smith-Lovin, L., Brashears, M.E. (2006) Social isolation in America: changes in core discussion networks over two decades, *American Sociological Review*, 71(3), 353–375.

McPherson, M., Smith-Lovin, L., and Cook, J.M. (2002) Birds of a feather: homophily in social networks, *Annual Review of Sociology*, 27, 415–444.

Media Awareness Network (2005) Canadians in a Wired World – Phase II. Available at: https://mediasmarts.ca/sites/mediasmarts/files/pdfs/publication-report/full/YCWWII-trends-recomm.pdf.

Meghanathan, N. (2019) Unit disk graph-based node similarity index for complex network analysis, *Complexity*, 1–22.

Mehdizadeh, S. (2010) 'Self-presentation 2.0: narcissism and self-esteem on Facebook', *Cyberpsychology Behaviour, and Sociology Networking*, 13(4), 357–364.

Mehra, B., Merkel, C., and Bishop, A.P. (2004) The internet for empowerment of minority and marginalized users, *New Media and Society*, 6, 781–802.

Meishar-Tal, H., Kurtz, G., and Pieterse, E. (2012) Facebook groups as LMS: a case study, *The International Review of Research in Open and Distance Learning*, 13(4), 33–48.

Meneses, J. and Mominó, J.M. (2010) Putting digital literacy in practice: How schools contribute to digital inclusion in the network society, *The Information Society*, 26(3), 197–208.

Mesch, G.S. (2001) Social relationships and Internet use among adolescents in Israel, *Social Science Quarterly*, 82(2), 329–339.

Mesch, G.S. (2003) The family and the internet: the Israeli case, *Social Science Quarterly*, 84, 1038–1050.

Mesch G.S. (2006) The family and the internet: exploring a social boundaries approach, *Journal of Family Communication*, 6(2), 119–138.

Mesch, G.S. (2007) *Internet use, family boundaries and the perception of parent adolescent conflicts*, unpublished manuscript, Israel: University of Haifa.

Mesch, G.S. (2009a) Social context and adolescents' choice of communication channels, *Computers in Human Behavior*, 25(1), 244–251.

Mesch, G.S. (2009b) Parental mediation, online activities and cyberbullying, *Cyberpsychology and Behavior*, 12(4), 387–393.

Mesch, G.S. (2009c) Social bonds and Internet pornographic exposure among adolescents, *Journal of Adolescence*, 32(3), 601–618.

Mesch, G.S. (2012) Youth and technology, *New Directions in Youth Development*, 135, 97–105.

Mesch, G.S. (2016) Ethnic origin and access to electronic health services, *Health Informatics Journal*, 22(4), 791–803.

Mesch G.S. (2018a) Race, ethnicity and the strength of Facebook ties, *Journal of Youth Studies* 21(5), 575–589.

Mesch, G.S. (2018b) Parent–child connections on social networking sites and cyberbullying, *Youth and Society*, 50(8), 1145–1156.

188 Bibliography

Mesch, G.S., Fishman, G., and Eisikovits, Z. (2003) Attitudes supporting violence and aggressive behavior among adolescents in Israel: the role of family and peers, *Journal of Interpersonal Violence*, 18, 1132–1148.

Mesch, G. and Frenkel, M. (2014) Family imbalance and adjustment to information and communication technologies, in K.B. Wright and L.M. Webb (Eds,), *Computer-Mediated Communication in Personal Relationships*, New York: Peter Lang.

Mesch, G.S. and Levanon, Y. (2003) Community networking and locally based social ties in two suburban localities, *City and Community*, 2, 335–351.

Mesch G.S. and Talmud, I. (2006a) Online friendship formation, communication channels, and social closeness, *International Journal of Internet Sciences*, 1(1), 29–44.

Mesch, G.S. and Talmud, I. (2006b) The quality of online and offline relationships, the role of multiplexity and duration, *The Information Society*, 22(3), 137–148.

Mesch, G.S. and Talmud, I. (2007a) Similarity and the quality of online and offline social relationships among adolescents in Israel, *Journal of Research in Adolescence*, 17(2), 455–465.

Mesch, G.S. and Talmud, I. (2007b) Introduction, *Information, Communication and Society*, Special Issue, Transcending Boundaries in the Network Society.

Mesch, G.S. and Talmud, I. (2007c) Privacy and networking: ethnic differences in the use of cell phones and IM in Israel, in J. Katz (Ed,). *Mobile Communication and Social Change in a Global Context*, Cambridge, MA: MIT Press, pp. 313–325.

Mesch, G.S. and Talmud, I. (2010) Internet connectivity, community participation, and place attachment: a longitudinal study, *American Behavioral Scientist*, 53(8), 1095–1110.

Mesch, G., Talmud, I., and Kolobov, T. (2013) Explaining digital inequalities in Israel: juxtaposing the conflict and cultural perspectives, in M. Ragnedda and G.W. Muschert (Eds.), *The Digital Divide: The Internet and Social Inequality in International Perspective*, London: Routledge, pp. 220–234.

Mesch, G.S. Quase-Han, A., and Talmud, I. (2012) IM social networks: individual, relational and cultural characteristics, *Journal of Personal and Social Relationships*, 29(6), 736–759.

Milioni, D.L., Doudaki, V., and Demertzis, N. (2014) Youth, ethnicity, and a 'reverse digital divide': a study of internet use in a divided country, *Convergence*, 20, 316–336.

Miller, D. (2016) What is social media?, in D. Miller, E. Costa, T. Haynes, R. McDonald, J. Nicolescu, J. Sinanan, S. Spyer, S. Venkatraman, and X. Wang (Eds.), *How the World Changed Social Media*, London: UCL Press. Available at: www.jstor.org/stable/j.ctt1g69z35.8.

Milner, H. (2006) The digital divide: the role of political institutions in technology diffusion, *Comparative Political Studies*, 39(2), 176–199.

Bibliography 189

Mitchell, K.J., Ybarra, M., and Finkelhor, D. (2007) The relative importance of online victimization in understanding depression, delinquency, and substance use, *Child Maltreatment*, 12(4), 314–324.

Mitchell, K.J., Wolak, J., and Finkelhor, D. (2007) Trends in youth reports of sexual solicitations, harassment and unwanted exposure to pornography on the Internet, *Journal of Adolescent Health*, 40(2), 116–126.

MNET (2001) Young Canadians in a wired world. MNET survey. Available at: www.mediaawareness/ca/english/special _initiatives/surveys/index.cfm.

Monge, P.R. and Contractor, N.S. (2003) *Theories of Communication Networks*, Oxford: Oxford University Press.

Moody, J. (2001) Race, school integration, and friendship segregation in America, *American Journal of Sociology*, 107(3), 679–716.

Morahan, M.J. (2005) Internet abuse, Addiction? Disorder? Symptom? Alternative explanations? *Social Science Computer Review*, 23, 39–48.

Mouttapa, M., Valente, T., Gallaher, P., Rohrbach, L.A., and Unger, J.B. (2004) Social network predictors of bullying and victimization, *Adolescence*, 39(154), 315–335.

Nachmias, R., Mioduser, D., and Shemla, A. (2001) Information and communication technologies usage by students in an Israeli high school: equity, gender, and inside/outside school learning issues, *Education and Information Technologies*, 6(1), 43–53.

Nahapiet, J. and Ghoshal, S. (1998) Social capital, intellectual capital, and the organizational advantage, *Academy of Management Review*, 23, 242–266.

Nansel, T.R., Ovepeck, M., Pilla, R.S., Ruan, W.J., Simons-Morton, B., and Chedit, P. (2001) Bullying behaviors among US youth: prevalence and association with psychological adjustment, *Journal of the American Medical Association*, 285, 2094–2100.

Neal, J.W. (2007) Why social networks matter: a structural approach to the study of relational aggression in middle childhood and adolescence, *Child and Youth Care Forum*, 36, 195–211.

Neuman, S. (1991) *Literacy in the Television Age*, Hillsdale, NJ: Ablex Publishing.

Nicholas, D.B., Darch, J., McNeill, T., Brister, L., O'Leary, K., Berlin, D., and Koller, D. (2007) Perceptions of online support for hospitalized children and adolescents, *Social Work in Health Care*, 44(3), 205–223.

Nicole, B.E., Steinfield, C., and Lampe, C. (2007) The benefits of Facebook "friends": social capital and college students' use of online social network sites, *Journal of Computer-Mediated Communication*, 12, 1143–1168.

Nie, N.H., Hillygus, D.S., and Erbring, L. (2002) Internet use, interpersonal relations and sociability: a time diary study, in B. Wellman, and C. Haythornthwaite (Eds.), *Internet in Everyday Life*, Oxford: Blackwell, pp. 215–244.

OECD (2001) *Understanding the Digital Divide*. Paris: OECD.

OECD (2018) Bridging the digital gender divide include upskill, innovate. Available at: www.oecd.org/internet/bridging-the-digital-gender-divide.pdf.

190 *Bibliography*

OECD (2019) Broadband statistics. July. Available at: www.oecd.org.

OFCOM (2008) *Annual Report*. Available at: www.ofcom.org.uk/__data/assets/ pdf_file/0021/6159/annrep0809full.pdf.

Olson, D.H., Russel, C.S., and Sprenkle, D.H. (1983) Circumflex model of marital and family systems, *Family Processes*, 22, 69–83.

Olweus, D. (1994) Bullying at school: long term outcomes for the victims and an effective school-based intervention program, in L.R. Huesmann (Ed.), *Aggressive Behavior: Current Perspectives*, New York: Plenum, pp. 97–130.

Olweus, D. and Limber, S.P. (2018) Some problem with cyberbullying research, *Current Opinion in Psychiatry*, 19, 139–143.

Ooka, E. and Wellman, B. (2006) Does social capital pay off more within or between ethnic groups? Analyzing job searchers in five Toronto ethnic groups, in E. Fong (Ed.), *Inside the Mosaic*, Toronto: University of Toronto Press, pp. 199–226.

Orben, A., Dienlin, T., and Przybylski, A.K. (2019) Social media's enduring effect on adolescent life satisfaction, *PNAS*, 116(21), 10226–10228.

Orben, A. and Przybylski, A. (2019) The association between adolescent well-being and digital technology use. *Nature Human Behaviour* 3(2) Online.

Orthner, D.K. and Mancini, J.A. (1991) Benefits of leisure experiences for family bonding, in B.L. Driver (Ed.), *Nature Human Behaviour*, 3, 173–182.

Papacharissi, Z. (2005) The real-virtual dichotomy in online interaction: new media uses and consequences revisited, *Communication Yearbook*, 29, 215–237.

Papacharissi, Z. and Easton, E. (2013) In the habitus of the new, in J. Hartley, J. Burgess, and A. Bruns (Eds.), *A Companion to New Media Dynamics*, Chichester: Wiley-Blackwell, pp. 167–184.

Parayil, G. (2005) The digital divide and increasing returns: Contradictions of informational capitalism, *The Information Society*, 21(1), 41–51

Pardum, C.J., L'Engle, K.L., and Brown, J.D. (2005) Linking exposure to outcomes: early adolescents' consumption of sexual content in six media, *Mass Communication and Society*, 8(2), 75–91.

Parks, M.R. and Floyd, K. (1996) Making friends in cyberspace, *Journal of Communication*, 46, 80–97.

Parks, M.R. and Roberts, L. (1998) Making moosic: the development of personal relationships online and a comparison to their off-line counterparts, *Journal of Social and Personal Relationships*, 15, 517–537.

Pasquier, D. (2001) Media at home: domestic interactions and regulation. In A.S. Lenhart and M. Madden (Eds.), *Teens, Privacy and Online Social Networks*, Washington, DC: Pew and American Life Project. Available at: http:// pewresearch.org/pubs/454/teens-privacy–online-social-networks.

Patchin, J. (2002) Bullied youth lash out; strain as an explanation of extreme school violence, *Journal of Criminology and Social Psychology*, 7, 22–43.

Patchin, J. and Hinduja, S. (2006) Bullies move beyond the schoolyard, *Youth Violence and Juvenile Justice*, 4(2), 148–169.

Bibliography 191

Pearson, M. (2010) Dynamic networks and behavior: separating selection from influence, *Sociological Methodology*, 40, 329–393.

Pearson, M. and Michell, L. (2009) Smoke rings: social network analysis of friendship groups, smoking and drug-taking, *Drug: Education, Prevention and Policy*, 7(1), 21–37.

Pearson, M., Steglich, C., and Snijders, T. (2006) Homophily and assimilation among sport-active adolescent substance users, *Connections*, 27(1), 47–63.

Pellegrini, A.D. and Smith, P.K. (1998) Physical activity play: the nature and function of a neglected aspect of play, *Annual Progress in Child Psychiatry and Child Development*, 69, 5–36.

Peter, J. and Valkenburg, P.M. (2006) Research note: individual differences in perception of internet communication, *European Journal of Communication*, 21(2), 213–226.

Peter, J. and Valkenburg, P.M. (2016) Adolescents and pornography: a review of 20 years of research, *The Journal of Sex Research*, 53(4–5), 509–531.

Pew Research Center (2019a) Internet use by gender. Available at: www.pewinternet.org/chart/internet-use-by-gender/.

Pew Research Center (2019b) Internet use by age. Available at: www.pewinternet.org/chart/internet-use-by-sge/.

Pfeil, U., Arjan, R., and Panayiotis, Z. (2009) Differences in online social networking-a study of users profiles and the social capital divide among teenagers and older users in Myspace, *Computers in Human Behavior*, 25, 643–659.

Pittman, M., and Reich, B. (2016) Social media and loneliness: why an Instagram picture may be worth more than a thousand Twitter words, *Computers in Human Behavior*, 62, 155–167.

Ploderer, B., Howard, S., and Thomas, P. (2008) Being online, living offline: the influence of social ties over the appropriation of social network sites, *CSCW'08*, November: 8–12.

Preciado, P., Snijders, T.A.B., Burk, W.J., Stattin, H., and Kerr, M. (2012) Does proximity matter? Distance dependence of adolescent friendships, *Social Networks*, 34(1), 18–31.

Prensky, M. (2001) Digital natives, digital immigrants, *On the Horizon*, 9, 1–6.

Putnam, R. (1995) Tuning in, tuning out: the strange disappearance of social capital in America, *Political Science*, 28, 664–683.

Putnam, R. (2000) *Bowling Alone: The Collapse and Revival of American Community*, New York: Simon & Schuster.

Racz, S.J., Lindstrom Johnson, S., Bradshaw, C.P., and Cheng, T.L. (2017) Parenting in the digital age: urban Black youth's perception about technology based communication with parents, *Journal of Family Studies*, 23(2), 198–214.

Rafaeli, S., Barak, M., Dan-Gur, Y., and Toch, E. (2003) Knowledge sharing and online assessment. Paper presented at E-Society Proceedings of the 2003 IADIS conference IADIS e-Society.

192 *Bibliography*

Rainie, L. Smith, A., and Duggan, M. (2013) Coming and going on Facebook. Washington, DC: Pew Internet and American Life Project, February 5. Available at: www.pewinternet.org/Reports/2013/Coming-and-going-on-facebook.aspx.

Raza, S.A., Qazi, W., and Umer, A. (2016) Facebook is a source of social capital building among university students, *Journal of Educational Computing Research*, 55(3), 295–322.

Rice, R.E. (1980) The impacts of computer-mediated organizational and interpersonal communication, *Annual Review of Information Science and Technology*, 15, 221–250.

Rice, R.E. and Love, G. (1987) Electronic emotion: socioemotional content in a computer-mediated communication network, *Communication Research*, 14, 85–108.

Robinson, J.P., Kestnbaum, M., Neustadtl, A., and Alvarez, A. (2000) The Internet and other uses of time, in B. Wellman, and C. Haythornthwaite (Eds.), *The Internet in Everyday Life*, Oxford: Blackwell, pp. 244–262.

Robinson, L. (2008) *Living and Learning with New Media*, Boston: MIT Press.

Robinson, L. (2011) Information-channel preferences and information-opportunity structures, *Information, Communication and Society*, 14(4), 472–494.

Rodkin, P.C., Farmer, T.W., Pearl, R., and Van Acker, R. (2000) Heterogeneity of popular boys: antisocial and prosocial configurations, *Developmental Psychology*, 36(1), 14.

Rogers, E.M. (1995) *The Diffusion of Innovations*, 2nd edn, New York: Free Press.

Rosen, L.D. (2007) *Me, MySpace, and I: Parenting the Net Generation*, Basingstoke: Palgrave Macmillan.

Rosen, L.D., Cheever, N.A., and Carrier, L.M. (2008) The association of parenting style and child age with parental limit setting and adolescent MySpace behavior, *Journal of Applied Developmental Psychology*, 29, 459–471.

Rothfuss-Buerkel, N.L. and Buerkel, R.A. (2001) Family mediation, in J. Bryant and A.J. Bryant (Eds.), *Television and the American Family*, Hillsdale, NJ: Lawrence Erlbaum Associates, pp. 335–375.

Rudi, J., Dworkin, J., Walker, S., and Doty, J. (2015) Parents' use of information and communications technologies for family communication: differences by age of children, *Information, Communication and Society*, 18(1), 78–93.

Ruppel, E.T. and Burke, J. (2015) Complementary channel use and the role of social competence, *Journal of Computer-Mediated Communication*, 20(1), 37–51.

Saarento, S. and Salmivalli, C. (2015) The role of classroom peer ecology and bystanders' responses to bullying, *Child Development Perspectives*, 9(4), 201–205.

Sabik, N.J., Falat, J., and Magagnos, J. (2019) When self-worth depends on social media feedback: associations with psychological well-being, *Sex Roles*. https://doi.org/10.1007/s11199-019-01062-8.

Sajuria, J., Van Heerde-Hudson, J., Hudson, D., Dasandi, N., and Theocharis, Y. (2014) Tweeting alone? An analysis of bridging and bonding social capital in online networks, *American Politics Research*, 43, 708–738.

Bibliography 193

Sanders, C.E., Field, T.M., Miguel, D., and Kaplan, M. (2000) The relationship of internet use to depression and social isolation among adolescents, *Adolescence*, 35, 237–242.

Sassen, S. (2002) Toward a sociology of information technology, *Current Sociology*, 50, 365–388.

Sasson, H., and Mesch, G.S. (2014) Parental mediation, peer norms and risky online behavior among adolescents, *Computers in Human Behavior*, 33, 32–38.

Sasson, H. and Mesch, G.S. (2016) Gender differences in the factors explaining risky behavior online, *Journal of Youth and Adolescence*, 45(5), 973–985.

Sasson, H. and Mesch, G.S. (2017) The role of parental mediation and peer norms on the likelihood of cyberbullying, *The Journal of Genetic Psychology*, 178(1), 15–27.

Sasson, H. and Mesch, G.S. (2019) Parental mediation, in *The International Encyclopedia of Media Literacy*, New York: Wiley, pp. 1–6.

Scholz, C., Jovanova, M., Baek, E.C., and Falk, E.B. (2020) Media content sharing as a value-based decision, *Current Opinion in Psychology*, 31, 83–88.

Schouten, A.P., Valkenburg, P.M., and Peter, J. (2007) Precursors and underlying processes of adolescents' online self-disclosure: developing and testing an "internet attribute-perception" model, *Media Psychology*, 10, 292–315.

Seabrook, E.M., Kern, M.L., and Rickard, N.S. (2016) Social networking sites, depression, and anxiety: a systematic review, *Journal of Mental Health* , 3(4), e50. https://doi.org/10.2196/mental.5842.

Seepersad, S. (2004) Coping with loneliness: adolescent online and offline behavior, *Cyber-psychology and Behavior*, 7(1), 35–40.

Semon, D.J. and Gerris, J.R.M. (2002) Longitudinal changes in the time parents spend with their adolescent children as a function of child age, pubertal status and gender, *Journal of Family Psychology*, 16(4), 415–427.

Seto, M.C., Maric, A., and Barbaree, H.E. (2001) The role of pornography in the etiologic of sexual aggression, *Aggression and Violent Behaviour*, 6, 35–53.

Shah, D.V., Kwak, N., and Holbert, R.L. (2001a) "Connecting" and "disconnecting" with civic life: patterns of internet use and the production of social capital, *Political Communication*, 18(2), 141–162.

Shah, D.V., McLeod, J.M., and Yoon, S.H. (2001b) Communication, context, and community: an exploration of print, broadcast, and internet influences, *Communication Research*, 28(4), 464–506.

Sharma, M.K., Menon, I.S., and Marimuthu, P. (2017) An exploration of use of social networking sites amongst users with psychological problems, *ASEAN Journal of Psychiatry*, 18, 22–31.

Shaw, A., DeScioli, P., Barakzai, A., and Kurzban, R. (2017) Whoever is not with me is against me: the costs of neutrality among friends, *Journal of Experimental Social Psychology*, 71, 96–104.

Shek, D.T.L. and Ma, C.M.S. (2014) Using structural equation modeling to examine consumption of pornographic materials in Chinese adolescents in Hong Kong, *International Journal on Disability and Human Development*, 13(2),

194   *Bibliography*

Shklovski, I., Kiesler, S., and Kraut, M.R. (2006) The internet and social interaction: a meta-analysis and critique of studies 1995–2003, in R. Kraut, M. Brynin, and S. Kiesler (Eds.), *Domesticating Information and Communication Technology*, Oxford: Oxford University Press, pp. 765–807.

Shpigelman, C.N. (2017) Leveraging social capital of persons with intellectual disabilities through Facebook participation: the perspectives of family members and direct support staff, *Intellectual and Developmental Disabilities*, 55, 407–418.

Shrum, W., Cheek Jr, N.H., and Hunter S. (1988) Friendship in school: gender and racial homophily, *Sociology of Education*, 61, 227–239.

Shutts, K. (2015) Young children's preferences: gender, race, and social status, *Child Development Perspectives*, 9, 262–266.

Shutts, K., Roben, C.K.P., and Spelke, E.S. (2013) Children's use of social categories in thinking about people and social relationships, *Journal of Cognition and Development*, 14, 35–62.

Silverstone, R. and Haddon, L. (1996) Design and the domestication of information and communication technologies: technical change and everyday life, in R. Silverstone and R. Mansell (Eds.), *Communication by Design: The Politics of Information and Communication Technologies*, Oxford: Oxford University Press.

Simmel, G. (1990) *The Philosophy of Money*, edited by D. Frisby, trans. T. Bottomore and D. Frisby, London: Routledge.

Sinikka, S. (2005) Cultural differentiation or social segregation? Four approaches to the digital divide, *New Media and Society*, 7(5), 684–700.

Šmahel, D. and Machovcova, K. (2006) Internet use in the Czech Republic: gender and age differences, in F. Sudweeks, H. Hrachovec, and C. Ess (Eds.), *Cultural Attitudes towards Technology and Communication*, Perth, Australia: Murdoch University, pp. 521–533.

Smetana, J.G. (1988) Adolescents' and parents' conceptions of parental authority, *Child Development*, 59, 321–335.

Smetana, J.G. and Asquith, P. (1994) Adolescents' and parents' conceptions of parental authority and personal autonomy, *Child Development*, 65, 1147–1162.

Smith, A. and Anderson, M. (2018) *Social Media Use in 2018*, Washington, DC: Pew Research Center. Available at: www.pewinternet.org/2018/03/01/social-media-use-in-2018/.

Smith, L. (2007) Online networkers who click to 1000 friends. *The Times*. Available at: www.thetimes.co.uk/tol/news/science/article2416229.

Smith, M.R. (1985) *Military Enterprise and Technological Change: Perspectives on the American Experience*, Boston, MA: MIT Press.

Smith, P., Mahdavi, J., Carvalho, M., and Tippet, N. (2006) *An Investigation into Cyber Bullying: Its Forms, Awareness, and Impact, and the Relationship between Age and Gender in Cyber Bullying*, Unit for School and Family Studies, Goldsmith College, University of London.

Smith, P.K. (2015) The nature of cyberbullying and what we can do about it, *Journal of Research in Special Education Needs*, 15, 176–184.

Bibliography 195

Soukup, C. (1999) The gendered interactional patterns of computer-mediated chat rooms: a critical ethnographic study, *The Information Society*, 15(3), 169–176.

Spears, R. and Lea, M. (1992) Social influence and the influence of "social" in computer mediated communication, in M. Lea (Ed.), *Contexts of Computer Mediated Communication*, New York: Harvester Wheatsheaf, pp. 30–65.

Spears, R. and Lea, M. (1994) Panacea or panopticon? The hidden power of computer mediated communication, *Communication Research*, 21, 427–459.

Spies, S.L.A. and Margolin, G. (2014) Growing up wired: social networking sites and adolescent psychosocial development, *Clinical Child and Family Psychology Review*, 17(1), 1–18. https://doi.org/10.1007/s10567-013-0135-1.

Spooner, T.H., Rainie, L., and Meredith, P. (2001) *Asian-Americans and the Internet: the young and the connected*, Washington, DC: The Pew and American Life Project.

Sproull, L. and Kiesler, S. (1986) Reducing social context cues: electronic email in organizational communications, *Management Science*, 32, 1492–1512.

Sproull, L. and Kiesler, S. (1991) *Connections*, Cambridge, MA: MIT Press.

Sproull, L., Subramani, M., Kiesler, S., Walker, J.H., and Waters, K. (1996) When the interface is a face, *Human-Computer Interaction*, 11(2), 97–124.

Stanton-Salazar, R.D. and Spina, S.U. (2005) Adolescent peer networks as a context for social and emotional support, *Youth and Society*, 36(4), 379–417.

Stavrinides, P., Nikiforou, M., and Georgiou, S. (2015) Do mothers know? Longitudinal associations between parental knowledge, bullying, and victimization, *Journal of Social and Personal Relationships*, 32(2), 180–196.

Steglich, C., Sinclair, P., Holliday, J., and Moore, L. (2012) Actor-based analysis of peer influence in A Stop Smoking in Schools Trial (ASSIST), *Social Networks*, 34(3), 359–369.

Steglich, C., Snijders, T.A.B., and Pearson, M. (2010) Dynamic networks and behavior: separating selection from influence, *Sociological Methodology*, 40, 329–393.

Steinberg, L. and Silk, J.S (2002) Parenting adolescents, in M.H. Bornstein (Ed.), *Handbook of Parenting, vol. 1: Children and Parenting*, Mahwah, NJ: Erlbaum, pp.103–133.

Steinfield, C., Ellison, N.B., and Lampe, C. (2008) Social capital, self esteem, and use of online social network sites: a longitudinal analysis, *Journal of Applied Developmental Psychology*, 29, 434–445.

Stephenson, P. and Smith, D. (1989) Bullying in junior schools, in D.P. Tattum, and D.A. Lane (Eds.), *Bullying in Schools*, Stroke-on-Trent: Trentham, pp. 45–58.

Stern, S.R. (2004) Expressions of identity online: prominent features and gender differences in adolescents' world wide web home pages, *Journal of Broadcasting and Electronic Media*, 48(2), 218–243.

Stoller, E.P., Miller, B., and Guo, S. (2001) Shared ethnicity and relationship multiplexity within the informal networks of retired European American sunbelt migrants: a case study, *Research on Aging*, 23(3), 304–325.

196 *Bibliography*

Su, C.C. and Chan, N.K. (2017) Predicting social capital on Facebook: the implications of use intensity, perceived content desirability, and Facebook-enabled communication practices, *Computers in Human Behavior*, 72, 259–268.

Subrahmanyam, K. and Greenfield, P. (2008) Online communication and adolescent relationships, *The Future of Children*, 18(1), 119–146.

Subrahmanyam, K., Kraut, R.E., Greenfield, P., and Gross, E.G. (2000) The impact of home computer use on children's activities and development, *The Future of Children*, 10, 123–144.

Subrahmanyam, K., Kraut, R.E., Greenfield, P., and Gross, E.G. (2001) The impact of computer use on children's and adolescents' development, *Journal of Applied Developmental Psychology*, 22(1), 7–30.

Suitor, J.J., Pillemer, K., and Keeton, S. (1995) When experience counts: the effects of experiential and structural similarity on patterns of support and interpersonal stress, *Social Forces*, 73, 1573–1588.

Suler, J. (2004) The online disinheriting effect, *Cyber-Psychology and Behavior*, 7, 321–326.

Sullivan, H.S. (1953) *The Interpersonal Theory of Psychiatry*, New York: Norton.

Sutherland, R., Furlong, R., and Facer, K. (2003) *Screenplay: Children and Computing in the Home*, London: Routledge-Falmer.

Taipale, S. and Farinosi, M. (2018) The big meaning of small messages: the use of WhatsApp in intergenerational family communication, paper presented at International Conference on Human Aspects of IT for the Aged Population ITAP 2018: Human Aspects of IT for the Aged Population, Acceptance, Communication and Participation, pp. 532–546.

Takeuchi, L., (2011) *Families Matter: Designing Media for a Digital Age*, New York: The Joan Ganz Cooney Center at Sesame Workshop.

Tapscott, D. (1998) *Growing Up Digital: The Rise of the Net generation*, New York: McGraw Hill.

Temdee, P. (2019) Smart learning environment for enhancing digital literacy of Thai youth: a case study of ethnic minority group wireless, *Personal Communication*. https://doi.org/10.1007/s11277-019-06637-y.

Terlecki, M. and Newcombe, N. (2005) How important is the digital divide? The relation of computer and videogame usage to gender differences in mental rotation ability, *Sex Roles*, 53(5–6), 433–441.

The Economist (2009) Science and technology, February 26.

Tian X (2015) Network domains in social networking sites: expectations, meanings, and social capital, *Information, Communication and Society*, 19, 188–202.

Tichon, J.G. and Shapiro, M. (2003) With a little help from my friends: children, the internet and social support, *Journal of Technology in Human Services*, 21(4), 73–92.

Tidwell, L.C. and Walther, J.B. (2002) Computer-mediated communication effects on disclosure, impressions, and interpersonal evaluations: getting to know one another a bit at a time, *Human Communication Research*, 28, 317–348.

Bibliography 197

Tocqueville, A. de (1954) [1835]. *Democracy in America*, New York: Schocken.

Treem. J., Dailey, S.L., Pierce, C.S., and Biffl, D. (2016) What we are talking about when we talk about social media?: A framework for study, *Sociology Compass*, 10(9), 768–778.

Turkle, S. (1996) Parallel lives: working on identity in virtual spaces, in D. Grodin, and T.R. Lindlof (Eds.), *Constructing the Self in a Mediated World: Inquires in Social Construction*, Thousand Oaks, CA: Sage, pp. 156–175.

Turkle, S. (2011) *Life on the Screen*, New York: Simon & Schuster.

Turkle, S. (2015a) *Alone Together*, New York: Basic Books.

Turkle, S. (2015b) *Reclaiming Conversation: The Power of Talk in the Digital Age*, New York: Penguin Press.

Turow, J. (2001) Family boundaries, commercialism, and the internet, a framework for research, *Applied Developmental Psychology*, 22, 73–86.

Turow, J. and Nir, L. (2000) *The Internet and the Family 2000: The View from the Parents, the View from the Kids*, Philadelphia, PA: The Annenberg Public Policy Center at the University of Pennsylvania. Available at: www.appcpenn.org/Internet/.

Twenge, J.M., Spitzberg, B.H., and Campbell, W.K. (2019) Less in-person social interaction with peers among U.S. adolescents in the 21st century and links to loneliness, *Journal of Social and Personal Relationships*, 36(6), 1892–1913.

Tynes, B., Reynolds, L., and Greenfield, P. (2004) Adolescence race and ethnicity on the internet: a comparison of discourse in monitored vs unmonitored chat rooms, *Applied Developmental Psychology*, 25, 667–684.

Ueno, K. (2005) The effects of friendship networks on adolescent depressive symptoms, *Social Science Research*, 34(3), 484–510.

Underwood, H. and Findlay, B. (2004) Internet relationships and their impact on primary relationships, *Behaviour Change*, 21(2), 127–140.

Uusiautti, S. and Maatta, K. (2014) I am no longer alone—how do university students perceive the possibilities of social media? *International Journal of Adolescence and Youth*, 19, 293–305.

Valcour, P.M. and Hunter, L.W. (2005) Technology, organizations, and work-life integration, in E.E. Kossek and S.J. Lambert (Eds.), *Managing Work-Life Integration in Organizations: Future Directions for Research and Practice*, Mahwah, NJ: Erlbaum, pp. 61–84.

Valentine, G. and Holloway, S.L. (2002) Cyberkids? Exploring children's identities and social networks in on-line and off-line worlds, *Annals of the Association of American Geographers*, 92(2), 302–319.

Valkenburg, P.M., Krcmar, M., Peeters, A.L., and Marseille, N.M. (1999) Developing a scale to assess three styles of television mediation: "instructive mediation", "restrictive mediation" and "social co viewing", *Journal of Broadcasting and Electronic Media*, 43, 52–66.

Valkenburg, P.M. and Peter, J. (2007a) Preadolescents' and adolescents' online communication and their closeness to friends, *Developmental Psychology*, 43(2), 267–277.

198 Bibliography

Valkenburg, P.M. and Peter, J. (2007b) Online communication and adolescent wellbeing: testing the stimulation versus the displacement hypothesis, *Journal of Computer-Mediated Communication*, 12, 1169–1182.

Valkenburg, P.M. and Peter, J. (2008) Adolescent 'identity experiments on the internet: consequences for social competence and self-concept unity, *Communication Research*, 35(2), 208–231.

Valkenburg P.M. and Peter, J. (2009) The effects of Instant Messaging on the quality of adolescents' existing friendships: a longitudinal study, *Journal of Communication*, 59, 79–97.

Valkenburg, P.M. and Peter, J. (2013) The differential susceptibility to media effects model, *Journal of Communication*, 63(2), 221–243.

Valkenburg, P.M., Peter, J., and Schouten, A. (2006) Friend networking sites and their relationship to adolescents' well-being and social self-esteem, *Cyberpsychology and Behavior*, 9(5), 584–590.

Valkenburg, P.M. and Soeters, K.E. (2001) Children's positive and negative experiences with the internet an exploratory survey, *Communication Research*, 28(5), 652–675.

Valkenburg, P. and Taylor Piotrowski, J. (2017) *Plugged In: How Media Attract and Affect Youth*, New Haven, CT: Yale University Press.

Van Cleemput, K. (2010) "I'll See you on IM, text, or call you": a social network approach of adolescents' use of communication media, *Bulletin of Science, Technology and Society*, 30(2), 75–85.

Van Deursen, A.J. and Van Dijk, J. (2010) Internet skills and the digital divide, *New Media and Society*, 13(6), 896–911.

Van Deursen, A.J. and Van Dijk, J.A. (2014) The digital divide shifts to differences in usage, *New Media and Society*, 16(3), 507–526.

Van Deursen, A.J. and Van Dijk, J.A. (2015) Toward a multifaceted model of internet access for understanding digital divides: An empirical investigation, *The Information Society*, 31(5), 379–391.

Van Deursen, A.J., Van Dijk, J.A., and Peter, M. (2015) Increasing inequalities in what we do online: A longitudinal cross sectional analysis of Internet activities among the Dutch population (2010 to 2013) over gender, age, education, and income, *Telematics and Informatics*, 32(2), 259–272.

Van Dijk, J. (2005) *The Deepening Divide: Inequality in the Information Society*, London: Sage Publications.

Van Dijk, J. (2006) Digital divide research, achievements and shortcomings, *Poetics*, 34(1), 221–235.

Van Dijk, J. and Hacker, K. (2003) The digital divide as a complex and dynamic phenomenon special issue: remapping the digital divide, *The Information Society*, 19, 315–326.

Van Dijk, J.A. and Van Deursen A.J. (2014) *Digital Skills Unlocking The Information Society*, New York: Palgrave Macmillan.

Van Ingen, E., and Wright, K.B. (2016) Predictors of mobilizing online coping versus offline coping resources after negative life events, *Computers in Human Behavior*, 59, 431–439.

Bibliography 199

Van Rompaey, V., Roe, K., and Struys, K. (2002) Children's influence on internet access at home, adoption and use in the family context, *Information, Communication, and Society*, 5(2), 189–206.

Van Zoonen, L. 2002. Gendering the internet: claims, controversies and cultures, *European Journal of Communication*, 17(1), 5–23.

Vaterlaus, J.M., Barnett, K., Roche, C., and Young, J.A. (2016) "Snapchat is more personal": An exploratory study on Snapchat behaviors and young adult interpersonal relationships, *Computers in Human Behavior*, 62, 594–601.

Vehovar, V., Sicherl, P., Husing, T., and Dolnicar, V. (2006) Methodological challenges of digital divide measurements, *The Information Society*, 22(5), 279–290.

Vilhelmson, B., Thulin, E., and Elldér, E. (2017) Where does time spent on the Internet come from? Tracing the influence of information and communications technology use on daily activities, *Information, Communication and Society*, 20(2), 250–263. https://doi.org/10.1080/1369118X.2016.1164741.

Vitak, J. and Ellison, N.B. (2012) 'There's a network out there you might as well tap': exploring the benefits of and barriers to exchanging informational and support-based resources on Facebook, *New Media and Society*, 15, 243–259.

Vriens, E. and Van Ingen, E. (2018) Does the rise of the Internet bring erosion of strong ties? Analyses of social media use and changes in core discussion networks, *New Media and Society*, 20(7), 2432–2449.

Vryzas, K. and Tsitouridou. M. (2002) The home computer in children's everyday life: the case of Greece, *Learning, Media and Technology*, 27(1), 9–17.

W3Techs (2015) Languages used on the Internet. Available at: http://w3techs. com/technologies/overview/content_language.

Wajcman, J., Bittman, M., and Brown, J.E. (2008) Families without borders: mobile phones, connectedness and work-home divisions, *Sociology*, 42(4), 635–652.

Wajcman, J., Rose, E., Brown, J.E., and Bittman, M. (2010) Enacting virtual connections between work and home, *Journal of Sociology*, 46, 257–275.

Walther, J.B. (1996) Computer-mediated communication: impersonal, interpersonal and hyperpersonal interaction, *Communication Research*, 23(1), 3–43.

Walther, J.B. (2011) Theories of computer-mediated communication and interpersonal relations, *The Handbook of Interpersonal Communication*, 4, 443–479.

Wang, G., Zhao, J., and Shadbolt, N. (2019) What concerns do Chinese parents have about their children's digital adoption and how to better support them? KOALA Project Report 3.5, University of Oxford.

Wang, N., Roaché, D.J., and Pusateri, K.B. (2018) Associations between parents' and young adults' face-to-face and technologically mediated communication competence: the role of family communication patterns, *Communication Research*, 46, 1171–1196.

Wang, R., Bianchi, S.M., and Raley, S.B. (2005) Teenagers' internet use and family rules: a research note, *Journal of Marriage and Family*, 67(5), 1249–1258.

Wasserman, S. and Faust, K. (1995) *Social Network Analysis*, Cambridge: Cambridge University Press.

200 Bibliography

Watt, D. and White, J.M. (1994) Computers and the family life: a family developmental perspective, *Journal of Comparative Family Studies*, 30, 1–15.

Wei, H.S. and Jonson-Reid, M. (2011) Friends can hurt you: Examining the coexistence of friendship and bullying among early adolescents, *School Psychology International*, 32(3), 244–262.

Wellman, B. (2001) Computer networks as social networks, *Science*, 293, 2031–2034.

Wellman, B. and Haythornthwaite, C. (2002) *The Internet in Everyday Life*, Oxford: Blackwell.

Wellman, B., Quan-Haase, A., Boase, J., and Chen, W. (2003) The social affordances of the internet for networked individualism, *Journal of Computer Mediated Communication*, 8(3).

Wellman, B., Salaff, J., Dimitrova, D., Garton, L., Gulia, M., and Haythornthwaite, C. (1996) Computer networks as social networks, *Annual Review of Sociology*, 22, 213–238.

West, A., Lewis, J., and Currie, P. (2009) Students' Facebook 'friends': public and private spheres, *Journal of Youth Studies*, 12(6), 615–627.

White, K.J.C. and Guest, A.M. (2003) Community lost or transformed? urbanization and social ties, *City and Community*, 2(3), 239–259.

Williams, A. and Merten, M.J. (2009) Adolescents' online social networking following the death of a peer, *Journal of Adolescent Research*, 24(1), 67–90.

Williams, J.R. (2019) The use of online social networking sites to nurture and cultivate bonding social capital: a systematic review of the literature from 1997 to 2018, *New Media and Society*. https://doi.org/10.1177/1461444819858749.

Willis, S. and Trante, B. (2006) Beyond the 'digital divide' internet diffusion and inequality in Australia, *Journal of Sociology*, 42(1), 43–59.

Wilson, B. and Atkinson, M. (2005) Rave and straightedge, the virtual and the real: exploring online and offline experiences in Canadian youth subcultures, *Youth and Society*, 36(3), 276–311.

Wilson, K.R., Wallin, J.S., and Reiser, C. (2003) Social stratification and the digital divide, *Social Science Computer Review*, 21(2), 133–143.

Wing, C. (2005) Young Canadians in a wired world. Available at: www.media-awareness.ca.

Wohn, D.Y. and Birnholtz, J. (2015) From ambient to adaptation: Interpersonal attention management among young adults, in *Proceedings of the 17th International Conference on Human-Computer Interaction with Mobile Devices and Services*, pp. 26–35.

Wolak, J., Mitchell, K.J., and Finkelhor, D. (2002) Close online relationships in a national sample of adolescents, *Adolescence*, 37, 441–456.

Wolak, J., Mitchell, K.J., and Finkelhor, D. (2003) Escaping or connecting? Characteristics of youth who form close online relationships, *Journal of Adolescence*, 26, 105–119.

Wolfradt, U. and Doll, J. (2001) Motives of adolescents to use the internet as a function of personality traits, personal and social factors, *Educational Computing Research*, 24(1), 13–27.

Bibliography 201

Woolcock, M. (1998) Social capital and economic development: toward a theoretical synthesis and policy framework, *Theory and Society*, 27(2), 151–208.

Yan, Z. (2006) What influences children's and adolescents' understanding of the complexity of the internet? *Developmental Psychology*, 42(3), 418–428.

Yates, S.J. and Lockley, E. (2008) Moments of separation; gender, (not so remote) relationships, and the cell phone, in S Holland, *Remote Relationships in a Small World*, New York: Peter Lang, pp. 74–116.

Ybarra, M.L. and Mitchell, K.J. (2004) Online aggressor/targets, aggressors and targets: a comparison of associated youth characteristics, *Journal of Child Psychology and Psychiatry*, 45(7), 1308–1316.

Ybarra, M.L. and Mitchell, K.J. (2008) How risky are social networking sites? A comparison of places online where youth sexual solicitation and harassment occurs, *Pediatrics*, 121(2), e350–e357.

Youniss, J. and Smollar, J. (1985) *Adolescent Relations with Mothers, Fathers and Friends*, Chicago: The University of Chicago Press.

Youniss, J. and Smollar J. (1996) Adolescents' interpersonal relationships in social context, in T. Berndt and G.W. Ladd (Eds.), *Peer Relationships in Child Development*, New York: Wiley, pp. 300–316.

Yynes, B.M. (2007) Internet safety gone wild? Sacrificing the educational and psychosocial benefits of online social environments, *Journal of Adolescent Research*, 22(6), 575–584.

Zabrieskie, R.B. and McCormick, B.P. (2001) The influences of family leisure patterns on perceptions of family functioning, *Family Relations*, 50(3) 281–289.

Zhao, K., Stehlé, J., Bianconi, G., and Barrat, A. (2011) Social network dynamics of face-to-face interactions, *Physical Review E*, 83, 056109.

Ziegele, M. and Reinecke, L. (2017) No place for negative emotions? The effects of message valence, communication channel, and social distance on users' willingness to respond to SNS status updates, *Computers in Human Behavior*, 75, 704–713.

Index

Note: Page numbers in *italics* refer to figures; those in **bold** refer to tables.

Abbas, R. 131
access to ICT 9–10, 32, **34**, 59, 66, 75, 97, 114–124, **116**, 126, 130, 158, 159, 161, 165; restricting 4, 34, 45, 46
activity displacement 51, 52–54, **52**, 58–60, 65–66
activity, foci of 20–21, 91, 156, 157
activity multiplexity 103, 104
activity rules 36–37, 40
adolescence as developmental life stage 1, 4–5, 10–12, 23, 31–32, 48, 52, 56, 61, 62, 68, 70, 83, 89–90, 107, 155, 162
African Americans 75, 76, 119, 138
age differences of online/offline friends 77, 84, 104–105, 107
algorithms 167
amplification 82, 108, 116–118, **126**, 130, 133, 161, 165
anonymity 6, 33, 74, **93**, 94, 96, 112, 124; and bullying 141, 143, 144, **144**, 147, 148, 149, 151
Antheunis, M.L. 80
anxiety, social 51, 57, 72, 73, 74, 96, 133, 152
apps 11, 14, 17, 25, 90, 95, 97, 108–109, 119; *see also individual apps*
Arab teenagers 63, 64, 98–99
"art of association" 125, 126
asynchronous communication 4, 25, 84, 147–148
Attewell, P. 121, 122
Australia 30–31, 44, 150

authoritarian parenting 47, 48
authoritative parenting 47, 48
authority, hierarchies of 13, 14, 37, 39, **43**
autonomy 13, 14, 28, 37, 39, 40, 41, **43**, 47, 98, **106**, 107, 110, 126, **131**, 155, 157, 164; structural 125, 132, 133

Bargh, J.A. 96
Barnett, K. 167
Battle, J. 122
bedroom culture 28, 50, 51
Belgium 103–104
Blais, J.J. 105
blogs 9, 55, 65, 75, 97, 150, 159
Boase, J. 69
Bolton, R.N. 8
bullying 139–141, 142, 144, **144**, 147, 148–149, 153, 163; online 32, 107, 110, 136, 137–139, 141, 142–149, **144**, 151–153; *see also* harassment
Burt, R.S. 132
Butler, B. 125
Bybee, C. 45

Cacioppo, J.T. 111
California 75
Canada 43, 44, 47, 142, 148, 150
Carvalho, J. 37
categorical divide 117–118
cell phones (mobile phones) 26–27, 30–31, 44, 63, 76, 86, 97, 100, 104, 124, 150, 161, 164; *see also* smartphones

centrality 17–18, **19**, 126, 140
Chae, Y.G. 36
Chan, D.K.S. 127–128
channel, choice of 9, 67–68, 70, 84, 98, 101–105, **106**, 123, 163, 164
chat rooms 41–42, 71, 79–80, 97, 100, 105, 142, 143, **144**, 146, 148, 149, 150, 151, 152
Cheng, G.H.L. 127–128
China 120
Christakis, N.A. 111
closeness 18, 19, **19**, 74, 77, 78–79, 80, 81, 86, 89, 96, 99, 100–101, 104, 130; family 36, 42, **43**, 59; *see also* proximity
Coleman, J. 126
computer location **43**, 45
computer-mediated communication (CMC) 3, 5, 70, 75, **85**, 102, 108, 118, 123–124, 133, 134, 154; and intimacy 82, **93**, 95, 112; theoretical perspectives on 91–97, **93**, 160–161; *see also* online communication
conflict, parent-adolescent 13, 35–36, 38–43, **43**, 49
content multiplexity 103, 104
contextual rules 36, 37, 40
Cooper, R.B. 92–93
creativity 4, 8, 120, 158
Crimes Against Children research center 142, 149
cues-filtered-out theory **93**, 94–95, 96–97
cues, non-verbal 74, 92, **93**, 94, 95, 112, 141, 148
cultural capital 117, 122, 161
Cummings, J.N. 125
cyberbullying 32, 107, 110, 136, 137–139, 141, 142–149, **144**, 151–153; *see also* harassment
Cyprus 75–76

density of social networks 18, **19**, 114, 125, 126–127, 128–130, *129*, 132, 136, 139, 163
depression 110, 127, 137, 139, 144
descriptive norms 138
developmental-ecological approach 29–30, 48

digital divide 76, 114–124, **116**, **117**, 125, **126**, 130, 133, 134, 161–162, 164, 165–166
digital natives 7–8, 90, 97; *see also* net-generation
disabled people 119–120
disclosure of personal information 11, 18, 31, 39–40, 74, 78, 81, 96, 101, 110, 133, 143, **144**, 147, 150, 166; *see also* intimacy
disconnection 159
disinhibition effect 147, 148
displacement 16, **34**, 35–36, 50, 51, 52–56, **52**, **56**, 58–60, 64–67, 68, 160
dissociative imagination 147, 148
Doll, J. 73
dominance theory 139–140
Dunbar, R.I.M. 16
Durkheim, E. 125
dystopian perspective 73, 124, 125, 132, 161

Ellison, N.B. 74, 128
email 4, 17, 25, 33, 41–42, 44, 64, 65, 70, 81, 97, 98, 104, 124, 146
embeddedness of ICT 9, **22**, 23, 81, 84, **85**, 104, 107, 122, 157, 161
Enemybook 145
ethnicity/race 74–75, 76, 87, 115–116, 117–118, **117**, 119, 121, 123, 126, 138, 156; *see also* racism
expectation gaps 14, 41–42
expertise, adolescent 13, 14, 29, 37, 39, 41, **43**, 157
extracurricular activities 11, 45, 51, **52**, 57, 58, 59, 66, 98, 140
extroverts 72–73, 76–77, 133; *see also* personality

face-to-face communication 12, 92–93, 94, 102, 103, 162; convergence with online 17, 63, 70, 80, 81, 83, 98, 99–100, 102, 106–109, **106**, 112, 113, 123, 160; inhibited nature of 73, 95, 100; reduced by online **52**, **56**, 58; supplemented by online 86, 103–104, 108, 130, 165; *see also* offline relationships
Facebook 14, 16, 27, 28, 67, 75, 76, 83–84, 101, 128, 131, 132, 145

204 Index

families 22, 118; boundaries in 24, 25, 29, 30–34, **34**, 35, 49, 162; closeness of 36, 42, **43**; family time 29, 30, 34–38, 42, 45, 48–49, 158; hierarchies of authority 13, 14, 37, 39, **43**; tensions over the Internet 1, 12–14, 23, 24, 37, 162; *see also* parents
Farmer, T.W. 140
Feld, S.L. 20–21
Finland 26
flaming **93**, 95, 101
Flickr 158–159
foci of activity 20–21, 91, 156, 157
Fowler, J.H. 111
friending between parents and children on SNS 27, 28, 29, 146
friendships 10–12, 56, 57, *61*, 71, 80–81, 83–85, 89–91, 103, 111, 128, 137–138, 139, 160; mixed mode 79, 80–81; quality of 71, 72, 78–79, 80, 105, 109, 110, 114, 127; reciprocal 140; sex segregation in 77, 87; *see also* offline relationships; online relationships
functional similarity **52**, 53, 54–56, **56**

gaming 20, 30, 38, 41–42, **56**, 57, 64–65, 69–70, 79–80, 101, 105, 106–107, 142
Gen Y 8
gender differences 44, 57, 59, 62, 87, 97, 101, 104, 109, 111, 117, 121–122, 150
Germany 73
Gershuny, J. 59
globalization 116, 124
Granovetter, M. 125, 127
Greece 119
Greenspan, R. 119

Halligan, R.P. 137
Hampton, K.N. 124
harassment 32, 101, 107, 136, 137, 141, 146, 149–151, 152, 163; *see also* bullying
hate content 33, **34**, 48, 142, 145; *see also* bullying
Hatebook 145
hierarchies of authority 13, 14, 37, 39, **43**
Hispanics 75, 119
Holland 73, 74, 78, 80–81, 101
Holloway, S.L. 82

HomeNet study 72–73
homework 11, 13, 31, 33–34, 38, 41, 42, 46, **56**, 69, 97–98, 158
homophily 12, 16, **19**, 20, 77, **85**, 86, 90–91, 92, 103, 105, **106**, 107, 112, 128, 130, 165, 167; *see also* similarity
Horvitz, E. 107
household chores 42, 49, 54
human ecology theory 25, 28
hyperpersonal interation model **93**, 95

ICQ 105
ICTs (Information and Communication Technologies) 1, 4, 10, 36, 67–68, 70, 88, 154, 155, 157–167; and existing relationships 89–113, **93**, **106**, 162–163, 165; and families 25–34, **34**, 38–43, **43**, 68, 69, 162; and social network structure 114, **116**, **117**, **126**, *129*, **131**, 157; theories of 22–23, **22**, 154–155, 160; *see also* Internet
identity 6, 7, 30, 35, 83, 87–88, **93**, 147; common 138, 160; false 137, 141, 144; formation of 32, 81, 107, 108, 109, 110, 155, 159, 163; offline 5, 82, 107; social 74, 82, **93**, 95, 136–137
Igarashi, T. 76, 86
IM (Instant Messaging) 3, 4, 17, 25, 41–42, **56**, 63, 64–65, 67, 79, 81, 97, 98–101, 104, 105, 137, 149, 152, 162
inequalities 4, 20, 115–116, 117–124, **117**, **126**, 130, 156, 161
information age 2–5, 12–13, 23, 114, 164
injunctive norms 138
Instagram 97, 158–159
intergenerational interactions 14, 26, 41
Internet 1–10, 11, 155–156, 158, 159, 162, 164; as cultural artefact 5, 6–9, 154, 155; as culture 5–6; early days of 16, 110, 121; and family tensions 3, 12–14, 24, 28, 30, 31, 34, **34**; at home 24–49, 157; and sociability 50–68; *see also* ICTs; online communication; online relationships
intimacy 12, 17, 18, **19**, 31, 57, 89, 100, 103, 104, 107, 132, 133; in online relationships 6, 19, 74, 78, 82, **93**, 95, 96, 99–100, 101, 105, 112, 124, 133, 143, **144**, 166; *see also* personal information, disclosure of

introverts 72–73, 76–77; *see also*
    personality
isolation 33, 52, 55–56, 60, *61*, 62–63,
    65, 66–67, 76, 85, **85**, 110, 124, 127,
    130, 140, 159, 163; within households
    31, 36, 38; *see also* loneliness
Israel 37, 42, 44, 58, 59, 61–62, *61*,
    63–64, 66, 78–79, 98–99, 104–105,
    122, 131–132
Italy 26
Ito, M. 127

Japan 76, 86
Jewish adolescents 63–64, 98–99
job-hunting 115, 121, 159; *see also* work
    activities/employment

Kahai, S.S. 92–93
Katz, J.E. 157, 163
Kiesler, S. 94
Kim, H.H.S. 131
Korea/Koreans 46, 84, 109, 119, 131
Kozarian, L. 75
Kraut, R. 125

lack of contextual clues approach 92,
    93, 95
Lampe, C. 128
language barriers 11, **117**, 119
language skills improved 41, 50–51, 65
Larson, R.W. 10
Latinos 75, 119
LaVoie, D. 119
Lea, M. 95–96
Lee, S.J. 36, 105
Lee, Y. 14
Leskovec, J. 107
Lin, N. 116, 127
literacy 4, 7, 8, 10, 69, 70, 81, 83, 115,
    116–117, **116**, 118, 120, 122, 123,
    134, 152, 159, 166; new kind of 154,
    164–165
loneliness 73, 82, 99, 104, 111, 140, 144;
    see also isolation
Los Angeles 119

marginal fringe activities **52**, 53, 55–56
marketing 33, 118, 159
material access 118
math skills 50–51, 122

Mazur, E. 75
McKenna, K.Y.A. 96
media convergence 67–68, 96–97, 99;
    see also multimedia
media multiplexity 17, **19**, 71, 98,
    103–104, **106**, 112
media multitasking 52, 64–67, 68,
    157–158
media privatization 7, 28, 50, 51
media production 7, 8, 35, 38, 50, 65,
    120, 154–155, 158
media richness **22**, 23, 92–94, **93**
Meier, Meigan 137
mental health issues 10, 109, 110–111,
    125, 127, 131, 137, 139, 144
Merten, M.J. 36
Mesch, G.S. 29, 42, 76, 77, 98–99,
    131
"millennium generation" 7, 154
Miller, D. 108–109
Minnesota Adolescent Community
    Cohort Study 14
Mitchell, K.J. 142
mixed mode friendships 79, 80–81
mobile phones *see* cell phones (mobile
    phones); smartphones
moral panic 109
motivational access 118
multimedia 4, 7, 33, 50, 51, 54, 67;
    producers, adolescents as 8, 35, 50,
    65, 120
multiplexity 16–17, 103, 162–163;
    activity 103, 104; content 103, 104; of
    media 17, **19**, 71, 98, 103–104, **106**,
    112; resource 17, **19**; *see also* face-to-
    face communication: convergence
    with online
multitasking 52, 64–67, 68, 157–158
MySpace 16, 47, 137, 149, 158–159

National Educational Longitudinal
    Survey (NELS88) 122
negative social ties 136–153; *see also*
    cyberbullying
net-generation 7, 8, **22**, 50, 120, 134,
    154, 164–165; *see also* digital natives
network effect 97–98, **106**
"network integration" 126–127
network society 1, 2–3, 4, 23; *see also*
    social networks

206 Index

networked individualism 1, 2–5, **22**, 23, 83–85, 124, 127, 130, 164–165
normalization 114–118, **126**, 161, 165–166
norms 6, 21, 22, 28, 32, 56–57, 71, 83, 84, 123, 130, 136, 138, 156, 166

OECD (Organisation for Economic Co-operation and Development) 122–123
offline relationships 81, 104, 125, 127–128, 160–161; homogeneity of 84, 157; integration with online 51, 68, 71–72, 77, 82, 83, 99, 106–107, **106**, 108, 109, 130, 166; quality of 78–79, 80, 81, 105; sex segregation of 77, 84, 87; stronger than online **85**, 133, 160, 166; *see also* face-to-face communication
offline social networks 16, 17, 84, 102, 131
O'Neill, H. 119
online communication 6, 62–63, 70, 71, 73, 82, 84, 87, 127, 128, 133; asynchronous 4, 25, 84, 147–148; convergence with face-to-face 17, 63, 70, 80, 81, 83, 98, 99–100, 102, 106–109, **106**, 112, 113, 123, 160; and diversification 75, 107; in existing relationships 89–113; lack of non-verbal cues 74, 92, **93**, 94, 95, 112, 141, 148; and negative social ties 136–153; synchronous 4, 25, 84; theoretical perspectives on 92–97, **93**, 112; *see also* computer-mediated communication (CMC)
online relationships 11, 12, 19, 125, 127–128, 155, 157, 166; compensate for lack of off-line 19, 74, **85**, 108, 123, 128, 130, 133, 151, 163, 165; effects on social networks 76–77, 85–87, **85**; existing relationships 89–113; formation of 21, 66–67, 69–88, 102, 123, 138, 157; maintenance of 64, 106, **106**, 112, 123; and mutual friends 82, 166; quality of 78–79, 80, 81, 105; sex segregation of 77, 87; with strangers 51, 81–82, 97, 99, 100, 132, 133–134, 138, 143, 146, 148, 152, 163, 166;

weaker than offline **85**, 133, 160, 166; *see also* face-to-face communication: convergence with online
Orben, A. 111–112

Palestinian teenagers 131–132
parents 10, 11, 13–14, 26–29, 33, 34–49, 59, 61–62, 89–90, 98–99, 157; and bullying 136, 140–141, 145, 149; conflict with adolescents 13, 35–36, 38–43, **43**, 49; and control 13, 24, 28, 29, **34**, 36–37, 39–40, 43, 49, 157; educational level of 29, 38, 48, 59, **117**, 118, 122; expectation gap of 13–14, 41–42, **43**, 69; friending children 27, 28, 29, 146; and online communication 26, 27, 44, 67–68, 90; parental mediation 45–48, 49; parenting styles 47–48; socio-economic status of 13, 29, 59, **117**, 118, 121, 122, 123; *see also* families
Pearl, R. 140
peer relationships 4–5, 10–11, 28–29, 32, 59, 60–63, *61*, 71, 83, 89–90, 99, 123, 127, 132, 157, 162, 163, 165; activities 51, 55, 57, 58, 67, 83, 84–85; and bullying 136, 137, 138, 139–140; lack of 10, 90, 140, 159; peer pressure 83, 84, 92, **106**, 107, **131**, 134, 138; reinforced by online activities 51, 67, 101, 106, 107, 130, 132, 134, 146–147, 157–158, 159
periphery of social networks 92, 111, **117**, 140
permissive parents 47, 48
persistence 124
personal information, disclosure of 11, 18, 31, 39–40, 74, 78, 81, 96, 101, 110, 133, 143, **144**, 147, 150, 166; *see also* intimacy
personality 32, 57, 59, 72–73, 76–77, **85**, 133, 148, 152, 163
Peter, J. 74, 78, 80, 99, 101, 105, 133
Pew Research Center 60, 76, 97, 100, 101, 116, 121–122, 142–143
Pittsburgh 72–73
play 53, 55, 56–57, **56**, 69
pornography 32–33, **34**, 48
pre-adolescents 39, 100–101
privacy 27, 29, 31

privatization, media 7, 28, 50, 51
proximity 6, 12, 20, **52**, 53, 69–71, 78, 80–81, 84, 91, 92, 102–103, 105, 108, 112, 128, 130, 141, 156, 165, 167
proximity-similarity hypothesis 11–12, 90
Przybylski, A. 112
Putnam, R. 21–22, 126

quality of friendships 71, 72, 78–79, 80, 81, 105, 109, 110, 114, 127

racism 6, 33, 107, 149, 151; *see also* ethnicity/race
radio **52**, 55, 60
Rafaeli, S. 126
"rape myth" 32
reading newspapers 54, 55, **56**, 64
reciprocity 18, **19**, 21, 73, 130, 140, 163
reconfiguration of social networks **22**, 23, 82, 114, 134, 162, 164
Rice, R.E. 157, 163
Robinson, D. 45
Roche, C. 167
Rodkin, P.C. 140
romance 25, 100–101, 105, 138
Rosen, L.D. 149
rules 36–37, 39–40, 41, **43**, 46, 47, 48; activity rules 36–37, 40; contextual rules 36, 37, 40

schools 11, 34–35, 41, 42, **43**, 49, 60, 68, 69, 70, 87, 120, 140–141, 156; and adolescent friendships 11, 12, 13, 20, 63, 64, 70–71, 77, 79, 91, 99, 101, 102, 104–105; *see also* homework
Seepersad, S. 82
self-esteem 19, 57, 74, 83–84, 109, 128, 133, 151
self-regulation, adolescent 13–14, 41, **43**, 47, 57
sensation seeking 32, 73, **85**
Seoul 84
sex segregation of online/offline friends 77, 84, 87, 98
sexual harassment 141, 146, 148, 149–151
sexually explicit material 32–33, **34**, 36–37, 48

SIDE (social identity and de-individuation) **93**, 95–96
similarity 16, 20, 21, 66–67, 71, 80, 81, 104–105, 128, 162, 163, 165; functional **52**, 53, 54–56, **56**; proximity-similarity hypothesis 11–12, 90; *see also* homophily
Simmel, G. 125
Singapore 40, 84
skills access 118
Slovenia 26
smartphones 10, 13, 25, 30, 31, 36–37, 67, 68, 83, 97, 101, 121, 122; *see also* apps; cell phones (mobile phones)
Smollar, J. 11, 57
SMS (short message service) 17, 98, 149, 158, 162; *see also* text messaging
Snapchat 101, 167
Snapshot 158–159
Snubster 145
sociability 5, 15, 16–17, 50–68, 69, 73, 79, 84, 154, 156, 157, 162, 163, 166
social affordance **22**, 68, 84, **85**, 108, 164, 165
social anxiety 51, 57, 72, 73, 74, 96, 133, 152
social apps 11, 14, 17, 25, 90, 95, 97, 108–109, 119; *see also individual apps*
social capital 1–2, 19, 21–22, **22**, 24, 74, 75, 83, 97, 110, 114–115, 129–130, 131–132, 155–156, 161–162, 163; bonding 114, 126–127, *129*, 130, **131**, 134–135, 162–163; bridging 83, 114, 126, 127, 128, *129*, 130, **131**, 133, 134–135, 162; definition of 21, 156; differential use of 124–128; expansion of 75, 134, 157, 162
social compensation hypothesis 74
social constructivism 22, **22**, 123, 124, 160–161
social control 95, 126, **131**, 132, 133
social diversification 18–23, **19**, 74–83, 107, 137, 154, 155
social network analysis 15, 16, 19, **85**, 103–104, 133, 136–137, 140
social networking sites (SNS) 3, 4, 9, 16, 27–28, 46–47, **56**, 75–76, 80, 97, 98, 99, 128, 134, 147–148, 152, 159, 162, 165; and bullying/ harassment 137, 141, 142, 143, **144**,

208 *Index*

145, 146–147, 149, 150, 152, 153; family connections on 25, 27, 28, 29, 146; public profiles on 30, 46–47, 97, 100, 143, **144**, 150; and strangers 51, 100, 137, 142; *see also* social networks; *individual networking sites*
social networks 3–4, 14–18, 19–20, **19**, 22, 23, 25, 27, 30, 47–48, **56**, 66, 71, 76–78, 83, 158, 163; centrality 17–18, **19**, 126, 140; density 18, **19**, 114, 125, 126–127, 128–130, *129*, 132, 136, 139, 163; effects in media adoption 97–101; expansion of 22, 23, 66–67, 69, 75–77, 83, **85**, 86, 123, 128, 130–131, 134, 152, 155, 156, 157, 163, 165; heterogeneity of 15, 77, 87, 114, 128, 130, 146, 163; homophily in 12, 16, **19**, 20, 77, **85**, 86, 90–91, 92, 103, 105, **106**, 107, 112, 128, 130, 165, 167; impact of ICT on 89–113; offline 16, 17, 84, 102, 131; online relationship formation and 85–87, **85**; periphery of 92, 111, **117**, 140; sizes of 15–16, **19**, 21, 56, 63–64, 75, 76, 85–86, 100, 128, 156, 165; structure of 19–20, 22–23, 66, 76–78, 83, 114–135, 137, 160, 162, 164, 166–167; transitivity of 18, 70, 84, **85**, **106**, 107, 112, 126, 128–129, **131**, 133, 165, 166; *see also* network society; social ties
social norms theory 138; *see also* norms
social presence 70, 79, 92, **93**, 94
social psychology 73, 95
social ties 10–12, 15, 16–17, 19, 21, 22–23, 69, 70, 75, 76–79, 85–87, **85**, 125, 128, 130, 131, **144**, 162–164, 165, 167; existing 20, 70, 86, 89–113, **106**, 146, 155, 157, 158; negative 136–153, 163; segmented 126; strong ties 9, 18, 31, 74, 76, 102, 103, 123, 124, 127, 133, 134, 138; transitive 126, 128, **131**, 132, 133; weak ties 9, 18, 31, 74, 75, 76, 83, 104, 124, 125, 127, **131**, 134, 138, 160; *see also* offline relationships; online relationships
socialization 29, 87, 105, 120, 155, 158, 159, 167
SoundCloud 158–159
South Korea 84

Spears, R. 95–96
Spina, S.U. 87
Sproull, L. 94
Stanton-Salazar, R.D. 87
Steinfield, C. 128
strangers, online 51, 81–82, 97, 99, 100, 132, 133–134, 138, 143, 146, 148, 152, 163, 166
strong ties 9, 18, 31, 74, 76, 102, 103, 123, 124, 127, 133, 138
structural holes theory 125, 126, 129–130, 132
substitution effect 55, **56**
suicide 10, 109, 125, 131, 137, 139, 144
Suler, J. 147
synchronous communication 4, 25, 84

Taipei 84
Takai, J. 76, 86
Talmud, I. 77, 98–99
technological determinism 5, 8–9, 22, **22**, 123–124, 160–161
telephone 72, 80, 99, 104, 108, 163–164; *see also* cell phones (mobile phones)
television (TV) 22, 36, 45, 49, 52, 53, 54, 55, 60, 64, 65, 161
text messaging 26–27, 30, 44, 67, 76, 86, 97, 100, 104; *see also* SMS (short message service)
"thick communicative action" 104
time displacement 35–36, 51, 52–53, **52**, 59, 60, 66
time, family 29, 30, 34–38, 42, 45, 48–49, 158
TIME (telecommunications, information technologies, media, entertainment) 67
Tocqueville, A. de 125
Toronto 43
transformation **52**, 53
transitivity 18, 70, 84, **85**, **106**, 107, 112, 126, 128–129, **131**, 133, 165, 166
trust 11, 18, **19**, 21, 22, 40, 81, 89, 96, 103, 104, **131**, 132, 156, 162
Turkle, S. 6, 109–110
Turow, J. 45

UGC (user-generated-content) 158–159
UK (United Kingdom) 39, 44, 100, 150

US (United States) 8, 14, 29, 39, 43, 47–48, 60, 64–65, 72–73, 97, 138; bullying/harassment 137, 142, 147, 149–150; ethnicity 75, 76, 119, 121, 138; family time 35, 36, 43; gender 101, 121; online communication 44, 62–63, 64–65, 100; online friendships 11, 100, 138
usage access 118
utopian perspective 4, 124, 161

Valentine, G. 82
Valkenburg, P.M. 74, 78, 80, 99, 101, 105, 133
Van Acker, R. 140
Van Cleemput, K. 103–104
Van Dijk, J. 117
Vaterlaus, J.M. 167
Verma, S. 10
video conversations 26, 95, 96–97
virtual reality 5–6, 7, 9, 15, 19, 31, 72, 81, **85**, 87, 107, 108, 120–121, 144, 151, 166–167; virtual relationships 6, 116, 161, 164
volunteering 14, 21–22

W3Techs 119
Walther, J.B. 95
Watt; D. 25, 28
weak ties 9, 18, 31, 74, 75, 76, 83, 104, 124, 125, 127, **131**, 134, 138, 160
weblogs 159
well-being 10, 73, 83–84, 90, 101, 109, 110, 111–112, 125, 131, 132, 133, 136, 152
Wellman, B. 3, 69, 124
WhatsApp 25–26, 67, 79, 90, 99
White, J.M. 25, 28
Williams, A. 36, 134
Wilson, K.R. 123
Wolfradt, U. 73
Woolcock, M. 126
work activities/employment 30–31, **34**, 35, 115, 118, 121, 159

Ybarra, M.L. 142
Yoshida, T. 76, 86
Young, J.A. 167
Youniss, J. 11, 57
YouTube 143, 158–159

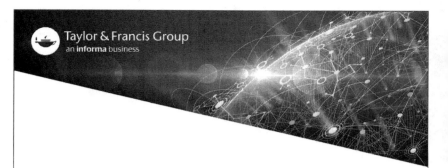